Industrial Democracy

Industrial Democracy

THE SOCIOLOGY OF PARTICIPATION

Paul Blumberg

Schocken Books · New York

First SCHOCKEN PAPERBACK edition 1973
Second Printing, 1976

Copyright © 1968 by Paul Blumberg
Library of Congress Catalog Card No. 69-12382

Manufactured in the United States of America

For my father

Preface

The reader will not find herein a model of value-free sociology. I have become increasingly convinced that the best sociologists among us are not those who artificially excise the moral component from their works, who attempt to play God and raise themselves above their fellows, or who invoke the old dogma that because science cannot establish the validity of values, that values, insofar as possible, should be excluded from science.

Much of this, of course, is sham. As Morris Cohen wrote long ago in *Reason and Nature*: 'Those who boast that they are not, as social scientists, interested in what ought to be, generally assume (tacitly) that the hitherto prevailing order is the proper ideal of what ought to be. . . .' But even in those cases where the sociologist does approximate the ideals of value-neutrality, he thereby voluntarily surrenders a part of him which makes him distinct and unique as a man. When a man becomes a sociologist, he too often *subtracts* the moral component from himself and, as sociologist, he then becomes something less than what he was. Preferably, when a man becomes a sociologist, he should not subtract from himself, but *supplement* what he is with scientific methods of enquiry, which are not as incompatible with the frank and honest expression of widely held values of democracy, freedom, equality, and community, as is customarily believed.

What gives strength and energy and a lasting human as well as scientific quality to our best sociological works is just this infusion of moral commitment which is so lacking in those works of bloodless detachment.

Thirty years ago, Robert Lynd wrote in his *Knowledge for What?* that the proper role of the social sciences is 'to be troublesome, to disconcert the habitual arrangements by which we manage to live along, and to demonstrate the possibility of change in more adequate directions'. This seems as true today as when Lynd wrote it.

All this is not to imply, of course, that I have in any sense intentionally biased the analysis in the direction of a prior moral commitment. As C. Wright Mills said, 'I have tried to be objective. I do not claim to be detached.'

For their advice at various stages of preparation of this manuscript, I should like to thank Lewis S. Feuer of University of Toronto, Paul Halmos of the University College of South Wales and Monmouthshire, Bernard Karsh of the University of Illinois, S. M. Lipset of Harvard University, and Franz Schurmann of the University of California, Berkeley. Naturally, I take full responsibility for the final product. To my wife, Barbara, I owe a special debt of gratitude: for her sensible suggestions and criticism, her aid in editing the manuscript, and, above all, her inexhaustible patience and understanding.

I should like to thank the following publishers and journals for permission to quote from their works: *Human Relations* for L. Coch's and J. R. P. French's 'Overcoming Resistance to Change'; *Personnel Psychology* for E. A. Fleishman's and E. F. Harris' 'Patterns of Leadership Behavior Related to Employee Grievances'; Harvard University Press for F. J. Roethlisberger's and W. J. Dickson's *Management and the Worker* and T. N. Whitehead's *The Industrial Worker*; Doubleday & Co, Inc. for D. Riesman's 'Leisure and Work' in *Abundance for What?*; Messrs Basil Blackwell Ltd for Hugh Clegg's *Industrial Democracy and Nationalization* and *A New Approach to Industrial Democracy*.

Contents

1. Introduction: The Relevance and the Future of Workers' Management

In many respects, the issue of workers' management seems peculiarly irrelevant to the world of our own day, dominated by such overriding issues as war and peace, capitalism and Communism, the emergence of new independent nations, the crisis of economic development, the population explosion, the advent and consequences of automation, the quest for racial equality, and so on. The idea of 'workers' control' seems curiously antiquated today, merely a quaint slogan of historical interest, based on political movements now defunct or impotent, on issues long forgotten, on premises which were perhaps even initially unsound, and on conditions which no longer exist. In short, history seems to have bypassed the issue of workers' management entirely.

My own view is that this historical judgment may be premature, and that workers' management may well become an increasingly important issue as we move into the final third of our century. This view is based upon certain signs and trends of our time, some overt but misunderstood, others more obscure and unrecognised. In this introduction, I shall summarise briefly what might be considered the major forces pushing in the direction of a renewal of the issue of workers' management, some of which will be treated at length in later chapters.

I

The alienating character of much industrial labour, discussed so often since the days of Marx and still of prime importance in our world, seems to be substantially *mitigated* by the introduction of various forms of direct workers' participation. An impressive panoply of research findings (discussed in Chapters 2, 3, 5 and 6) demonstrates consistently that satisfaction in work is significantly enhanced by increasing workers' decision-making powers on the job. Under a great variety of work situations and among workers of vastly different levels of skill, work satisfaction has been shown to increase even though the technical processes of production and the workers' tasks themselves remain unchanged. The cumulative weight of this research is slowly beginning to change the sociologists' image of the worker; to a growing number of writers, the modern worker is perhaps best understood as being oriented and responsive to participation.

Meanwhile, other 'solutions' to the work alienation problem—such as a turn towards leisure, automation, anti-industrialism, and job enlargement—have all proved wanting, for one reason or another (see Chapter 4).

It must be noted, however, that although this research constitutes a major argument for a reconsideration of the issue of workers' management, scientific findings of this nature do not usually generate social or political movements and, in themselves, may have negligible impact on the course of history. At the same time, however, scientific evidence occasionally may be incorporated into ongoing social or political movements, witness, for example, the role of sociological findings in the movement to abolish racial segregation in American schools.

II

The growth and significance of public ownership *outside* the Communist world, both in the industrialised West and in the developing regions,* has been accompanied by a search for appropriate administrative forms. The manifest failure of the public corporation to arouse the British workers' enthusiasm on the job stands as apt testimony that any kind of administration of the public sector which does not involve the worker directly in management, but only via remote representatives at the top, cannot hope to affect significantly the workers' attitudes towards their work or their company. This fact has been demonstrated on a wide scale: in West Germany (codetermination), in France (tripartite—government, employees, public—administration of nationalised enterprises), and in Israel (the Histadrut or trade union-owned sector). The basic failure of all these schemes to change the meaning of work for the worker can best be understood by an

* Public ownership in such 'capitalist' countries as France, for example, is extensive: coal mining, electricity, gas, many banks, numerous insurance companies, railroads, aircraft, the Renault automobile works, radio and television networks, and much more. The public sector accounts for about 25 per cent of the national gross fixed investment. For other Western countries, the percentages are as follows: Britain, 32; Italy, 27; West Germany, 15–20; Sweden, 15; Norway, 14; Netherlands, 13; Belgium, 10. [Cited in Perry Anderson, 'Problems of Socialist Strategy', in Anderson and Robin Blackburn (eds), *Towards Socialism* (Cornell University Press, NY 1966), p. 232]. In many areas of the developing world, especially in Africa and Asia, public ownership is even more extensive.

observation G. D. H. Cole made years ago, comparing the psychology of *political* democracy with the psychology of *industrial* democracy.[1] In politics, it is the events at the highest (national or international) level which matter most to the citizen, and about which he is most likely to be informed and interested. In industry, on the other hand, it is what occurs at the lowest level, on the factory floor, that matters most to the worker. A simple change in the locus of ownership at the highest level, from private to public, with no democratisation of the workers' immediate situation in the shop and with no rights of direct participation, is likely to have a minimal impact on traditional problems of work alienation. This, more than anything, explains why these diverse forms of 'industrial democracy at the top' have been failures from the point of view of the worker.

Nevertheless, workers' indifference cannot be overcome simply by involving them directly. And here we must take note of the record of joint consultation bodies, miscellaneous plant committees and other advisory councils in England, France, Belgium, Sweden, India, Israel, and elsewhere. While these have involved workers directly or through representatives close to home, they have generally proved very disappointing, and have failed to arouse workers' sustained interest. Perhaps because they are form without much content and have sharply circumscribed power and jurisdiction, workers often regard them simply as a waste of time. In Britain, France, Israel and India, these bodies have achieved the most meagre results, at best, and discussions of these forms sound like nothing so much as funeral orations.[2]

Finally, producers' co-operatives, which do involve workers significantly in management, have repeatedly been proved both economically and socially an inappropriate vehicle for workers' management. Economically, they have always been plagued with chronic shortages of capital, stemming from their inadequate initial resources, and the hostile milieu in which they operate makes borrowing from the private capital market quite difficult. In the Western world, they are economically inconsequential, especially when compared to the flourishing consumers' co-operative movement.

Socially, producers' co-operatives have a tendency to 'degenerate', as the Webbs and others observed long ago, due in part to the lack of outside public control of their activities. This 'degeneration' takes some of the following forms: transforming the co-operative into a simple profit-making, profit-seeking business, indistinguishable from

[1] See notes at end of book.

a private enterprise; exploitating a monopoly situation, often to public disadvantage (as has happened in Israel); closing off of co-operative membership; raising the cost of membership to a prohibitively high level; and resorting to the anti-co-operative device of taking on hired labour.[3]

One co-operative form which has been successful, economically and socially, but which has been almost totally ignored by Western writers, is kibbutz *industry* in Israel. These factories in the fields (about 150 in 1959 employing over 5,000 workers) account for an ever-increasing share of kibbutz employment and income, and they are generally organised according to kibbutz principles of democratic election of managers and rotation of offices. Although much attention has been given to the organisation of kibbutz agriculture and communal life, research on the fascinating social organisation of the kibbutz factory, which might have relevance to the industrial and the industrialising world, is almost non-existent.[4] With the exception of this unique form, however, the experience with producers' co-operatives has been largely a disappointing one.

The lessons of all the foregoing disappointments seem to be as follows: the failure of the public corporation suggests that direct involvement of workers is essential if the meaning of work is to be changed; the failure of advisory councils suggests that direct involvement of workers must take place within institutions which have significant powers; and the failure of producers' co-operatives suggests that the interests of the public must be safeguarded within the framework of any system of workers' participation.

As a consequence of these failures, there has been noticeable discontent with present systems of administering public property. For decades, this discontent has expressed itself in a recurring quest, in the Labour and Socialist movements, for new forms and new ideas. The issue, to what extent should workers participate in the management of the enterprises in which they are employed, runs like a thread through twentieth-century European politics; it disappears only to appear again, for it has never really been resolved satisfactorily. It is clearly part of Socialism's unfinished business. And in this continuing discontent and failure to resolve the issue fully and finally, lies the dynamic for further change and experiment with various forms of workers' management.[5]

III

The internal dynamics of Socialist ideology itself also seems to point to an ultimate return to the idea of workers' management.[6] As Socialists are generally committed to the reduction or the elimination of class differences, and as class involves inequalities of power as well as inequalities of economic position and status. Socialists are inevitably drawn back to the need to eliminate power inequalities, in industrial as well as in political settings: to abolish bureaucratic and unrepresentative industrial (as well as political) hierarchies, to eliminate arbitrary and unchecked authority in industry, to reduce rigid superior-subordinate, command-obedience industrial relationships, and so on. Thus, the internal logic of Socialist ideology itself tends to point ultimately in the direction of a renewed emphasis on some kind of industrial or workshop democracy.

More concretely, recent changes in European capitalism and the ideological bankruptcy of European Social Democracy have made appeals for workers' management more practical and even necessary than ever before.

There was a time when radical parties in Europe could base their appeals on the destitution, the misery, and the bitter deprivations of the working class, in short, on economic issues basic to life itself. However, the neo-capitalist European economies since World War II have made obsolete political appeals based on the urgent economic problems of the past. Partial nationalisation, planning, Welfare State measures, increases in productivity, and so on have lifted the mass of citizens above the poverty level. The apparent ability of neo-capitalism to satisfy the needs of individual consumption has made it imperative that appeals for a radical transformation now be diverted from quantitative deprivations to qualitative deprivations. As André Gorz says in a new book in the work alienation tradition:

> ... in a developed society, needs are not only quantitative: the need for consumer goods; but also qualitative: the need for information, for communication, for fellowship; the need to be free not only from exploitation but from oppression and alienation in work and leisure.[7]

Specifically, Gorz sees the qualitative deprivations of neo-capitalism as consisting, first, of unmet collective needs of society. Because these collective needs cannot be expressed in market terms, because they do not respond to the profit motive, and because the vast majority of economic resources lie with the market- and profit-oriented sector, contemporary capitalism experiences a vast social imbalance expressed, in Galbraith's terms, as private affluence amid public squalor. Concretely this takes the form of urban decay, financial crisis and lack of planning, rural decline and underdevelopment, crises in public education, hospitals, parks, libraries, public transportation, low cost housing, air, water, and noise pollution, and so on. Glutting the market with private goods and services, contemporary capitalism has been accused of creating distorted priorities and providing the 'superfluous before the necessary'.

According to European Left Socialists, other qualitative needs unmet by neo-capitalism are for the widening and deepening of democratic forms in social and economic life, without which the alienation of the citizens and the worker continues. On work in the contemporary world, Gorz writes:

> On the margin of civil society, with its formal liberties, there . . . persists behind the gates of factories, a despotic, authoritarian society with a military discipline and hierarchy which demands of the workers both unconditional obedience and active participation in their own oppression.[8]

Thus, demands for workers' participation, which once seemed idealistic, remote, abstract and visionary, suddenly become immediately relevant, as the issue of mass poverty recedes. To European Left Socialists, workshop democracy is both an immediate demand, to be put forward now within the framework of neo-capitalism, and an ultimate aspiration.[9]

If the European Left is to survive, it cannot be assimilated ideologically and politically into the neo-capitalist framework, but neither can it continue to base its appeals on outmoded issues of working class misery. It must focus on new issues, based on the qualitative deficiencies of contemporary society, such as the inadequate satisfaction of collective needs plus the necessity for broadening democratic forms in social and economic life.

In this sense, the survival of the European Left is partly linked to its ability and willingness to resurrect the old, idealistic appeals for workers' participation and transform them into immediate political issues.

IV

Just as the dynamics of Socialist ideology points in the direction of a renewal of interest in workers' management, so liberal ideology plus other social forces not usually considered part of the socialist tradition occasionally act to extend participation beyond strictly political boundaries. The anti-poverty legislation in the United States in the mid-1960s which originally provided for the 'maximum feasible participation of the poor' in diverse forms of community programmes is an example—albeit small, short-lived, and controversial—of the gradual extension of the concept of democracy into an economic and social sphere. This moderate proposal for participation has been extended and radicalised in recent years by diverse community organisers and especially by Black Power advocates who call for control of the institutions of the city ghetto or the rural black community—the schools, housing, businesses, politics, organisations—by the black residents themselves.

Additionally, in the emerging New Left movement in the United States, there is a strong emphasis on what has been termed 'participatory democracy'.[10] This active and vocal group of young radicals has a vocabulary and a set of concerns that put it in marked contrast to their political forbears in the traditional Left. The new radicals are less interested in the usual class struggle rhetoric and interminable debates over the nature of the Soviet state. They are far more concerned, in a non-theoretical and non-ideological manner, with the moral and philosophical issues involved in war, racial prejudice, poverty, and what is more pertinent here—their own sense of alienation from the impersonal, centralised, unresponsive, and unaccountable bureaucracies that have come to dominate modern life. Although their solutions are vaguely formulated, the New Left answers the problems of bureaucracy with an appeal for thoroughgoing democratic decision-making from below—whether 'below' means associations of the poor in their own ghetto organisations or students sharing power with faculty and administration in the multiversity.

The themes of student power and participatory democracy in the American academic community are being echoed by student groups and young people in Europe. The Dutch Provos—short for '*Provocateurs*'—young anarchists with a sense of humour, call for the organisation of an international provotariat, which they see as the last hope for a contemporary revolutionary class in the West. In revolt against a society of manipulated consumers and pseudo-democratic forms, they claim that 'democracy is not a set of rules but a feeling', and the West has the rules but has lost the feeling.[11]

In England, the unprecedented student demonstrations and sit-ins at the London School of Economics in 1967 ultimately involved issues of student participation.[12]

In the early 1960s, Italian architecture students conducted university sit-ins ' . . . demanding a voice in the determination of their programmes and of the subjects taught. They won their case'.[13] In 1967–8, an epidemic of student strikes and sit-ins swept through Italian universities at Turin, Milan, Pisa, Florence, Rome, and Naples. Students demanded reform of the Italian university system, long dominated by small groups of absolutist senior faculty members, broader rights of student participation, and the like. The Left Wing 'Red Guards' at Turin, where the movement began, attempted to abolish traditional authority, elect professors, and to base students' grades and promotions on the judgment of student committees.[14]

West Germany has its own so-called 'student problem'. The movement originated in the mid-1960s at the Free University in Berlin with the aim of achieving academic reform. It was ultimately taken over by the Association of Socialist German Students and others which constitutes now an 'extraparliamentary opposition' to what they consider the West German authoritarian establishment.[15] Orators, theorists and leaders such as Rudi Dutschke and Ekkehard Krippendorf have called for 'a new social form based on workers' councils and continuous democratic decision'.[16]

Probably the clearest statement of the American New Left's vision of a participatory democracy is contained in the founding manifesto of the small but influential Students for a Democratic Society (SDS), founded in the early 1960s.

> We seek the establishment of a democracy of individual participation governed by two central aims: That the individual share in those social decisions determining the quality and direction of his life; that society be organised to encourage independence in men and provide the media for their common participation.

Regarding the organisation of economic life, they argue

> that work should involve incentives worthier than money or survival. It should be educative, not stultifying; creative, not mechanical; self-directed, not manipulated; . . . that the economic experience is so personally decisive that the individual must share in its full determination; that the economy itself is of such social importance that its major resources and means of production should be open to democratic participation and subject to democratic social regulation.[17]

There is evidence that the ideology of participation is not confined simply to the modest membership (7,000) of the SDS. The waves of student discontent which began in Berkeley late in 1964 and have swept across the land ever since, can be realistically interpreted as an academic counterpart of industrial demands for 'workers' control'. Although the Berkeley Free Speech Movement (FSM) was triggered by a relatively minor infringement of students' rights, the whole scope and vision of the movement became enormously enlarged, with student leaders eventually driven to the conclusion that nothing less than faculty-student self-government would cure the evils of the anomic, bureaucratic, unreachable multiversity. Recalling the ideas of the old Guild Socialist movement, one began to hear much of the virtues of the medieval university system where an essentially self-governing community of scholars and students dispensed altogether with the services of Chancellors, Provosts, and Presidents.

Barbara Garson, author of the controversial play, *Macbird!*, and a student activist in the Free Speech Movement, captured the emerging political mood in Berkeley as she wrote in the FSM *Newsletter* during the hectic days in the fall of 1964:

> . . . I dream of some day living in a democracy. On campus, committees of students and faculty will make the minimum regulations needed to administer (not rule) our academic community. I hope to see democracy extended to the offices and factories, so that everyone may have the satisfaction of making the decisions about the use of his productive energies.
>
> I look past government by the grunted consent of the governed. Some day we will participate actively in running our own lives in all spheres of work and leisure.[18]

At its 1967 convention, the National Student Association, representing more than three hundred student governments on campuses having nearly two million students, adopted a resolution for the first time calling for student power. The organisation demanded complete student control over dormitory hours and other social and housing rules, but, more important and quite unprecedented, came out for student participation in setting basic academic policies such as course requirements, admission standards, and the hiring and dismissal of faculty members.

v

It has been said that ideologies of workers' management arise during periods of political, social, or economic unrest. More specifically, however, it seems that these ideologies take root and grow when, for one reason or another, the legitimacy of an established economic élite is called into question and when the status of that group suffers a serious decline.[19] Looking into the recent history of Yugoslavia, West Germany, and Israel, for example, one may observe that systems of workers' or trade union management, albeit of different kinds, are common to all three countries: in Yugoslavia the institution of workers' councils; in Germany, the experiment in codetermination; and in Israel, the widespread ownership and control of the economy by the huge General Federation of Labour (Histadrut). What is also common to these three countries, which in all other respects have such diverse histories, is that in each the legitimacy of an established economic élite was shaken and repudiated, creating what one might call an entrepreneurial vacuum of legitimacy into which has stepped a particular ideology of workers' management.

In Yugoslavia, for example, it was in part the Soviet attempt to exploit that country economically after World War II through the use of so-called joint stock companies which would have given the USSR strategic control over major sectors of the Yugoslav economy that led to the rejection of the Soviet managerial and political élite and the ultimate repudiation of the entire Soviet system of central planning. In West Germany, the leading role of the business élite in giving moral and financial support to Hitler led to the disgrace of that class in the eyes of large sections of the German public, political parties from Left to Right, the Allies, and the reconstituted trade union movement immediately following the war. Such universal repudiation of the legitimacy of this class provided fertile ground for the partial triumph of the dormant ideology of codetermination, as labour declared that the economic power of the business élite, exercised irresponsibly before and during the Third Reich, must now be shared by a democratic and responsible Labour movement. The establishment of codetermination, particularly in the steel and coal industries following the war, was directly attributable to the moral bankruptcy into which the German business élite had fallen.

The Israeli case is slightly more complicated. The early Zionists who came to live and work in Palestine believed that the Jewish occupational structure in the lands of the Diaspora was lopsided and unnatural in the sense that Jews were heavily concentrated in commercial and financial occupations and were vastly underrepresented in manual occupations and especially in agriculture. Adopting some of the ideology of European anti-Semites, many Zionists considered Jewish life in the Diaspora parasitic and immoral because the Jews were not firmly rooted in what was judged the basic and most essential work of the world, manual and agricultural labour. Because of these beliefs, Zionists, whether Socialists or not, tended to denigrate the status and authority of the Jewish businessman, for he was the symbol of the abnormality of Jewish life in Europe. At the same time, the status of simple manual labour was enhanced enormously, epitomised by the life, labour and writings of the pioneer, A. D. Gordon, the acclaimed prophet of the religion of labour.

One may easily infer that this ideology of individual and collective regeneration through manual toil was not highly conducive to grant-ing the bourgeois Jewish economic élite its accustomed place in the context of settlement in Palestine. On the contrary, Zionist ideology, by rejecting the legitimacy of the traditional economic élite, laid the groundwork for the development of the economy outside the usual capitalist framework. It permitted the emergence and development of an ideology of workers' management that was unique and became in-stitutionalised in the large economic holdings of the Labour movement.

What has this repudiation of economic élites to do with the future of workers' management? In many parts of the Third World today there is an analogous repudiation of economic élites. On a fairly wide scale there exists an all-pervasive anti-capitalist ideology, a partial con-sequence of the experience of these nations with Western imperialism in the nineteenth and twentieth centuries.[20] Capitalism has been widely repudiated simply because it is regarded as synonymous with hated imperialism, of which the peoples of the Third World were the chief victims. Then, too, an unanticipated consequence of Western im-perialism was that by seeking to dominate the economies of the colonies, they often prevented the development of a strong, indigenous capitalist class; and when the Western nations pulled out, the enfeebled forces of domestic capitalism were hopelessly unequal to the task of developing and modernising their society. Ironically, then, Western capitalism ultimately became a force, not for the spread of capitalism in the underdeveloped world, but for the spread of various forms of socialism. In many of the developing lands, capitalism was not only politically and morally impossible, because of its association with colonialism, but it was economically impossible as well.

Consequently, one nationalist leader after another has adopted some form of 'Socialism' as a guiding economic premise—whether it be

Nehru's 'Democratic Collectivism', Senghor's 'African Socialism', Nyerere's 'Communitarianism', Sékou Touré's 'Communocracy', or Nasser's 'Democratic, Socialist, Co-operative Democracy'. As these new nations have rejected not only the economic élite of capitalism but the very institutions of capitalism itself, we should not be surprised to see in these developing countries various experimental forms of workers' management. Certainly the great interest which the African nations have shown in both Israeli experiments in co-operation and the Yugoslav system of workers' management is significant here. Indeed, the experiments with workers' management on some 22,000 nationalised farms and 500 factories in Algeria, and other tentative beginnings in Burma and elsewhere, may represent signs of an important movement which may spread in the developing world.

VI

A final and very different strand of evidence concerning the possible future importance of philosophies of participation is the tentative success of the Yugoslav system of workers' management, both economically and in terms of involving a great proportion of the labour force in some degree of managerial decision-making. This experiment is discussed in some detail in Chapters 8 and 9.

Also important along these lines is the gradual evolution of the economic institutions of the USSR and Eastern Europe toward various forms of decentralised economic arrangements. Although workers' management such as exists in Yugoslavia has not been introduced anywhere else in the Communist world, the direction is clear. Almost all the countries in the Soviet bloc are moving towards greater autonomy of the individual firm with regard to production, marketing, financing, and pricing, at the expense of the centralised planning machinery. None of this decentralisation has involved the workers yet. But with the interest and occasionally even the guarded admiration expressed by the Soviet leaders for the Yugoslav system of workers' management, it seems moderately likely that the trend in the European Communist world is toward something resembling the Yugoslav model, and away from the kind of detailed administrative planning characteristic of the USSR since the end of the NEP period.

The multiplicity of forces summarised above points tentatively in the direction of a renewal of interest in various systems of workers' management. As we have seen, the democratic capitalist West, the Communist East, and the developing countries are all subject to different though unmistakable pressures for experiments with workers' participation. Whether these pressures will overcome the obviously potent forces militating against a revitalisation of workers' management of course remains to be seen; but it must be with some caution that we relegate the entire subject of workers' participation to the trash heap of history. It may yet have its day.

2. The Forgotten Lessons of the Mayo Experiments: I

'There aren't so many bosses making it miserable for you [in the Test Room], why don't they let the girls all work this way?'— *Worker in the Relay Assembly Test Room*

It is now just over forty years since the Mayo experiments began, and although their methodology and value premises have often been criticised, these studies have nevertheless had an extraordinary impact. They literally gave birth to the field of industrial sociology as well as to the Human Relations in Industry Approach, and they began what was to be a thorough transformation of the behavioural science image of industrial man. The Mayo studies have become part of the core subject matter of contemporary sociology, to which every student, almost without exception, is exposed early in his training. Because of this enormous influence, I believe that a reappraisal of the exact meaning of the Mayo studies is very much in order.

The purpose of this chapter is not to discuss, evaluate, or criticise the ideology underlying either the Mayo studies or the Human Relations in Industry approach which grew out of those studies. That is a task which began over a quarter of a century ago, and over the years a veritable army of social scientists has conducted a prolonged war on the doctrines of this school.[1] These critics have with much justification condemned, among other things, *1*, this school's naïve harmony approach to social relations in industry and in society; *2*, their managerial bias demonstrated by their admitted goal of attempting to secure the co-operation of workers for goals defined and approved by a managerial élite in harmony with the general interests of the firm; *3*, their neglect of trade unionism as a factor in an industrial setting.

Rather than discussing the ideological foundations of the Mayo school, which have received exhaustive criticism from all quarters, we shall instead be concerned with the *empirical* aspects of the Mayo experiments which have been relatively neglected by the critics in the general onslaught against this school's doctrinal premises. The major focus of this chapter will be an interpretation—or rather a re-interpretation—of the Hawthorne Studies and, in particular, of the initial experiment in that series, the Relay Assembly Test Room study. The ideology of the Mayo school will be treated indirectly and only where necessary in the course of a re-examination of this experiment.

Our thesis is easily stated. It is that one of the most important conclusions which one may draw from the Relay Assembly Test Room experiment has been consistently underplayed or even ignored by: *1*, the experimenters themselves; *2*, the chief biographers of this experiment (Mayo[2] and Roethlisberger and Dickson[3]); and *3*, a generation of writers of introductory sociology and industrial sociology textbooks. I believe that some of the most important implications of this study were largely lost sight of in the mass of data collected by the researchers, were buried again in an avalanche of information presented by Roethlisberger and Dickson, and were thus partially obscured from those who have since used this work as a source in describing the Western Electric research.

Most authors who have written on the Hawthorne Studies have described the importance of the Relay Assembly Test Room experiment as demonstrating primarily that an informal network of interpersonal relations arises within the framework of the formal organisation which may either assist the formal organisation in fulfilling its goals or, as in the case of the Bank Wiring Room experiment, may subvert these goals. These writers have largely explained the improvements in morale and productivity in the Relay Assembly Test Room either in terms of this cohesive primary group which the workers formed or, alternatively, by the workers' enhanced status as a result of being selected for the experiment and accorded special treatment and privileges by the company (the so-called 'Hawthorne effect'[4]). However important these factors are, there is, nevertheless, another lesson of this experiment which has been largely forgotten. But to understand that lesson one must first understand the exact nature of the experiment itself.

The Relay Assembly Test Room experiment began in 1927 at the Hawthorne Works (Chicago) of the giant Western Electric Company which is the largest producer of telephone equipment in the United States. The experiment grew out of previous studies, begun in 1924 in the same plant, which were designed to discover the effects of variations in illumination upon worker output.[5] The researchers' general hypothesis was derived from common sense: they expected that productivity would rise as illumination increased (to an optimum point) and would probably fall as illumination decreased. This simple hypothesis was shattered, however, when, after several experiments in large departments of the plant, it was discovered that changes in productivity occurred quite independently of the level of illumination. In most cases output tended to increase over time as the experiment proceeded, whether the level of illumination was raised or lowered. In certain notable instances, productivity was maintained even down to a point where it became so dark the workers could scarcely see.

From these experiments, the researchers, now somewhat perplexed, concluded tentatively that variations in levels of illumination, within a reasonable range, did not seem to be appreciably related to industrial output. But they were generally unsatisfied with the design of the illumination experiments, for they had been conducted in large departments where a number of extraneous factors such as turnover of personnel and changes in work performed had gone uncontrolled. The investigators also believed that further studies should be undertaken which would examine the effects of a greater number of variables.

For these reasons, the Western Electric researchers—now joined by members of the Harvard Graduate School of Business Administration —decided to experiment with a number of different variables upon a small group of workers. In order to control the test situation as carefully as possible, the researchers removed the workers from their regular department entirely and placed them in a special test room. The result was the Relay Assembly Test experiment. In the broadest sense, it was undertaken in order to assess the effects of certain experimentally induced conditions upon industrial fatigue and monotony which, in turn, were thought to affect worker output and morale. The independent variables which the researchers initially believed would be important in the experiment were physical or technical, not sociological. Indeed, it would not be amiss to say that at this stage sociological variables simply did not exist in the minds of the investigators. They were concerned exclusively at this time with the effects of: *1*, introducing rest pauses of different lengths and different frequencies during the working day; *2*, supplying small lunches to the workers during mid-morning; *3*, changing the length of the working day (shorter hours) and the length of the work week (fewer days).

The job performed in the test room consisted of assembling telephone relays,* a rather simple task which required approximately one minute per relay for each worker working alone, and involved putting together about thirty-five small parts and securing them with machine

* A relay is simply a switch operated by remote control.

screws. Six workers were chosen to participate in the Relay Assembly Test Room experiment, two selected by the researchers and the others chosen by these two workers.[6]

The researchers divided the experiment into a number of periods of different lengths during which time they introduced the variables, charted output, and, by means of the test room observer's daily history log, recorded behaviour and selected conversation. Before the workers were actually moved into the test room, their output was recorded for two weeks in the regular department. This was considered Period I in the experiment. In Period II the workers were moved into the test room but no other changes were introduced at this time. In Period III the workers' piece rate system was changed so that compensation was determined on the basis of the output of the five test workers, rather than as members of their former department of about one hundred workers. This change was not initially conceived as an experimental variable but it was later discovered to have had some positive effect on worker output, and subsequent studies (Second Relay Assembly Group and Mica Splitting experiment) were designed to assess its importance.[7] During Period IV the workers received two five-minute rest pauses each day, and with this change the first of the experimental variables was introduced. Periods V–VII continued the rest pauses but they varied as to length and frequency. In Period VII, in addition, a small lunch was served to the workers during the morning. Periods VIII–XIII involved variations in the length of the working day and in the length of the work week. A summary of the changes introduced through to Period XIII is reproduced below.[8]

Period	Length in weeks	Experimental conditions of work
I	2	Standard (i.e. 48 hrs., no rests, a.m. lunches; Sat. a.m. work)
II	5	Standard (moved to test room)
III	8	Standard (piece rate changed)
IV	5	Two 5-minute rests
V	4	Two 10-minute rests
VI	4	Six 5-minute rests
VII	11	15-minute a.m. rest and lunch; 10-minute p.m. rest
VIII	7	Same as VII, but 4.30 stop
IX	4	Same as VII, but 4.00 stop
X	12	Same as VII
XI	9	Same as VII, but Saturday a.m. off
XII	12	Standard (i.e. same as Period III)
XIII	31	Same as VII

What were the effects of the experiment upon productivity and worker morale? With respect, first, to productivity, they were startling. From Period I through Period XIII there was a general, secular upward trend in output, regardless of the introduction or withdrawal of rest periods, lunches, short days, short weeks, etc. (See Figure 1.) This unanticipated result strongly suggested that the changes in the physical conditions of work had little if anything to do with the improvements in output.[9] The following specific evidence supported this conclusion:

1. When in Period XII, after more than a year of experimental changes, the original conditions of work were restored and all previous privileges withdrawn—at this stage, 'the daily and weekly output rose to a point higher than at any other time. . . '.[10] In Period III, where 'standard' conditions prevailed (a full 48-hour week, no rest pauses or lunches), the five workers assembled less than 2,500 relays a week. In Period XII, under identical conditions, weekly output reached 2,900, a gain of nearly 20 per cent.[11] Increased skill in assembling the relays was not the answer as only experienced assemblers were chosen for the experiment in order to avoid the possible complications of learning.

2. In Periods VII, X, and XIII, physical conditions of work were once more identical and yet output rates varied widely, with higher figures for the later periods.

3. In Periods, X, XI, and XII, conditions varied enormously. In Periods XI, workers had two rest periods, lunches, and Saturday mornings off. During Period XII, standard conditions prevailed with no rests, lunches, or free Saturdays. Despite the differences in the physical conditions of these adjacent periods, output was roughly similar in all three.

Having concluded that there could be no simple and direct relationship between these physical conditions and productivity, the researchers proceeded to examine all of the following hypotheses: *1,* that productivity had increased over time due to a *gradual* relief from cumulative fatigue as a result of rest pauses, shorter hours, etc.; *2,* that productivity had increased over time due to a gradual relief from the monotony of the tasks due, once more, to the introduction of the experimental conditions; *3,* that the improvements were due to changes in the piece rate system; *4,* that increased output resulted from the superior material conditions and methods of work in the test room as compared with the regular department. All of these hypotheses were carefully explored and all were ultimately rejected.[12]

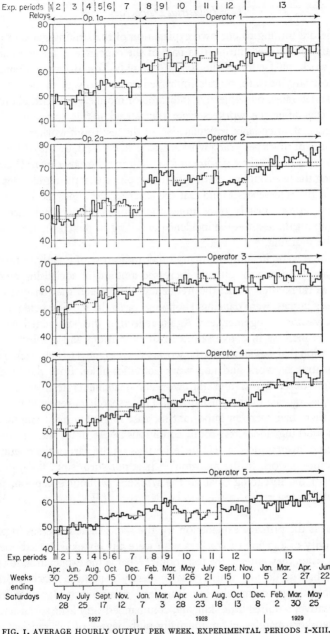

FIG. I. AVERAGE HOURLY OUTPUT PER WEEK, EXPERIMENTAL PERIODS I-XIII.
RELAY ASSEMBLY TEST ROOM.

(Source: F. J. Roethlisberger and W. J. Dickson, *Management and the Worker* [Harvard University Press, Cambridge, Mass., 1939], p. 76).

Before turning to our own explanation of the striking gains in productivity achieved during this part of the experiment, let us examine
the work satisfaction of the Relay Assembly Test Room workers. By
almost any measure, morale improved enormously in the test room.
Absentee rates, one objective indicator of morale, decreased about 80
per cent after the workers were transferred to the test room. The
number of 'attendance irregularities' of the test room workers (i.e. the
number of times per year a worker was sick, excused, or late) decreased
from 15·2 before the experiment to 3·5 during the experiment.[13] Comparing the test room workers with the employees in the regular department, the researchers found that the latter had $3\frac{1}{2}$ times the amount of
illness, approximately three times the number of personal absences,
and about three times the incidence of failing to punch the time clock
in the morning.[14]

There were, in addition, many other indicators of greatly improved
morale. One was the sharply increased amount of socialising among
the workers after work: the frequency with which they visited each
other's homes, went dancing, shopping, or to the movies, held parties,
took vacations together, etc. Again reflecting the heightened morale
was an increase in conversation in the test room and a spirit of co-
operation that was shown in the workers' willingness to help each other
in matters of work and non-work activities alike. Both the investigators' observations and the workers' statements testified to the
changed morale of the participants. The researchers repeatedly noted
that there had been 'an important increase in contentment among the
girls working under test-room conditions'.[15] At times the test room
observer even noticed a definite 'eagerness on the part of the operators
to come to work in the morning'.[16] It is not surprising, then, in the
light of the foregoing, that all the workers, without exception, preferred the test room to the regular department.[17]

What is the primary explanation for the remarkable increases in productivity of a group of workers who were already experienced operatives when they entered the test room? What is the explanation for the
fact that on a job which was endlessly repetitive (each worker
assembled approximately five hundred relays each day), entirely
uncreative, required little skill, and commanded very little social status,
the workers manifested an unusually high degree of job satisfaction?
I believe that a *major*, although of course not the exclusive, explanation
for the remarkable increases in productivity and morale lay in the

crucial role which the test room workers played in determining the conditions under which they worked. The operatives, from the very beginning of the experiment, were drawn into the decision-making process and achieved a large measure of direct and active control over their tasks and working conditions. In other words, a small but genuine dose of workers' participation was introduced into the test room, for reasons I shall discuss presently, along with the physical and technical changes. And unknown to the investigators, it was this element of participative management which helped to account for the improvements in the test room. What were crucial was not the physical changes themselves but the manner in which they were introduced.

In the following discussion I should like first to indicate just *why* the workers were brought into the decision-making process. Second, I shall describe the nature and extent of workers' participation in the test room. Finally, I shall discuss how the major chroniclers of this experiment, Roethlisberger and Dickson, have treated this element of workers' participation and how they lost sight of it after an initial recognition of its importance.

I

Why was workers' participation introduced into the test room? Needless to say, it cannot be traced to any syndicalist leanings of either the Harvard Business School or the Western Electric Company. Actually, it arose accidentally, as a result of the experimenters' desire to achieve what they considered a 'controlled experiment'. The study was originally designed to test the effects of various experimentally induced conditions (rests, lunches, shorter hours, etc.) upon efficiency and morale. In order to achieve valid results, the investigators believed that it was crucial not to upset or antagonise the workers in any way, and every effort had to be made to secure their complete co-operation in the experiment. As one writer said:

> . . . it was explicitly known that if the morale of the workers varied greatly, and specifically if they failed to be co-operative, the experiment could not be a success, so great pains were taken to secure and hold the co-operation of the workers.[18]

This superficially logical argument is actually methodologically fallacious, for the effect of trying to gain the workers' co-operation was *to introduce another variable* into the experiment and not, as the investigators assumed, to assure a more rigorously controlled situation.

Unaware of this, the researchers did carefully proceed to make every effort to gain the co-operation of the participants. And, significantly, the method chosen for securing the workers' co-operation was to give them, for the first time in their working lives, a substantial voice in the determination of their work situation in all its aspects. Thus, the introduction of workers' participation was due originally to an error in the research design of the experiment. By introducing a significant amount of worker self-determination, the researchers inadvertently changed the nature of the entire experiment, by bringing into play one of the most important independent variables of the study.

II

What were the nature and extent of this work group participation? In the Relay Assembly Test Room, workers' participation meant essentially that the operatives had frequent contact (through conferences, informal conversation and interviews) with supervisory and managerial personnel. The workers were consulted about the nature of the experimental changes, not merely informed of them. Their advice and counsel were sought, their suggestions and criticisms were heeded. In essence,

> ... each of the six operators ... was raised to the status of a chosen collaborator with a number of executives including a superintendent. This attitude of collaboration had been carefully fostered, and the operators were specifically told that they would be consulted about experimental changes and that their preferences would carry weight.[19]

Another account describes the changed patterns of authority as follows:

> The operators were advised of and consulted about changes to be made, and several plans suggested by the experimenters were not introduced because they met with the disapproval of the operators. The operators were questioned sympathetically about their reactions to the different conditions of work. Many of these discussions, in the beginning of the test, took place in the office of the superintendent.[20]

In the test room the traditional structure of industrial authority was altered. Formal control over the workers shifted more and more away from management at all levels to the experimenters who, for the sake of a 'controlled experiment', permitted the development of a measure of self-determination among the workers previously unknown and unheard of to them. At first, nominal control over the test room workers was vested in a foreman, but as his duties were principally in the regular department, jurisdiction fell increasingly to the test room observer. However, the function of the test room observer was not to exercise authority, but merely: '*1*, to keep accurate records of all that happened; and *2*, to create and maintain a friendly atmosphere in the test room.'[21]

The marked change in the pattern of industrial authority was evident from the very first meeting of the superintendent with the workers at the beginning of the experiment. According to the superintendent's notes of that occasion:

> We told them [the workers] that we had in mind trying out several changes in working conditions, such as rest periods, lunches, the various lengths of the working days and weeks, and that any changes of this sort would be discussed with the operators with the idea of getting their thoughts and comments before making the changes.[22]

In this manner the adoption of subsequent rest pauses, lunches, short days and weeks, etc., came about with the knowledge, advice, consent and collaboration of the test room workers. Mayo's account of the experiment, as well as that of Roethlisberger and Dickson, is peppered with references to the transformation of the authority pattern as discussed above. Mayo writes, for example: 'The question [of rest pauses] had been discussed beforehand with the operatives—as all subsequent changes were. . . .'[23] 'By arrangement with the workers' certain changes were introduced.[24] '. . . it had already been agreed between the workers and the officers in charge' that other conditions would be introduced.[25] And he speaks of the 'recurrent conferences with high executive authorities', and so on.[26]

Of course, the rights and powers of the test room workers were never formally set down, and in practice they fluctuated from one period to another. At certain times the workers had merely the right to obtain information from the experimenters, and from the company. More often they enjoyed the right of suggestion and advice. At other times their powers approached the opposite end of what might be called the control continuum, with the test room workers having the right of temporary veto, permanent veto, and occasionally even the right of sole jurisdiction.[27]

I should like now to quote briefly from the accounts of various conferences between the workers, the experimenters and the management in order to convey a more vivid picture of the specifics of the consultative process. A typical conference concerned the introduction of rest pauses. The meeting began with the supervisor discussing output curves for each of the operators.

The subject of the rest periods was then discussed. This led to a return to the curve charts for information concerning performance, and the low and high points of the day's activity [output rate] was pointed out. From this it was decided to fix rest periods. The girls were asked for any suggestions in this respect. The superintendent: 'How long do you think the rest periods should be?' Operator 2a suggested ten minutes and the other girls gave assent to this length of time.... Layout operator thought one minute periods each half hour better than five minutes at a time. The superintendent: 'When do you girls feel the rest periods should come, and when do you feel the most need of them?' Op. 1a: '10.00'. Op. 2a: '10.00' [etc].[28]

The morning rest pauses were finally set at 10.00 in line with the suggestions of the test room workers.

When it came to changes in the length of the working day (beginning with Period VIII), the workers were again consulted.

At a meeting of investigators and operators before beginning this period, the operators were given the opportunity of choosing between either starting work one-half hour later in the morning or stopping work one-half hour earlier in the afternoon. They unanimously chose the latter alternative. Consequently, the working day was shortened by stopping work at 4.30 p.m., instead of at 5.00 p.m. during Period VIII.[29]

For the next experimental period, number IX, it was decided to reduce hours still further, and the general plan was to cut another thirty minutes from the working day. However:

Before these plans were introduced, following the customary test room practice, they were presented to the operators for their approval. The operators expressed themselves in favour of shortening the day still further, apparently having confidence that their earnings would not be affected. At this meeting they were also given the choice of taking the additional time off by either starting work one hour later in the morning or stopping one hour earlier in the afternoon. Again they chose the latter alternative.[30]

Even when lunches were to be introduced, the workers were consulted, along with the company doctors, as to what should be served.[31]

The workers got so used to determining their own conditions of work that when their suggestions were occasionally overruled, they complained vociferously to management and to the investigators. At one meeting the question arose as to whether rest pauses in the coming period should take the form of six five-minute breaks scattered through the day or two fifteen-minute pauses, one in the morning and one in the afternoon. The workers unanimously preferred the fifteen-minute breaks but the investigators this time vetoed their decision and chose the five-minute breaks. The comments made by the workers to the observer-supervisor when the changes were introduced illustrate both their attitude toward authority and how they reacted to conditions introduced against their will.

> Op. 1a: 'I don't like these rest periods. I just get started to work, then have to stop. When I come back, I don't feel like working.'
> Op. 2a: 'I don't like it either.'
> Op. 3: 'I feel the same as Op. 2a does about it.'[32]

The observer then remarked that perhaps they would like it better after they had got used to it, whereupon Op. 4 replied frankly, 'I didn't like it yesterday or today, so why should I like it tomorrow?'.

The workers' attitude toward authority changed completely in the test room. The official observer in the room was also the workers' nominal supervisor but, as we have said, he was on strict instructions to avoid giving the impression that he was an authority figure, and his prime social function was to observe, record the workers' behaviour and conversation, and to oil the wheels of the experiment by doing everything possible to secure their co-operation.

The atmosphere of freedom in the test room was reflected in the workers' frank and informal manner toward their nominal supervisor. Many incidents typified this climate of freedom. One of them took place at one of the small 'parties' which the workers were granted as a concession for undergoing physical examinations every six weeks. At the party the workers mentioned to the supervisor that they hoped the experiment would continue for a long time because they preferred working in the test room to working in the regular department. When the supervisor remarked that conditions in both places were nearly alike, one worker disagreed strongly. Another agreed with the first, saying

> Op. 3: 'Yes, there are too many bosses in the [regular] department.'
> Op. 1: 'Yes, Mr. — [the observer] is the only boss we have.'
> Op. 2: 'Say, he's no boss. We don't have any boss.'
> Observer (starting to speak): 'But you know . . .'
> Op. 3: 'Shut up' [said good-naturedly].
> Op. 2: 'Look at that. Look at the way she tells her boss to shut up.'[33]

These examples, of course, could be multiplied, and all of them point to the fact that for these workers, the nature of industrial authority had been completely transformed. It was not merely a question of 'lenient supervision'; it went beyond that, as Mayo himself observed: 'Many times over, the history sheets and other records [in the test room] show that in the opinion of the group all supervision had been removed.'[34]

This radical transformation of authority and the introduction of a strong measure of self-determination among the workers were all the more significant because they were introduced suddenly into an industrial situation where a climate of fear and suspicion of authority had long prevailed. Even a cursory reading of *Management and the Worker* reveals a milieu where workers constantly feared the imposition of arbitrary discipline and punishment, including fear of dismissal and even being cheated out of their wages by the company.[35] The phenomenon of output restriction in the classic Bank Wiring Room experiment, to take merely one example, can be explained largely in terms of the workers' fear that any change in their productivity, up or down, might provoke an arbitrary, unpredictable, and undesirable response from the authorities. In that sense, fear froze their responses, as they believed that

> If we exceed our day's work by any appreciable amount, something will happen. The 'rate' might be cut, the 'rate' might be raised, the 'bogey' might be raised, someone might be laid off, or the supervisor might 'bawl out' the slower men.[36]

In such a context worker self-determination as it functioned in the test room represented a radical change from conditions existing elsewhere in the factory.

But this self-determination, nevertheless, had limits. What were these limits? In the German literature on co-determination there have evolved three categories of managerial decision-making in which labour may seek a role. These three areas of potential workers' participation at the enterprise level are:[37]

1. Personnel Decisions (including hiring, firing, promotions, transfers, on the job training, etc.);

2. Social Decisions (including administration of welfare programmes, health and safety regulations, pension funds, regulation of hours of work, vacation schedules, rest periods, etc.);

3. Economic Decisions (including; *a.* technical issues such as new methods of production, production planning and control and *b.* business matters such as product lines, sales, expansion or contraction of operations, rationalisation, capital investment, distribution and use of profits, changes in plant organisation, mergers, etc.).

Applying these categories to the test room situation, we see that the workers there had jurisdiction over Social Decisions only. They had no jurisdiction over Personnel Decisions (hiring, firing, and promotion), and none over Economic Decisions whether of a technical or a commercial nature. The self-determination of the test room workers was thus sharply circumscribed and yet it had significant effects.

How did the workers themselves explain their satisfaction with the test room situation and their increased productivity in it? It is not surprising that they tended to account for it in terms of the alteration of the authority patterns and the introduction of worker self-determination in a limited yet important area. At first puzzled by their own improvement, the workers eventually began to understand it in terms of 'a freedom from constraints or "interferences" which operated' in the experimental situation.[38] As a result the workers lost 'what came to be called their "apprehension of authority" '.[39] They began to interact more spontaneously with each other and with management as the experiment progressed and they developed new enthusiasm for their work as they lost their shyness and fear.[40] Agreeing unanimously that they preferred working in the test room to working in the regular department, the workers, when questioned, mentioned such factors as 'no bosses', 'less supervision', 'freedom', 'the way we are treated'.[41]

In short, this rather modest experiment in workers' participation introduced inadvertently by the researchers 'was hailed by the operators as a major revolution in their whole situation; it had the force of a Magna Carta or of a Declaration of Independence . . .'[42] and accounted in large measure for their improvements in efficiency and their heightened job satisfaction. Self-determination helped to account for the improvements by acting upon the workers in at least two ways: *1*, it increased their sense of responsibility toward and identification with their jobs, as they were now deeply involved in helping to set the conditions under which they would work most satisfactorily; *2*, it enhanced their social status as they now spoke with an authoritative voice with management, and the social distance between management and the workers, once enormous, suddenly shrank to near insignificance. Thus, changes in the structure of power (self-determination) acted through a psychological dimension (increased sense of responsibility and identification with job) and a status dimension (decreased social distance from management) to effect the improvements noted. However important these intervening conditions were, though, it was the alteration in the structure of authority that was the determining factor.

We have seen that the workers themselves tended to explain their
improvements in terms of the introduction of a limited measure of industrial self-determination. How did the researchers account for these
changes? Ironically, what was quite clear to the workers was not nearly
so apparent to the investigators whose conclusions were indefinite and
prone to vacillate over time. Initially, the experimenters did seem to
agree with the workers that the element of self-determination was
largely responsible for the observed changes and improvements. For
example, the officer in charge of the experiment reported quite early
that:

> Important factors in the production of a better mental attitude and
> greater enjoyment of work have been the greater freedom, less strict
> supervision and the opportunity to vary from a fixed pace without
> reprimand from a gang boss.[43]

And Roethlisberger and Dickson say at one point:

> According to one hypothesis [presumably accepted by the authors but
> here, as elsewhere, left rather vague], the altered type of supervision in
> the Relay Assembly Test Room had been the change which seemed to
> be more closely associated with the continued improvement in the out-
> put of the workers than any other. A new supervisor-employee relation-
> ship had developed in which there existed a spirit of co-operation with
> the experimenters and management.[44]

However, this is not to say that the experimenters ultimately drew
conclusions similar to those presented here. This is most certainly not
the case and in this regard three observations must be made.

1. First, it must be carefully noted that the prime mover here was
not conceived of by the experimenters as anything so potentially
radical as industrial self-determination for workers. Rather, as the
terminology above suggests, the entire matter was conceptualised as a
problem in 'supervision', and the lessons to be learned were that what
was needed was merely the training of more understanding, patient,
and sympathetic supervisors. The inferences which were initially drawn
from the Relay Assembly Room Experiment were that the supervisory
system, as it existed, needed minor improvements. There was never a
major questioning of the *basic premises* of the system of industrial
authority itself. Thus, although the study pointed, at least in a tentative way within the rather narrow limits of its methodological sound-
ness, in quite a radical direction, the experimenters themselves

narrowed the implications of the study by conceptualising them in terms of a conservative or, at the most, a 'reformist' framework. In so doing the experimenters failed to grasp the potentially more far-reaching implications of their own research, and, despite suggestive evidence to the contrary, they stayed faithfully within the framework of their own traditional thinking.

Occasionally there is a breakthrough as when Mayo writes that 'what the company actually did for the group [of relay assembly workers] was to reconstruct entirely its whole industrial situation'. It created 'a new industrial milieu in which their own [the workers'] self-determination and their social well-being ranked first and the work was incidental'.[45] However, this line of thought is not continued and the thread is rapidly lost.

2. The fact that the experimenters did not fully treat the broader implications which their research suggested is not the major fault in their interpretation of the Relay Assembly Test Room experiment, however. What is more important is that even these moderate conclusions, i.e. regarding supervision, were lost sight of in the enormous mass of data collected by the experimenters and presented by Roethlisberger and Dickson. And it is a striking fact that by the end of the volume this modest explanation in terms of supervisory changes disappears; and, more important, there is finally no clear cut, consistent, and forthright statement as to the meaning or significance of the Relay Assembly Room experiment at all, in spite of the lavish amount of time, effort, and attention expended on it. In other words, in the final analysis, the researchers were unable to give any satisfactory explanation for the changes that occurred in the Relay Assembly Test Room. If one asks why the explanation in terms of supervision was abandoned, one must conclude, after a careful reading of *Management and the Worker*, that this explanation was actually forgotten rather than discounted after a systematic examination of the evidence. Let us see how this occurred.

After the first two years of the Relay Assembly Test Room experiment, the investigators had decided tentatively that the change in supervision was an important factor affecting the great improvement in morale and productivity. This initial conclusion, however, was very hesitantly stated and the researchers preferred to assign causation to the very vague factors of employee 'attitudes and pre-occupations'.[46] Nevertheless, it was decided to launch an ambitious interview programme among the workers at the Hawthorne plant in order to elicit their opinions and complaints on the matter of supervision with an eye to improving supervisory policy in line with the workers' suggestions. An official document on the original intent of the interviewing programme clearly places its genesis in the desire to improve the supervisory system.

> It was thought that if all employees could be interviewed and their honest complaints secured, they would give a comprehensive picture of the supervisory practices followed and of the desirability of these practices.[47]

But in spite of the fact that the original purpose of the interview programme, which ultimately reached 20,000 Hawthorne employees, was to ascertain the opinions of the workers regarding *supervision*, this original purpose was soon abandoned and the conclusions hesitatingly drawn from the Relay Assembly Test Room experiment were forgotten. How did this occur?

After the interviewing programme began the investigators saw that they could isolate three types of complaints commonly made by the workers. These types varied according to the extent to which they could be objectively verified. The first type referred to complaints easily verified, e.g. 'this machine is out of order', 'this tool is not sharp'. A second type of complaint was more difficult to assess by objective tests, such as 'the work is hard', 'it is too hot in the factory', 'the lockers are dirty', and so on. The third type of complaints consisted mainly of subjective judgments difficult to verify by objective measurement: 'piece rates are too low', 'ability doesn't count around here', etc. As the interviewing proceeded the investigators tended more and more to take into consideration and take at face value only those complaints of the first and sometimes second category which could be evaluated by a 'competent engineer'. All other complaints, particularly regarding persons (including supervisors especially) and company policy which necessarily involved more subjective conditions and value judgments, were discounted. Gradually the investigators began to refuse to take at face value the manifest content of these kinds of complaints, as the workers expressed them in interviews. It was decided that these complaints were really only external manifestations of problems which the worker was having in his private life.

> They are complaints which refer to the significant personal and social life of the worker, and apart from such a context they are meaningless. They cannot be assessed apart from the situation of the individual who makes them.[48]

In other words the manifest content of the complaints about supervision and company policy were largely ignored and were interpreted most commonly as an expression of some psychological malady. A distinction was readily made, therefore, between the manifest and the latent function of the workers' complaints. In making this distinction the interviewers felt that they

> had good reasons to believe that certain grievances, although directed toward some object or person, were not due to some deficiency in the object criticised but rather were expressions of concealed, perhaps unconscious, disturbances in the employee's situation.[49]

Thus, workers' complaints of low wages, long hours, autocratic supervisors, and unhealthy working conditions were now interpreted, not as having much basis in fact, but simply as irrational expressions of such things as domestic squabbles, 'overdominating fathers', and the like.[50]

The entire interview programme, which had initially been designed to explore the ramifications of work group participation, or altered supervision as it was conceptualised, was now diverted from its original purpose. In addition, the study at this point lost its sociological orientation as the investigators turned to an almost exclusively psychological interpretation of the interviews. Moreover, the experiment became markedly ideological at this stage as the investigators, consciously or unconsciously, began to employ a device often used to discredit social, political, or economic turbulence: seeking out and 'exposing' the psychological roots of this unrest and, in so doing, ignoring or belittling the manifest content of the grievances themselves.

Shortly after the interviewing programme began, then, the entire emphasis of the experiment changed, from considerations of workers' control to those related to bowel control. 'The important consideration' now according to the researchers, 'was not whether his [a worker's] complaint was justified but why he felt the way he did'.[51] What the investigators did not realise was that by discounting the workers' manifest complaints about supervision and by claiming that they had little intrinsic merit in themselves except as symptoms of deeper psychological disturbances or needs, they could no longer explain the improvements that had occurred in the Relay Assembly Test Room experiment. If workers had no legitimate complaints against supervision, as the investigators began to assume, then how was it possible to account for the great improvements in morale and productivity in the Relay Assembly Test Room where supervision had been so radically altered? How was it possible to explain the fact that outside the test room as well, workers tended to 'respond at once to any slight betterment in [their] social conditions of work'?[52]

The investigators soon began to realise the limitations of this purely psychological interpretation of workers' grievances. This approach tended to make the work situation entirely irrelevant to the workers' satisfaction as the work place became merely an arena where the workers' psychological symptoms were played out. It became increasingly difficult for the investigators to discount the work situation as a factor of importance in itself, especially after it was repeatedly demonstrated that changes in the work situation did affect the workers' state of mind and his productivity. Furthermore, when there was adequate cause for dissatisfaction in the workers' immediate work situation, it took the investigators too far afield, unnecessarily far afield, to seek the causes for dissatisfaction in the workers' personal life situation.

Eventually, therefore, this exclusively psychological approach was dropped. But what is crucial is that when the investigators turned away from this psychological orientation, they did not return to the original problem of the interview programme: the question of supervision and its reform. Since its inception, the interview programme had grown enormously. After 'only' 10,000 interviews were completed (there were an additional 10,000 before it was finished), the investigators had compiled some 86,000 comments on ninety different subjects aside from supervision. In this mass of data the issue of supervision was ultimately forgotten and along with it was also forgotten the major lesson of the Relay Assembly Test Room experiment, namely that changes in 'supervision' had had striking effects on worker morale and productivity although the technical processes of work remained unchanged. This was in the beginning partially recognised by the researchers, as we have seen, and the massive interview programme was designed to explore this theme further. Here the thread was lost, however. The attention of the investigators was soon diverted to psychological factors in the workers' statements of discontent. After this approach was found relatively unsatisfactory, the interviewing orientation turned away from excessive psychologising of complaints in favour of a diffuse study of in-plant social relations.

> It became clear that many employee comments which had formerly been interpreted in terms of the interviewee's personal situation could be better understood if they were interpreted in the light of the employee's existing social organisation of the group with which he worked

and his position in that group. The advantages of this concept, the investigators felt, was that it enabled them to return from the study of personal situations to the study of factory situations.[53]

Note the absence here of any consideration of the issues of supervision. That subject was somehow lost in the shuffle and lost, too, is any further attempt to explain the meaning of the changes that occurred in the test room. At any rate, this return to sociological considerations led, after a time, to the famous Bank Wiring Room experiment and from that, to the subsequent 'discovery' of the informal organisation operating within the framework of a formal organisation.

The focus on formal and informal organisation eventually led to a re-definition of the significance of the Relay Assembly Test Room experiment. Its final significance to the investigators lay merely in the fact that it illustrated the existence of an informal organisation which worked 'in harmony with the aims of management', in contrast to the Bank Wiring Room experiment where the primary group undermined management's goals. Earlier in the volume, Roethlisberger and Dickson had spoken of the importance of supervisory changes in accounting for the improvement in the test room. True, these references had been mild, hesitant, and restrained. But by the end of the volume the original conclusions of this study, which had been stated tentatively, were nearly forgotten altogether, lost amid the mass of material collected and presented. All that they felt could be said after years of experiment and nearly six hundred pages of text was that:

> What the Relay Assembly Test Room experiment showed was that when innovations are introduced carefully and with regard to the actual sentiments of the workers, the workers are likely to develop a spontaneous type of informal organisation which will not only express more adequately their own values and significances but also is more likely to be in harmony with the aims of management.[54]

What it means to introduce innovations 'carefully' and 'with regard to the actual sentiments of the workers' we are never told. However vague this statement is, it tells us in no uncertain terms that the investigators were, after all, unable to understand or explain the lessons of the Relay Assembly Test Room experiment.

3. The Forgotten Lessons of the Mayo Experiments: II

'Yes, they pampered us at first, and now they take everything away from us. You know, we used to like to come to work. Now we just come to get the money.'—*Test Room Worker*

In the previous chapter, we attempted to reappraise the meaning of the famous Relay Assembly Test Room experiment, the first of the Mayo studies. There, we recapitulated the general findings of the study: a remarkable increase in productivity and an equally impressive decline in work alienation among those workers employed in the test room itself. We traced the explanations of these findings which the major chroniclers of that study, Roethlisberger and Dickson, offered in their treatise on these experiments, and found that, in the final analysis, their explanations for the changes which occurred in the test room were diffuse, vague, inconclusive, and vacillating. Most important, we attempted to demonstrate that a 'forgotten variable', the 'accidental' introduction of a considerable measure of 'workshop democracy'—the workers' acquisition of the right to determine, in consultation with management and the researchers, their actual conditions of work—was undoubtedly a crucial factor in the improvements noted in the test room. On almost every issue of importance, the workers were consulted, their advice and consent sought, their opinions given equal weight with those of management, their decisions promptly acted upon—all this in conjunction with the almost total disappearance of externally-imposed discipline and supervision. In brief, the entire system of industrial authority which these workers had been accustomed to labouring under was transformed during the experiment, as the test room workers developed into an almost self-governing body. In spite of the momentous import of this social transformation, however, it was almost totally overlooked by the researchers and the major chroniclers of the experiment.

Our objectives in the present chapter are twofold. First, we shall trace the Relay Assembly Test Room experiment to its unhappy demise and attempt to demonstrate that, just as the rise of 'workers' participation' led in the initial stages of the experiment to a striking improvement both in morale and productivity, so the gradual withdrawal of the right of workers' participation later on led to disillusionment among the test room workers and to a corresponding increase in work alienation and stagnation in their performance.

Secondly, we shall attempt to describe the entirely inadequate treatment which a generation of sociology textbook writers have accorded this significant experiment, a treatment which in all ways matches the inadequacy of Roethlisberger and Dickson's original discussion.

The two most well-known accounts of the Relay Assembly Test Room experiment, found in Mayo[1] and Roethlisberger and Dickson,[2] describe the study only midway through 1929 and, as a result, it is commonly believed that the experiment ended at that time.[3] Even Henry Landsberger, who did a meticulous re-examination of the Hawthorne Studies, speaks of the Relay Assembly Test Room as a two and a half year experiment.[4] However, the experiment did not end in 1929 after thirteen test periods, but continued, albeit under entirely different conditions, until 1932. Actually, the last half of the experiment, which has been completely ignored by most writers, is just as significant as the first half which has received exclusive attention. A vivid account of this later period is given by T. N. Whitehead.[5]

What makes the period after 1929 so important is that one of the most crucial independent variables of the entire experiment, the workers' participation in the decision-making process, was seriously abridged and frequently eliminated altogether during this time. The termination of workers' participation was not consciously planned as an experiment to measure the effect of its absence upon the workers as was, for example, the termination of rest periods or lunches. Rather, it was an accidental, unintended, and even unnoticed consequence of two separate events occurring at about this time. The first event was the experimenters' gradual loss of interest in the Relay Assembly Test Room experiment; the second was the onset of the economic depression.

How did these two basically unrelated events operate to choke off workers' participation in decision-making which had developed over the previous two and a half years? The first event, the gradual loss of interest in the experiment, was a consequence of two things:

1. The experimenters' basic confusion and perplexity over the meaning of the improvements that had occurred in the test room. Ironically, despite the extraordinary amount of time, thought, attention,

and effort which had gone into the experiment, the investigators never really emerged with a firm, precise, definite, or convincing explanation for the observed changes. This is reflected most strikingly in Roethlisberger and Dickson's very vague, general, and changing interpretations of the experiment. It seemed to the researchers at first to be a matter of supervisory changes, but this was never accepted without reservation. Often, at this point, their explanation had recourse to factors of employee attitudes and pre-occupations which really meant very little. Finally, the experiment was deemed important because it demonstrated how a primary group within a large organisation could act to reinforce the goals of that organisation; but the investigators never really explained just why this had occurred in the Relay Assembly Test Room.

It was this basic confusion among the investigators that led, not, as perhaps it should have, to a heightened interest in the project and renewed efforts to locate the crucial variables, but instead to growing indifference and neglect of the experiment.

2. The second factor involved in the experimenters' loss of interest was an indirect consequence of the first. Not knowing how to interpret their results, the researchers, especially in the later stages, really lost control of the experiment. They introduced changes haphazardly, pointlessly, without any clear research design, without much expectation of what they might or might not find, and without really knowing what their findings might prove or disprove. This phase of the Relay Assembly Test Room experiment was the least rigorous of the none-too-rigorous Hawthorne Studies. Because the experiment had left the researchers adrift with, admittedly, a few leads, they turned their attention increasingly in other directions. After 1929 the interview programme and ultimately the Bank Wiring Room experiment began to capture more and more of the imagination and attention of the researchers.

How did this situation affect the participation of the test room workers in setting their own conditions of work? Gradually, as the researchers' interest in the experiment waned, they became less willing to consult the workers concerning the changes to be introduced into the test room. The workers in these later years saw and met with supervisory personnel less and less frequently. Changes were introduced arbitrarily from above, and often on very short notice. Here is one of many examples that demonstrates the remarkable changes that had come about during the second half of the experiment.

The operators' seating arrangements were changed during the morning of 9th February 1931, and they were only informed of this an hour or so beforehand. It is true that Operator 1 seems to have heard some rumour, but to the rest, the changes came as a complete surprise.[6]

This new method of introducing changes was contrary to the methods employed earlier in the experiment, and represented an almost complete erosion of the self-determination to which the workers had become accustomed. Whitehead makes this significant comparison between the earlier and the later phases of the experiment.

> For the first two years no changes took place without some sort of conference in which the operators participated and their opinions were asked and given weight. This procedure gradually died out and the collaboration between the operators and the supervisory ranks somewhat altered in character. At first, experimentally controlled situations were the keynote of the experiment and the co-operation of the operators was eagerly sought; but by 1931 the Test Room was continuing with no very clear notion as to its precise value. Willingness on the part of the operators was tacitly assumed, and changes in working routines were insensibly removed from their field of consideration.[7]

This, then, was one element in the decline of workers' participation in the test room after 1929. The other element, equally important, was the economic depression, which further disrupted the experiment and interfered with what little worker self-determination remained. After May 1930, the 'experimental changes' introduced into the test room came to be determined, not by the workers, nor even by the experimenters, but by the exigencies of the depression. Thus, the depression dictated short work weeks, shortened daily hours, lay-offs, and the like. When this happened, the workers' control over their jobs suddenly became more remote than it ever had before. Hours, wages, conditions, and the like were now controlled by large, impersonal economic forces which the workers were powerless to control and unable to understand. The test room in the early 1930s became America in microcosm and the observer's records of the workers' behaviour, conversation, and circumstances, is an interesting piece of American social history aside from the experiment itself. The workers became preoccupied with lay-offs and reduced working time, as rumours of catastrophe spread wildly through the plant. Announcements of lay-offs, short weeks, and short days came often and with little warning, all of which the test room workers received with various emotions ranging from fear, alarm, despair, and hysteria to resignation and courage. One by one the ranks of the test room operators were decimated by lay-offs, and ultimately, when the last worker was fired, the experiment which had lingered on for years with no apparent purpose finally came to an unhappy end.

What were the effects upon the workers of these two events—the investigators' loss of interest in the experiment and the onset of the depression—both of which so greatly reduced the workers' self-determination? In order to describe the significance of these events, it might be helpful to compare the attitudes of the test room workers in the first half of the experiment with their attitudes under subsequent conditions outlined above. During the first phase of the experiment (roughly until the middle of 1929), the operators regarded their jobs as far more important and significant than the mere assembling of telephone relays. The workers 'ceased to be factory hands in their own thinking and became collaborators, not only in the arrangement of their activities, but in a research of high future significance'.[8] Their entire work situation injected an element of meaning and purpose into their lives which had been absent heretofore. For the most intelligent, articulate, and ambitious of the test room workers, the experiment represented 'a progressive escape from the boredom of a routine occupation'.[9] For this worker the new situation promised to lead to 'the achievement of some unspecified position of significance, in which daily life should be transformed from a routine process into a complexity of interesting and important events. The low activity of relay assembling was to emerge as a life's adventure.'[10]

In the second half of the experiment everything changed. The workers' previously ill-defined but high hopes were smashed. Disillusionment and demoralisation set in as the control and the status which the workers had achieved earlier declined disastrously. The routine nature of the operators' job had been temporarily obscured during the early part of the experiment partly because of the control which the workers had come to exercise over their conditions of work. Once this was taken away, first by the experimenters' loss of interest in the test, and then by the depression, the intrinsically unfulfilling aspects of their jobs reasserted themselves and severe boredom set in. Comments by the workers expressing impatience and disinterest with their repetitive tasks became very common now, of which the following is but one example.

Op. 2: 'Relay after relay, day after day, year after year, won't there ever be anything different?'
Op. 4: 'That's all, relay after relay.'

Op. 1: 'Get married.'
Op. 2: 'Yea, get married, then I'll have to come back and make more relays.'[11]

Comments such as these were rarely, if ever, heard during the first two years of the experiment.

Besides this notable increase in the workers' boredom with their jobs, there were other manifestations of discontent at this time. The incidence of complaints about minor irritations (noises, temperature, visitors, the number of faulty parts) increased markedly.[12] Also, it was noted that the workers began to quarrel and argue among themselves much more frequently than they ever had before.[13]

After a temporary period of disillusionment and disorientation after 1929, the operators managed to achieve a new equilibrium and source of satisfaction, not in the job itself, but in sociability with the other members of the work group, and at this point dissension among the workers tended to diminish. However, as this pleasure in sociability was a substitute for the previous enjoyment they had taken in their work and their participation in setting the conditions of it, there remained a residue of disappointment and resentment which carried over until the very end of the experiment.[14]

The workers' productivity also showed marked changes during the second phase of the experiment. Whereas output had continued to rise during the first two years of the experiment, during the later stages it ceased to improve at all, though it never fell back to the level at the beginning of the experiment until the last disastrous months of the study when the operators began to be laid off. At this point output fell precipitously to a level lower than at any time during the five years of the experiment.

Those who have pointed to the factor of 'supervision' as being the key to the changes in the Relay Assembly Test Room experiment are not only depoliticising the study, but are misinterpreting it as well. We have seen that a form of alienation—boredom, unrest, disinterest, nervousness, irritability, disillusionment—set in among the workers during the second half of the experiment which contrasted greatly with the high morale of the operators during the first half of the study. It is difficult to understand how 'supervision' *per se* could have accounted for the adverse changes during the later part of the experiment, for supervision in the test room remained *constant*—lenient and permissive—throughout the five years of the experiment and did not change after 1929. The degree of direct workers' participation in decision-making, however, did undergo a marked change after 1929, and its decline was roughly coincidental with the rise of disaffection among the workers.

Of course it would be presumptuous in the extreme to attempt to explain all the changes in the test room by reference to this one variable. Threatened unemployment, especially toward the final days of the experiment, undoubtedly had an independently adverse effect upon productivity and morale. Also, as the interest of the investigators in the experiment declined, the so-called 'Hawthorne effect' upon the workers necessarily diminished, as the test room workers increasingly came to be treated no differently from all the other workers in the plant.

Nevertheless, we should like to argue that the importance of the Relay Assembly Test Room experiment consisted, not in what the study 'proved', but the direction in which it pointed. Unfortunately this direction was obscured by the inability of Mayo and Roethlisberger and Dickson to spell out clearly the possible importance of the factor of workers' self-determination in accounting for the remarkable changes that occurred during the entire five years of the experiment.

How has the Relay Assembly Test Room experiment been treated by a generation of sociology textbook writers? Have the lessons of that experiment, forgotten by Roethlisberger and Dickson, been remembered by subsequent textbook writers? Have they succeeded in clarifying the exact meaning of the experiment where the major chroniclers of it have failed?

Unfortunately, the ambiguities found in Roethlisberger and Dickson have been mirrored and even magnified by the sociology textbook writers of the last quarter century. I have selected a large sample of introductory sociology and industrial sociology textbooks (twenty-eight and nine respectively) written in the United States since 1940 and done a content analysis of their treatment of the Relay Assembly Test Room experiment. One of the major deficiencies of these texts in their analysis of the experiment is the diffuseness of the language they use in discussing the meaning of the study. The writers often refer to numerous social or social psychological factors which presumably produced the changes in the test room, but they do so in language which lacks specificity, concreteness, and precision. Unsure of the actual meaning of the experiment, many writers hide behind a screen of generalities. Miller and Form, a model of vagueness, say in a summary table

> . . . an experimental study of five girls assembling telephone relays in a test room has shown the importance of feelings and attitudes . . . it was the social organisation among the test room operators which caused the differences in production.[15]

Elbridge says, only a little more clearly, that

> The researches of Mayo and others have demonstrated the crucial importance of social relations in a plant—both those among the operatives and between the operatives and their supervisors. Mayo shows that a worker is not satisfied unless he understands the goal of his work—the purpose it is to serve—and that he wishes to serve an economic function deemed valuable to his group; they want to be trusted and given a measure of responsibility. The kind of fellowship permitted by plant relationships is also of much significance.[16]

Neither does Chinoy cast much light on the precise meaning of the experiment.

> It appeared clear that the attitudes of the girls and their feelings about their work were of strategic importance. Moreover, good relations with supervisors and the positive atmosphere inadvertently created in the experimental situation by soliciting co-operation and paying close attention to the girls had so improved their morale that they continued to increase their production even when rest periods were taken away and other advantages provided at various stages of the inquiry were eliminated.[17]

There is an elusiveness of meaning throughout these analyses which is disturbing. The vagueness, of course, cannot be blamed entirely upon these writers, for it is partly traceable to the uncertainty, ambiguity, and indecisiveness of Roethlisberger's and Dickson's own explanation of the exact meaning of this study.

If one seeks to explain the improvements in the test room *concretely*, and by recourse to sociological, rather than physical, factors as, of course, most sociology texts do, then it is possible to point to three social changes which might have been responsible:[18] *1*, the transformation of traditional patterns of industrial *power* or *authority* which permitted the workers to determine the conditions of their work; *2*, the creation among the workers of a cohesive *primary group*; *3*, the awareness among the workers of the importance of the experiment and the enhanced *status* they achieved from participating in it and performing well (the 'Hawthorne effect').

When we examine a great number of sociology textbooks to discover which of the three explanations is most commonly employed, we find that the textbook writers, following closely the Human Relations in Industry approach, have ignored almost all questions of industrial *power* which this experiment has seriously raised, and instead have concentrated almost exclusively upon the dimensions of status, prestige, and the primary group. One typical account of the experiment, for example, explains it as follows: 'Elton Mayo's famous Hawthorn [*sic*] study indicates the importance of the workers feeling important if the morale necessary to efficient production is to be maintained.'[19] More 'systematically', the author adds later that:

> The Hawthorne experiment . . . proved that the way to get employees to work hard and enthusiastically was to: *1*, make the worker feel that his work is important; *2*, make the worker feel that he is important; *3*, recognise the fact that workers develop a social system and that the factory is a part of society.[20]

This short quotation contains four elements which are typically found in textbook treatments of the Relay Assembly Test Room experiment: *1*, status considerations receive paramount attention ('make the worker feel that he is important'); *2*, there is little or no reference to matters of industrial power or control; *3*, there is an unexamined acceptance of the managerial *Weltanschauung*; *4*, there is a chronic diffuseness and ambiguity of language ('recognise . . . that the factory is a part of society'). Some or all of these elements can be found in the following quotations.

In the first edition of his introductory text, Green claims that morale improved in the test room because the workers 'had been made to feel important'.[21] He adds that the major lesson which industrial sociology teaches

> is that workers . . . are primarily motivated by sentiment and loyalty, by the desire to belong and to feel important to other people, rather than by rational considerations of wages, hours, efficiency, and physical comfort.[22]

Another introductory textbook author claims that the Relay Assembly Test Room experiment proved that '. . . the worker must be treated and respected as an individual personality if he is to be contented and efficient in his work'.[23] Still another author offers essentially the same explanation, while also pointing to the importance of the primary group.

> The fact that the workers became a team with high *esprit de corps*, that they had become important to management as part of a major experiment, and that they had attracted favourable attention from fellow workers who were not included in the study operated in subtle ways to affect their rate of production.[24]

Many authors abdicate an explanation of the experiment altogether and instead fall back upon quoting long passages from Stuart Chase's *Men at Work* whose popular account stresses changing workers' attitudes, enhancing their status by making them feel important and satisfying their need for belonging, and re-establishing in the modern factory a 'clan unity which the machine age has stripped away'.[25]

Long ago, C. Wright Mills criticised the emphasis on status rather than on power in the Human Relations school, a criticism which applies equally well to recent textbook writers. 'Not only is the analysis of power almost absent', says Mills, 'but the facts of power are obscured and blurred in the vocabulary of the human relations experts'.[26] 'Why', Mills asks in language which is reminiscent of his critique of Lloyd Warner, 'are class and power not only minimised and made subordinate to status, but even sponged up into it?'[27]

One answer is that this subtle shift from a discussion of the power and control dimensions to the status and prestige dimensions effectively depoliticises the implications of this particular experiment. It is far easier and less politically portentous to make the worker feel that he belongs and is important than it is to tamper with the structure of industrial authority. There is probably no direct and conscious political motive at work here; most writers merely take the present framework of industrial authority as given, and their sociological imagination operates only within the boundaries of this framework.

By pointing out that most textbook writers err in discussing this experiment solely in terms of status and prestige, I am not arguing the other extreme, namely that one should discuss power alone and not status, or that the two are incompatible as explanations. On the contrary, both factors are significant. But it is important to bear in mind that if enhanced status of the test room workers was a factor in their improved satisfaction and efficiency—and most certainly it was—then one must also recognise that it was the increased *power* of the workers which enhanced their status. Increased power put them for the first time on equal or nearly equal terms with their 'superiors', it made them collaborators instead of subordinates, it enhanced their feelings of importance by entrusting them with a key voice in the determination of crucial conditions. Power was the means by which job satisfaction was increased as it worked through the status dimension. In this sense, power (or control)———→increased status———→ improvements in morale and productivity. Thus, the mistake that most textbook writers have made in interpreting this experiment is that by treating only the factor of social status, they have focused exclusively upon an intervening variable, while neglecting a crucial antecedent variable.

Certainly the generalisations one can draw from the Relay Assembly Test Room experiment are limited. In fact, Argyle concluded after a careful examination of the study—including the size and selection of the sample, the uncontrolled effects of the experimental situation itself, inadequate consideration of the possibility that physical changes might have played a role after all, the fluctuations of external economic conditions, the inadequate standardisation of the control groups, the highly selective recording of the test room observer—that 'no valid conclusions can be drawn from the experiment in the Relay Assembly Test Room'.[28] But even with all these criticisms of the experiment itself, he nevertheless believes that altered 'supervision' played a significant but incalculable role in accounting for the changes in the test room, in spite of the fact that the methodology of the study is much too faulty to permit exact determination of the importance of one factor or another.

But in the final analysis, the importance of this ground-breaking experiment lies not in what it unalterably 'proved' but the direction in which it is pointed. Subsequent research should have explored further the trail which this experiment tentatively began.

Granted, for a decade or more following the appearance of *Management and the Worker*, the emerging Human Relations in Industry school did concentrate some attention on the problem of supervision.[29] Moreover, the Hawthorne studies also inspired a rash of books, pamphlets, and company manuals purporting to teach the techniques of successful supervision.[30] But it is crucial to note that these studies and other publications involved minor alterations in supervisory practices, and did not have any larger conception of basic changes in the structure of industrial authority. The publications stressed personality, not structural changes in supervision. In so doing this school sought to give the worker the *illusion* of control without giving him the reality of it; they thereby opened themselves up to the charge often made against them that by helping to alter superficial excesses of supervision they aid realisation of company goals by means of manipulation rather than by the more direct, but sociologically obsolete, methods of coercion. In this regard, Mills says that the final advice of this school to the industrial manager is to relax his authoritarian manner and widen his manipulative grip by understanding employees better and countering their informal solidarities against management by controlling and exploiting these solidarities for smoother and less troublesome managerial efficiency.[31]

In this critique of the Mayo school, Mills presents a model which seeks to relate worker satisfaction to participation in decision-making.[32]

		OBJECTIVE STRUCTURE OF POWER	
		participates	does not participate
	cheerful and willing	1 the unalienated worker	2 manipulated pseudo-morale; management's goal to gather workers here
SUBJECTIVE CONDITION OF INDIVIDUAL	uncheerful and unwilling	3 malcontent; the unadjusted worker	4 the alienated worker

In cell one, Mills places the self-managing craftsman, the unalienated worker, Whitman's 'man in the open air'. Cell two for Mills represents the worker who is a victim of manipulated or pseudo-morale. This, says Mills, is management's ideal: the cheerful and willing worker who does not participate. In cell three is the participating worker who is nonetheless dissatisfied. Mills calls him the malcontent, the unadjusted worker. For Mills, the natural state of any worker who 'participates' is cheerfulness and willingness, and any worker who does participate but is still uncheerful and unwilling is not understandable except in terms of that worker's abnormality. The fourth cell represents the truly alienated worker, one who does not participate nor is his attitude cheerful and willing toward his work.

Although this model represents a very oversimplified view, it nevertheless clarifies the orientation of the Human Relations approach. The treatment of 'supervision' begun by the Hawthorne experiments and continued by their Human Relations in Industry descendants represents a preoccupation with the right half of this model only. These researchers have been interested in discovering why workers are in cell four and they have been concerned with the methods and techniques of moving workers from cell four to cell two (personal interviews, pseudo-participation, etc.). At the same time, the left half of the model, the participative half, has been completely neglected.

In terms of Mills' paradigm, it has been our argument that one of the most important—and forgotten—lessons of the Relay Assembly Test Room experiment is the importance of a concern with the participative half of this model and the implications of moving workers from cell four to cell one.

4. Proposed Solutions to Work Alienation

Although modern discussions of work alienation begin with Marx's 1844 *Economic and Philosophical Manuscripts*, there is evidence that Western thinkers since the Greeks have believed that work—especially manual labour—is a pretty dreadful thing, either so debasing as to be incompatible with a contemplative life, or merely a form of penance for original sin.[1] And although, as Max Weber observed, the Reformation eventually lent sacred significance to work, the work ethic which evolved from ascetic Protestantism and which was to have the greatest impact upon Western life, stressed entrepreneurship rather than manual toil. At any rate, it is safe to say that this stimulus no longer inspires the contemporary manual worker—if indeed it ever did.

Some contemporary writers have argued that work alienation is merely a condition which the intellectual imputes to the worker as he projects what would be his own painful reaction were he to have to step into work clothes and enter the factory. I do not share the belief that alienation is merely a condition which the intellectual experiences when he contemplates manual labour. I believe, rather—and there is, after all, ample sociological evidence to confirm it—that there are objective alienating qualities about much labour and that these are *seen* and *felt* as such by the worker, although he perhaps does not articulate them explicitly. True, as Robert Blauner has ably demonstrated, alienation varies from job to job and from industry to industry, and it is not possible to speak of the alienation of a unitary 'industrial man'.[2] And yet, an underlying strain of work alienation, here greater, there lesser, seems to be endemic to the world of work.

The one economic and sociological problem that will remain after the *truly* affluent society is achieved will be: what can be done with this world of work to make it less alienating for the mass of men? Even today, with the shortest work day and work week in modern history, the worker's daily job still extends nearly from one end of his waking hours to the other, especially if transportation is included plus an essential allowance for recuperation from the mental and physical fatigue of work. And as work dominates the day, so it dominates the week. Work stands like an enormous, dominating giant astride our waking hours, making its constant, unrelenting demands upon our minds and bodies. One cannot merely 'forget' work if it is unpleasant: it is simply too much with us. It is a merry-go-round from which one gets such little respite that he has hardly recovered from his dizziness when he must climb aboard again.

And just as work is long, so it is often onerous. For many the bulk of time is spent in labour that is repetitive, routine, uncreative, unfulfilling, tedious, objectively and subjectively boring, deadening to the spirit and the imagination. This is true not only in the factory but in the office as well, and except for the happy few, work is often merely a means to another end (economic survival), or gratifying only in the non-work aspects of the job (e.g. sociability with the work group).

What sets modern discussions of work alienation apart from traditional views is that, beginning with Marx, writers have believed that something can and should be done about the problem, rather than seeing labour as merely contemptible, punishment for sin, or a calling in which one might glorify God and/or gain a clue to one's salvation. Contemporary discussions of work alienation can be grouped into four categories, I believe, on the basis of the 'solutions' which various writers have proposed. In this chapter I should like to outline these four solutions very briefly in order to provide the setting for a discussion of a fifth which will occupy the following two chapters. My intent here is not to treat these proposed solutions exhaustively, but merely to enumerate the kinds of remedies which have been suggested, sketch some of their major arguments, and describe why I feel each in its own way is inadequate and unequal to the task.

1. *Leisure*

In the first category are those who see the answer to work alienation in activities outside of work itself, in leisure, in consumption or other satisfying pastimes.[3] Proponents of this approach abandon the hope of discovering meaning and pleasure in work in the contemporary world, and instead turn their attention to other pursuits which can somehow compensate for the almost total loss of gratification which modern work presumably embodies. The focus here is on man as consumer, of time or goods, rather than as producer. According to this view, the modern worker should cease the futile task of trying to fulfill himself, to find freedom or creative expression on the job. Instead, the leisure proponents argue that:

> Man is free and creative only when he plays; he transcends himself only when his work serves no purpose; he fulfills himself only when he has no 'job' to do. He develops his personality only when he throws off the thraldom of labour. He creates 'works' only where he is not in the position of a 'worker'.[4]

This school sees the modern worker as a man whose 'central life interest' is not focused on his work,[5] but, on the contrary, one who is constantly 'striving to exert himself less, to spend less time inside the factory, has no pride in his work, and gets little satisfaction out of a job well done. . . '.[6] Indeed, this is as it should be and not a cause for remorse.

Furthermore, the irksome quality of work is a condition of *all* industrial societies, whether socialist or capitalist, for the root cause of this alienation is technology, not faulty social or economic organisation. The central goal, then, is to cut work down to its essential minimum and to allow men to take their pleasure in leisure, whether that leisure be put to constructive use or merely spent in idleness. In short,

> . . . not by thinking of better devices of organising *homo faber* shall we liberate him [man] from the realm of necessity, but by resolutely acknowledging his human ability to enjoy life and to act creatively in purposeless play.[7]

This theme emerges from the writings of Clark Kerr also. According to him, the new world emerging over the horizon is one of 'pluralistic industrialism' in which there will be a polarity in man's life between alienation at work and fulfilment at play. In the world nearly upon us, 'for most people, any true scope for the independent spirit on the job will be missing',[8] with the only compensation for man residing in his leisure.

> The great new freedom may come in the leisure of individuals. Higher standards of living, more leisure, more education make this not only possible but almost inevitable. This will be the happy hunting ground for the independent spirit. Along with the bureaucratic conservatism of economic and political life may well go a New Bohemianism in the other aspects of life and partly as a reaction to the confining nature of the productive side of society.[9]

Summarising the nature of human life in stark, grim, and bold terms, Kerr explains his grotesque vision:

The new slavery to technology may bring a new dedication to diversity and individuality. This is the two-sided face of pluralistic industrialism that makes it forever a split personality looking in two directions at the same time. *The new slavery and the new freedom go hand in hand.*[10]

An equally pessimistic view of man's work is represented on the socialist side by Paul Lafargue, who was not nearly so imbued with the ethic of work as his distinguished father-in-law, Karl Marx. Whereas Max Weber saw the modern work ethic as emerging quite accidentally out of the teachings of the ascetic Protestant sects, Lafargue, in an indignant essay, *The Right to Be Lazy*, accused the bourgeoisie of perpetrating a gigantic hoax and fraud upon the working class by drugging them with an ideology espousing the so-called virtues and blessings of toil.[11] What could be better for the exploiting classes than a self-disciplined, work-oriented proletariat, one that would toil willingly, even eagerly, out of a sense of duty, without requiring any external compulsion whatsoever? How functional an ideology for the ruling classes.[12] Outraged, Lafargue argued that the proletarian's only duty toward work was to avoid it. Singing the praises of indolence, he cried: 'O, Laziness, mother of the arts and the noble virtues, be thou balsam for the pains of mankind'.[13] Work as we have known it from the beginning of the nineteenth century, relentless and aimless,

> ... is the worst frightful scourge which mankind has ever known; ... only when work is regulated according to reason, and is limited to a maximum corresponding to the social needs will it be a spice to the pleasure of idleness, a useful exercise to the human organism. . . .[14]

Seeking historical confirmation for this view, he cites the Classical Greeks who despised manual labour, believed that it degraded and brutalised man and made him unfit for truly human and intelligent life.[15] The early Christian view of work was not so far from this. Christ on the Mount said:

> Consider the lilies of the field, how they grow; they toil not, neither do they spin, yet I say unto ye that Solomon in all his glory was not arrayed like one of these.

The Christian view of work as punishment for sin is, of course, well known, and the Lord Himself demonstrated His attitude when, after working for six days, He has been idle ever since.

Those who see the solution to work alienation in creative or pleasurable leisure overlook the pervasive influence which work has upon man in all facets of his life, the interaction between life and work, and the impossibility of isolating malaise in one sphere from other spheres of life. As Ferdynand Zweig has said, 'A man is not one person at home and a different person at his work, he is one and the same man. He projects his personal worries, frustrations, and fears on to his workplace, and vice versa from workplace to home.'[16] Kerr is on very weak ground, indeed, when he argues that man can at one and the same time be both slave and free, that man can somehow keep the 'slavery' of his job from washing over into other areas of his life. Man can no more be slave and free simultaneously than he can be ill and well at once.

The leisure proponents ignore the dominant and central place which work must occupy in the life of nearly every man. As Robert Blauner has written, a leisure solution

> underestimates the fact that work remains the single most important life activity for most people, in terms of time and energy, and ignores the subtle ways in which the quality of one's worklife affects the quality of one's leisure, family relations, and basic self-feelings.[17]

Or, as sociologist Bernard Karsh has tersely put it, 'Work is not *part* of life, it is literally life itself'.

David Riesman, once having placed his faith in leisure as an antidote to alienated labour, is no longer quite so sure.

> ... my collaborators and I in *The Lonely Crowd* took it for granted that it was impossible to reverse the trend towards automation; we assumed that the current efforts to make work more meaningful—which by and large succeeded only in making it more time-consuming and gregarious but not more challenging—might as well be given up, with the meaning of life to be sought henceforth in the creative use of leisure. We failed to see, in the famous Marxist phrase, that 'quantity changes into quality' and that there would come a point where additional increments of leisure would prove more stultifying than satisfying and that the mass of men would be incapable of absorbing any more.[18]

And he argues now that if leisure is to be meaningful, then work, too, must have meaning. 'What I am asking for now,' he writes, 'is hardly less than reorganising work itself so that man can live humanely on as well as off the job.'[19]

Unhappiness at work does not necessarily lead to a free and creative use of leisure, but instead may inspire a frantic, desperate, compulsive, and very much unfree effort to escape or forget work. In short, alienated labour may breed alienated leisure. Georges Friedmann has correctly pointed out that

> ... the fragmentation of labour does not always cause the worker to seek leisure activities of greater scope in order to compensate for his frustrations. It may tend instead to disorganise the rest of his life and to arouse aggressive tendencies and outbursts of savage self-assertion through indulgence in all kinds of stimulants, in alcohol, in games of chance or luck, or in habits or bouts of 'conspicuous consumption', brutal amusement ... mass spectacles disguised as 'sport' or 'artistic' events ... crime and horror films [and the like]. ... [20]

Even though Freud viewed work primarily as an onerous and inescapable necessity,[21] he nevertheless realised that its positive function lay in 'binding the individual more closely to reality'. Work helps to structure the activity of the day and the week. It gives a sense of rhythm, of cycle, of pattern to life. It provides a sense of personal necessity, of deadline, of discipline, of order and purpose so necessary to a balanced existence. Work prevents feelings of pervasive aimlessness, of drift, of dissipation and decline often experienced by the unemployed, the retired, and students at the end of a long summer vacation. Leisure is meaningless without work, for, as Margaret Mead has written, 'Leisure is *earned* by work'.

Moreover, work in the Western world is the principal component of the male's sense of self-respect and masculinity. For the husband and father, work is the source of status and authority within the family. We know from numerous studies of the unemployed that long-term leisure can have devastating effects upon the man's position in the family. The disorganised, matriarchal lower class Negro family in the United States is a prime example of what happens to the status and authority of the male when he is chronically separated from meaningful work. The Negro wife and children often regard the unemployed husband with pity, contempt, and exasperation.[22]

Although research has suggested that work is not the primary interest in the lives of industrial workers, other well-known studies have shown that, in spite of this, only a minority of workers would choose to quit work entirely if they inherited enough money to live comfortably without it. This is true even of workers far down the occupational ladder, one study indicating that more than 75 per cent of skilled and semi-skilled workers and over half of unskilled workers would continue working even if financial need were not present.[23] The two most frequent explanations for continuing work were, according to the workers themselves, that they felt a need to keep occupied and that they would feel lost somehow without work.

It is at some risk, then, that we casually abandon work as a focus for gratification and fulfilment in the modern world, and so eagerly dismiss it as of little importance.

2. *Automation*

A second answer to contemporary work alienation is the automation solution. According to this view, the labour force is now being revolutionised, and soon unskilled and semi-skilled workers will virtually disappear and along with them their repetitive, routine, atomised, and monotonous machine-tending and assembly-line labour. Just as the mass production system transformed the unskilled labourer into a semi-skilled machine operator, so now will automation transform the latter into a skilled, highly educated and trained worker-technician. Machine tenders and assembly-line workers will give way to skilled machine repairers, installers, builders, controllers, and programmers, etc. There will be a tremendous need for white collar workers at all levels—clerical workers, technicians, professionals, and managerial personnel.

Moreover, the nature of manual work will be altered in the direction of greater work satisfaction. It will become more like white collar work and the line between the two will blur, for in the automated factory the worker's job, like that of his white collar colleague, 'is clean, includes record keeping and other clerical tasks, and involves responsibility'.[24] In the automated factory, of which the continuous-process industries of today such as chemical plants and oil refineries are supposedly a prototype, the trend toward the endless subdivision of tasks is broken, as the worker's job encompasses more operations than heretofore. He tends to be concerned with the entire process of production rather than with a minute segment of it, even though he may never actually come into physical contact with the product itself, and, in some cases, may never even see the product at all.

In the automated factories of the future, workers will not be tied to their machines but will have much greater freedom than operatives of today—freedom to control work pace, freedom of physical movement, etc. The rhythm of the automated factory—what has been called a calm and crisis rhythm—will be much more conducive to work interest than the unrelieved tedium of the unending, unvarying assembly-line.

Peter Drucker has written that in the automated tomorrow

Nobody will 'tend' machines; the semi-skilled operations servicing the machine will be performed by the machine itself. As a result, the worker, instead of being paced by the machine, paces it. He will determine what it does and how well it does it—by setting it, directing it, and maintaining it. His control is complete, and, because the production process is integrated, the way each man controls his own job shapes the performance of the entire operation.[25]

Work under automation will be characterised by the 'human use of human beings', as Norbert Wiener has said, wherein machines will perform the drudgery and men will be free to do those things at which they are presumably best: think, invent, plan, direct, and co-ordinate.

Looking at the nature of work in historical perspective, Blauner observed that the objective conditions making for alienation have increased as industry has proceeded unevenly from craft to machine-tending to conveyor-belt technology, but he believes that

with automated industry there is a counter-trend, one that we can fortunately expect to become even more important in the future. The case of the continuous-process industries, particularly the chemical industry, shows that automation increases the worker's control over his work process and checks the further division of labour and growth of large factories. The result is meaningful work in a more cohesive integrated industrial climate. The alienation curve begins to decline from its previous height as employees in automated industries gain a new dignity from responsibility and a sense of individual function.[26]

The major defect of the automation solution is simply that it is no solution at all for our time or even for the foreseeable future for most workers in any country on earth. The exponents of this solution, when they wax most eloquent, often describe a world which resembles nothing so much as the dream of workers' heaven in an old labour song, where

> The mill was made of marble,
> The machines were made out of gold,
> And nobody ever got tired,
> And nobody ever grew old.
>
> This mill was built in a garden—
> No dust or lint could be found.
> The air was so fresh and so fragrant
> With flowers and trees all around. . . .
>
> When I woke from this dream about heaven
> I wondered if some day there'd be
> A mill like that one down below here on earth
> For workers like you and like me.

Many automation enthusiasts write as if the dream of workers' heaven is, if not upon us already, due to arrive tomorrow. Often carried away by their own rhetoric, they almost always exaggerate the number of jobs which are, even in the foreseeable future, possible of becoming automated. One study conducted in the United States in the 1950s indicated that a maximum of 8 per cent of the labour force was working at jobs that were in any sense ripe for automation.[27] And as Friedmann has pointed out, the automation propagandists usually overestimate the speed at which these transformations can take place, while under-estimating the enormous technical, financial, and manpower obstacles which confront automation.

In the United States, the costs of total automation are so astronomical as to relegate it to the remote future. Yale Brozen, Professor of Business Economics at the University of Chicago, claims that to automate as completely as possible the manufacturing sector of the American economy alone would require an investment exceeding $2·5 trillion, and even this assumes that output would remain constant.[28] Total spending on new plant and equipment in US manufacturing in the early 1960s was approximately $15 billion annually. Thus, Brozen estimates that to automate manufacturing completely even without increasing output would require two centuries, at current investment levels. But if output is to increase, as it almost certainly must to take account of an expanding population, then complete automation is relegated to the indefinite future, unless the costs of automation can be drastically cut.

Moreover, the automationists, by pointing to a nebulous but utopian future, tend to ignore or play down the realities of the present, specifically, that there continues to be an enormous number of un-skilled and semi-skilled workers in the labour force, even in the most economically developed nations. For example, semi-skilled operatives, most of whom are engaged in repetitive tasks, with very short work cycles, requiring very little training—classic alienating characteristics—constituted 19 per cent of the US labour force in 1967 (see Table 1).[29] This was the largest single occupational group in the entire country, comprising some fourteen million workers. Unskilled labourers added another 5 per cent or 3½ million workers to this number (not including farm labourers, another one million). Considering only these semi-skilled and unskilled workers—and omitting lower white collar groups whose work has alienating tendencies of its own—the automation solution is certainly no solution whatsoever for the bulk of these

TABLE I: OCCUPATIONAL STRUCTURE OF THE UNITED STATES, 1900 AND 1967

	Per cent		Thousands	
	1900	1967	1900	1967
Total	100·0*	100·0*	29,030	74,666
White collar workers	17·6	46·2	5,115	34,512
Professional and technical workers	4·3	13·3	1,234	9,967
Managers, proprietors, and officials, excluding farm	5·8	10·3	1,697	7,699
Clerical workers	3·0	16·5	877	12,303
Sales workers	4·5	6·1	1,307	4,543
Blue collar workers	35·8	36·7	10,401	27,369
Craftsmen and foremen	10·5	13·1	3,062	9,758
Semi-skilled operatives	12·8	18·8	3,720	14,026
Labourers, excluding farm and mine	12·5	4·8	3,620	3,585
Service workers, including private household	9·0	12·4	2,626	9,225
Farm workers, including farmers, farm managers, labourers and foremen	37·5	4·8	10,888	3,560

* Percentages may not add precisely to 100 because of rounding.

manual workers who continue to constitute such a large share of the working population.

It is true that in the United States the proportion of unskilled workers has been shrinking rapidly over the years, and, since 1950, the proportion of semi-skilled workers has declined a bit, from slightly over 20 per cent to slightly under 19 per cent. But in 1900, semi-skilled workers comprised only 13 per cent of the labour force, and so the secular trend in semi-skilled labour—routine, repetitive, alienating —has been *up*, not down. And due to the expansion of the labour force itself, there are nearly four times as many semi-skilled workers today as there were at the turn of the century. Taking this group as a whole, automation has scarcely begun to touch it.

The proportion of manual workers at *all* skill levels in the American labour force has not declined at all since 1900, which may come as a surprise to those who believe that the working class is rapidly becoming extinct. Manual workers have held their own since the turn of the century, constituting about 36 per cent of the labour force in 1900 and approximately 37 per cent in 1967. In absolute terms there were 2½ times as many manual workers in the United States in 1967 as there were in 1900—over 27,000,000 as compared to less than 11,000,000.

The tremendous expansion in white collar occupations over this period (from 18 per cent to 46 per cent of the labour force) has come, not at the expense of the working class, but at the expense of the farm population which has decreased since 1900 from nearly 40 per cent of the labour force to approximately 5 per cent in 1967.

We have said, then, that enormous numbers of semi-skilled and unskilled workers remain with us to this day, and that for the bulk of them automation provides and will provide no solution *en masse*. But we have been speaking of the world's most economically developed nation. Certainly, if automation provides only the remotest solution here, then it provides no solution whatsoever for those in the under-developed world where economic conditions make the introduction of automated technology truly a distant dream of a worker's heaven. Erich Fromm's observations here are especially pertinent.

> . . . it will still be many generations before . . . automatisation and reduction of working time is reached, especially if we think not only of Europe and America but of Asia and Africa, which still have hardly started their industrial revolution. Is man, during the next few hundred years, to continue spending most of his energy on meaningless work, waiting for the time when work will hardly require any expenditure of energy? What will become of him in the meantime?[30]

Automation, thus, is not nearly as imminent as we have been led to believe; in that sense, we have been given a false picture. But even the picture which we have been given of automation *today* is not completely accurate. One of the key assumptions of the visionaries is that automation inevitably leads to an upgrading of the skill of the labour force. Across the board, they claim, automation increases the demand for skilled workers: the operators of automated equipment require more training; there is a significant increase in the need for highly skilled maintenance men and those doing indirect labour associated with the complex equipment; there is an increase in the demand for trained men to design, construct, and install automated equipment.

Despite these assumptions, the whole notion that automation leads inevitably to upgrading of skill has been challenged by James Bright's exhaustive study of thirteen automated plants in the United States.[31] Those who believe that complex automated machinery demands increased skill of the machine operator have simply not thought the matter through thoroughly, and will thus be surprised at Bright's finding that automation—if it changes skill requirements at all—is more likely to *reduce* the level of skill than to increase it.

To oversimplify, the explanation of the paradox lies in the fact that as machines take over more and more of the job, there is less and less for the worker to do. This results, not only in a reduction in the need for manual effort, but often in a reduction in the need for trained skills as well.

What the automation propagandists have done is to confuse the sophistication of the machinery—and the complexity of its design and maintenance—with the simplicity of its operation.

To illustrate how automated equipment often leads to a down-grading of skill requirements, Bright has constructed what might be called a continuum of mechanisation. Beginning at the very simplest level, with man working with his hands alone, without tools of any sort, we move consecutively to: the hand tool stage (e.g. a pliers); the powered hand tool (portable drill); the mounted power tool (drill press); the power tool with a fixed cycle (a drill which, when manually started, punches a hole and retracts); the power tool that performs several functions on the work material without manual assistance; the same machine operated by remote control; the machine that measures and reports characteristics of the work piece; the machine that detects errors and reports them; the machine that records its performance; the machine that modifies its behaviour on the basis of its own measurements; and on and on.[32] As we proceed across the continuum, machines make more refined and discriminating decisions, and are able to anticipate and correct errors.

Now, it becomes obvious that as we move along this continuum of mechanisation, from the most simple tools to the most complex auto-mated machinery, the level of 'skill' (however defined), will first rise, reach an optimum point, but then, as the machines begin to embody more processes and more decisions, the skill requirement of the operator begins to *decline*, as human intervention becomes increasingly unnecessary.

After illustrating the decline in operator skill requirements in the automated factories he studied, Bright cites some readily understand-able examples from non-factory life, which point again to the con-clusion that as machinery increases in sophistication, the skill required of the operator often diminishes.

Is today's car, with automatic choke, automatic transmission, power brakes, power steering, harder or easier to drive than a Model T Ford? Why can a 7-year-old girl wash dishes as well as her mother? It is because she has only to load the dishwasher and push a button! Who needs the most skill and experience for successful performance: the housewife who bakes in an automatic oven, or her grandmother who had to learn the art and knack of baking temperature control for her coal-fired stove by lengthy experience and keen attention?

If we think carefully about the skill, education, and training required to become a suitable operator on the machinery around us, it becomes clearer that we tend to confuse the maintenance and design problems or exceptional operator jobs with the most common situation: namely, that *growing automaticity tends to simplify operator duties*.[33]

Bright noticed some counter-trends, such as occasional cases where automation required the operator to take responsibility for a larger section of the line, when he was given responsibility for additional higher level tasks (e.g. set-up work and/or inspection), or when automation required new specialised operator skills. These trends, however, were not significant enough to offset the generally downgrading effect of automated equipment upon direct labour.

Moreover, Bright discovered that the slight increase in the numbers and the skill which are *sometimes* required of maintenance men, workers in indirect labour jobs, and engineers and technicians to build the machinery, did not significantly counterbalance the general decline in skill requirements of the greater mass of operator jobs in the automated factories he studied. In short, summarising the overall impact of automation upon skill in the thirteen plants he investigated, Bright concluded that '. . . there is little evidence to show that large numbers of distinctly superior skills are required to man the automated plant'.[34]

Other research corroborates these findings. For example:

1. In a survey of automated metal working firms in the United States in the late 1950s, only 27 per cent reported that the new equipment demanded higher skills, while 30 per cent reported no change and 43 per cent claimed that less skill was necessary compared to the period prior to the introduction of the automated machinery.

2. In a study of a plant employing 450 workers in its central accounting division, automation affected 90 per cent of the employees but there was no appreciable change in the average job grade (see below for further material on white collar automation).

3. A study by the US Bureau of Labor Statistics in the 1950s of an oil refinery, an airline, a bakery, an electronics firm, and an insurance company revealed no significant upgrading. In most cases, in fact, 'the effect on skill requirements was a transfer from one relatively low-skilled job to another of similar grade. In some cases there was definite downgrading.'[35]

Granted, all this research has been concerned with the impact of automation upon skill at the level of the individual firm and not at the level of the national economy or labour force as a whole. Nevertheless these studies should give the automation enthusiasts pause and lead to a re-examination of some of their key assumptions about the relationship of automation to skill requirements.

But there is yet another crucial point which should not be overlooked. Those who have painted such rosy pictures of the nature of work under automation have tended to ignore the entire body of survey research conducted among workers (both blue collar and white collar) employed in automated factories or offices.[36] These data certainly do not imply, the automation propagandists to the contrary notwithstanding, that work is or will be an unmitigated joy in an automated environment.

On the contrary, the research which the automation enthusiasts have neglected to explore indicates that while there are aspects of work under automation which represent a clear improvement over previous conditions, there are, in addition, other features and tendencies of automated work which are strongly alienating. In the factory these include: destruction of the work group and ensuing social isolation; fewer promotional opportunities; continuous stress, anxiety, and tension arising out of fear of damaging expensive equipment; the need for constant alertness; increased production rates; increased levels of supervision, and so on.

A notable example is provided by the intensive research of Charles Walker several years ago among workers at the first continuous seamless pipe mill in the US.[37] There one sees clearly both the positive and negative effects of automation upon work satisfaction. As has often been noted, the objective working conditions were much improved: the new mill was more spacious than the old, had better lighting, and was safer, as the workers were less threatened by heat, dirt, and danger. For most workers—although not all—there was less physical effort demanded on the job. And, for the first time, workers were able to see the entire process of pipe production, rather than merely segments of it as previously. Finally, a kind of enjoyable work rhythm ultimately developed among the members of the nine-man crew.

However, offsetting these gains were other features of the automated mill. Although physical effort and strain typically decreased, there was a noticeable increase in mental strain, for the new jobs demanded the workers' almost constant attention. Despite the unremitting need for alertness, some workers reported this in conjunction with monotony. Also, the pace of work was increased, and because more pipe was being turned out than ever before in the non-automated mill, more physical effort was required of those workers whose jobs had not been automated.

Not only was there less time for conversation because of the increased pace of work and need for constant attention, but there was less opportunity for talk because work groups were shattered. Symbolising this was the public address system which the men now used to communicate and which substituted for previous face-to-face contact in the old mill.[38]

Contrary to popular assumptions, and in line with previously reported findings, automation in the pipe mill did not lead to a significant upgrading of skills. Furthermore, most men believed their chances for promotion were worse than when they worked in the old, non-automated mill. There were far fewer jobs now, smaller work crews, and a narrower range of job classifications. The men believed also that promotion to foreman was even more unlikely in the new mill, those positions increasingly pre-empted by college men and young engineers. Only a tiny proportion of the men in the automated mill said that plants such as their own were clearly good for the working man. Most saw them as increasing the profits and productivity of the company while basically threatening the security of the worker.

Although all the workers in Walker's study ultimately (after several years) said they had made the right move in coming to work in the automated mill, this might have partially reflected the fact that the engineers had inadvertently set an 'easy' rate and the workers were consequently making far more money in the new than in the old mill. Thus, sentiment in favour of the new mill might have been based largely on higher earnings rather than on intrinsic qualities of life in the automated mill. Finally, it is significant that the blessings of automation in the new pipe mill were not enough to satisfy the workers. Even in the new, cleaner, automated environment, the workers expressed a profound desire for participation in the decision-making process; and it was a source of deep and continuing unhappiness among them that their serious suggestions and proposals for true collaboration in this new experiment were frustrated by management almost from the very beginning.[39]

Let us leave the automated factory now and enter the automated office. Here, evidence tentatively points in the direction of a real proletarianisation of the lower white collar mass. Work in the offices where large computers have been introduced is increasingly 'routine, monotonous, pressured, and confining';[40] a factory atmosphere often prevails due to the noise and heat of the machinery, multiple shift operation, and the constant checking and re-checking of work. There are a reduced number of clerical jobs without an increase in the skill requirements, the interest, or the challenge of the remaining jobs. The standards of performance are higher than in the non-automated office, the pace of work is increased, time schedules are tighter, deadlines become more important, and tardiness and absences become increasingly disruptive. Tasks must be carried out more quickly and they must also be done with more precision and accuracy as mistakes are much more costly and serious than before. Strain and tension on the job naturally increase. This often leads to a breakdown in group cohesiveness among the workers. There is less consultation with supervisors. There are increased fears of lay-offs and dismissals.

For example, in her comprehensive study of the automated office in the United States several years ago, Ida R. Hoos discovered that the impact on overall work satisfaction bore little relation to that confidently predicted by the automation Pollyannas.[41]

Throughout her extensive interviews in a multiplicity of settings, she encountered conditions which were, if anything, antithetical to work satisfaction. There were white collar slowdowns, restrictions of output, and miscellaneous office 'sabotage'—all generated by the fear of being automated out of a job. There was anomie due both to job transfers and the frequent disruption and destruction of customary work relationships, caused by the introduction of automated equipment. The objective nature of many of the jobs in the automated office became *less*, not more, challenging. There was a greater subdivision of tasks, much repetition, simplification, fragmentation (such as preparing data for the computer) and great attention to minute detail. More jobs were subject to precise measurement and quantification, which meant that each worker's output could be easily measured, rated, and compared with others. As a result, the pressure was on, continuous and steady, for high, accurate, and sustained output. Moreover, there were new restrictions on physical movement—compare the pre-automated file clerk with the automated card puncher—with predictable consequences for fatigue and boredom.

For the rank and file positions in the automated office—such as tabulating machine and key punch operators—there was very little upgrading from previous jobs, whether in terms of skill or education required, salary, or challenge and intrinsic job interest. True, the jobs of analysts, planners, and programmers usually represented upgrading in these respects, but workers in these positions comprised the office élite and represented an insignificant proportion of the entire office force.

There was anxiety even among supervisors, whose departments might be transferred or abolished and whose subordinates consequently might diminish or disappear. Supervisors without subordinates were deprived of function and consequently subject to downgrading.

Boredom among key punch operators was one of the principal reasons for annual turnover rates of 55–75 per cent in one office. 'This job is no different from a factory job,' one girl complained, 'except that I don't get paid as much as the girls working on the line'. Indeed, the author argues that automation is making the office ever more factory-like, with the objective count on output, the minute sub-division of tasks, the moving belts carrying work from station to station, restrictions on conversation, time clocks, the din of the machinery, around the clock operation, and the like. All of this is a far cry from the personal and one-to-one relationship between clerk and employer in the small office of a century ago.[42] It is a far cry, too, from the optimistic projections of those like management consultant John Diebold who confidently assert that the automated office will eliminate 'a whole stratum of dull, repetitive, low-paid jobs. . . .'

The automationists often predict a kind of merger between the working class and white collar employees, and they see this process almost solely in terms of the levelling up of the manual labourer to the position of the white collar worker. If the gap between the two in job content is narrowing, however, it is just as much due to the levelling down of the office worker toward the condition of the manual worker.

Certainly, those enthusiasts who sing the praises of automation and speak of a brave new world of satisfaction in work should examine more closely some of the empirical research conducted in the automated factories and offices of today. True, sociologist Robert Blauner who places great faith in automation as an antidote to work alienation conducted a meticulous study of an automated chemical plant and found work satisfaction there considerably greater than in non-automated machine-tending or assembly-line industries.[43] The chief flaw in this otherwise fine work is that Blauner, after going to great lengths to demonstrate the impossibility of referring to the alienation of a generalised 'industrial man' and the necessity of differentiating between industrial *men* on the basis of the particular industrial or technological milieu in which they work, then goes on to make the facile assumption that the high work satisfaction found in continuous-process industries—a special and limited type—can be used as a model for all other forms of automation, in offices as well as factories. This assumption is unwarranted. As we have seen, for fulfilment in work, automation of all kinds is often a mixed blessing at best.

3. *Anti-Industrialism*

Another answer which was heard frequently during the early stages of the industrial revolution but gradually less and less often as the possibility of its realisation dimmed, looks to anti-industrialism or decentralisation, only a few of whose proponents can be mentioned here. Whereas the automationists look to the future for the antidote to work alienation, the anti-industrialists or the decentralisers look to the past, to a former, pastoral, unmechanised age where work and life presumably had greater meaning and man had not subordinated himself to machine rule and machine worship. These are, in short, the intellectual machine wreckers of our day.

Of the many men from diverse points of view who represent this tradition, Aldous Huxley comes to mind, many of whose novels, *Brave New World, After Many a Summer Dies the Swan, Island*, portray the triumph and the tyranny of science and technology over man, and point the way toward a partial solution for man in a life of contemplation and individual experience in a setting of small, agrarian or only semi-mechanised communities. Many of the novels of Huxley's friend, D. H. Lawrence, treat also the relationship of men and machines, as well as the relationship of men and women,[44] and Lawrence's solution bears strong resemblance to Huxley's. The anti-industrial theme in *Lady Chatterley's Lover* is quite explicit and needs no elaboration here, but two quotations summarise Lawrence's views quite concisely. The gamekeeper, symbol of the natural man, uncorrupted by city or factory, speaking for Lawrence, says to Constance Chatterley:

> Let's live for summat else. Let's not live ter make money, neither for us-selves nor for anybody else. Now we're forced to. We're forced to make a bit for us-selves, an' a fair lot for the bosses. Let's stop it! Bit by bit, let's stop it. We needn't rant and rave. Bit by bit, let's drop the whole industrial life, and go back. The least little bit o' money'll do. For everybody, me an' you, bosses and masters, even the king. The least little bit o' money'll really do. Just make up your mind to it, an' you've got out o' th' mess.[45]

And Lady Chatterley, echoing her lover, says to him later in the conversation:

> ... it's a shame what's been done to people these last hundred years: men turned into nothing but labour-insects, and all their manhood taken away, and all their real life. I'd wipe the machines off the face of the earth again, and end the industrial epoch like a black mistake.[46]

We may also cite the views of a very different man, William Morris, whose faith in socialism distinguishes him from either Huxley or Lawrence, but whose opinions of the modern urban industrial complex place him with the others. Morris believed that socialism was an important first step in re-establishing contentment in work. However, matching his dislike of capitalism and the waste, injustice, and inequity of class society, was his distaste of industrialism run amuck, with the noise, filth, ugliness, and confusion that accompanied it. Socialism had to correct the technological evils of capitalism as well as its social evils, according to Morris. An important goal of Morris' socialism was to make all labour pleasant for the working man. This could be achieved, not only by reducing the working day to a tolerable length, but by ensuring that all work was truly useful to society, and that each man was trained for a variety of occupations—manual and non-manual— which he worked at alternately, a proposal resembling Marx's brief description of the nature of work after the abolition of the division of labour. Above all, Morris advocated a complete reform of the surroundings in which work took place, depicted at length in *News from Nowhere*. Morris revolted against the 'crowded towns and bewildering factories' of his day and stated that 'the interior of a great weaving-shed is almost as ridiculous a spectacle as it is a horrible one'.[47] He argued that modern workers

> need by no means be compelled to pig together in close city quarters. There is no reason why they should not follow their occupations in quiet country homes, in industrial colleges, in small towns, or, in short, where they find it happiest to live.[48]

Co-founder with Ruskin of the arts and crafts movement, Morris gave only one, or perhaps two, cheers at the most for labour-saving machinery, endorsing it with the strictest reservations. Where used, it must be dedicated literally to the saving of human labour, to reducing the work day, and to eliminating the most onerous and difficult of man's work. But gradually, Morris believed, the use of most machinery would tend to die out. Its use, he wrote would probably, after a time, be somewhat restricted when men found out that there was no anxiety as to mere subsistence, and learned to take an interest and pleasure in handiwork which, done deliberately and thoughtfully, could be made more attractive than machine work.[49]

On the American scene, anti-urbanism and anti-industrialism run like a thread through the entire intellectual history of the nation.[50] In his *Notes on Virginia* written in 1784, Jefferson, recoiling from the early horrors of the industrial revolution across the Atlantic, implored his American compatriots to 'let our workshops remain in Europe'. And since then, some of America's greatest thinkers—philosophers like Thoreau, essayists like Emerson, literary figures like Hawthorne, Poe, Melville, and Howells, writers like Henry Adams, these and many, many more—have all expressed views of urban industrial life which ranged from dissatisfaction to outright and total repudiation.

It is almost superfluous at this point in history to say that, for better or worse, industrialism can never be repealed and, barring a total nuclear war, is here to stay. The world of today and tomorrow is the world of the city and advanced machine technology. If man is to find satisfaction and meaning in life and in work, he must now search for it within the framework of the urban, industrial world. And while it is still possible for isolated individuals here and there to escape and turn back their own private clocks, for the mass of men this is an impossible solution, a hopeless, utopian dream, and one which, even if realisable, might not restore the pleasures that our nostalgic intellectuals have sought.

4. *Job Enlargement*

Whereas the anti-industrialists seek to reverse the entire course of modern industrialism, those who seek a solution in job enlargement want to reverse only certain trends of industrial life, viz. these which have led since mass production to an increasing fragmentation and subdivision of labour, where jobs are simplified and atomised to the point where each worker performs a tiny task which contributes in some positive but infinitesimally small way to the manufacture of the product. Job enlargement counteracts the minuteness and repetiveness of industrial occupations by giving the worker a more extended and elaborate series of operations to perform. which enhance his skill and versatility, and enable him to make a more significant contribution to the entire manufacturing process. Successfully introduced, it lengthens the work cycle, introduces variety, allows the worker to set his own work pace, offers him greater independence in deciding on work methods, and gives him responsibility and recognition for the quality of his work.

The International Business Machine Corporation was the pioneer in formal job enlargement experiments. During World War II, one of their production plants introduced what was to become a widely acclaimed innovation.[51] The affected job originally involved a semi-skilled worker whose task it was merely to take a part, insert it in a drill, start the machine, drill the required hole, put the part aside, and begin anew. This job was then expanded so the worker could learn new skills and perform more operations. After it had been enlarged,

> the job was made to include tool sharpening, the setting up of the machine for each new series of blueprints, a knowledge of calibration, of how deviations from tolerances will affect the part subsequently, and, what was no doubt the most important addition of all, the complete checking of the finished part, which meant using test-plate, height gauge, and comparator.[52]

Since this ground-breaking project, other well-known experiments have been conducted in the United States at Detroit Edison (electric utility), the Colonial Insurance Company, the Maytag Company (laundry equipment manufacturers), and Sears, Roebuck and Company.[53] These and other job enlargement projects have usually resulted in enhanced job satisfaction for the affected workers. In every study, however, a minority of workers prefer the original over the enlarged job, and, in a few cases, a majority of workers prefer the non-enlarged job.[54] Some authors claim that the case for job enlargement has been overstated and argue that only certain types of workers (e.g. those from small towns or rural areas) respond favourably to job enlargement.[55] Nevertheless, most authors continue to believe that, in general, job enlargement has a beneficial effect upon employees.

For example, Conant and Kilbridge studied a factory producing home laundry equipment (not identified but probably Maytag).[56] A few years earlier the company had switched some of its operations from progressive assembly to single operator bench assembly in which each worker, formerly responsible for only a minute part of the total assembly process on the line, was now responsible for the complete sub-assembly of water pumps or top control panels for the machines. Of the sixty workers interviewed who had worked both on the line and at the bench, more than two-thirds preferred the enlarged job. What the workers liked about the new system was that: they now

had a variety of jobs to perform; they could complete an entire operation; they could take responsibility and be given credit for the quality of
their work; they weren't tied to a work station. Even though each bench
worker was now more isolated from his fellows and couldn't engage in
as much interaction as when stationed on the line, the other satisfying
aspects of the new job more than offset this minor disadvantage.

Thus, job enlargement does seem to represent an important step in
halting the almost endless process of the division and sub-division of
labour which has accompanied mass production methods, and does
seem to be a significant move toward eliminating the most objectively
alienating characteristics of modern work. There are, nonetheless,
limitations on its extended applicability. Charles Walker, a noted
exponent of job enlargement, writes that this method could diversify
and enrich the jobs of perhaps only 500,000 workers in the United
States in the immediate future.[57] When measured against the countless
millions of semi-skilled and unskilled jobs in the economy, this
represents a rather inconsiderable number.

But even this overstates the possibilities, because thousands of jobs
for which enlargement is technically feasible will not be enlarged for
other than technical reasons. For example, in a recent study of 210 of
the largest 500 firms in the United States (industrial, transportation,
insurance, and utilities), over 80 per cent did not have even one job
enlargement programme.[58] Furthermore, only six of these companies
reported definite plans for introducing more than two job enlargement
projects within the next couple of years. Finally, far and away the
major criterion the companies used in evaluating the success of the
relatively few job management projects already under way was their
effects on costs, not work satisfaction.

Even where job enlargement is introduced by the occasional enlightened firm, it may have the effect of displacing workers, thus
leading to resistance to its continuation. At IBM, for example, the
set-up men and inspectors were gradually replaced as semi-skilled
workers took over their jobs. It was only because IBM was a dynamic
and expanding company that it could absorb the employees who had
been displaced by job enlargement. If this had not been possible—as
it would not be in all industries where job enlargement is technically
feasible—the company would undoubtedly have run into strong opposition from the workers and/or the trade union.

Considering now these four solutions discussed briefly here, we see that they have several qualities in common. All four, leisure, automation, anti-industrialism, and job enlargement are based on a kind of *technological determinism*. That is, the premise of each is that a given degree of job satisfaction (or job *dis*satisfaction) inevitably accompanies a certain technological level, and that increased satisfaction in work is possible only by altering the technology. Because of this, all these schools have given up the idea of attempting to establish satisfaction in work under present conditions. One view looks to the future, one to the past, one looks away from work altogether and toward leisure and consumption, and one toward a modification of existing work methods. All share the belief that tendencies for alienation are rooted in the technology of modern industrialism itself and that this alienation —inherent in industry as we know it—is unaffected by any change in the *social organisation* of industry. In other words, technology is the major, if not the exclusive, independent variable affecting the amount and degree of work alienation.

What I should like to do in the following chapter is to go on from a technological determinism to argue that *within a given technology*, the level of alienation can vary depending upon certain elements in the *social organisation* of the firm, namely, the extent to which workers are able to share in important decisions which affect both the company and the nature of the workers' tasks. The underlying hypothesis is that even though there are strong alienating tendencies in much modern industrial work, these can be significantly offset by 'participation' which tends to transform the workers' definition of the work situation.[59] In essence, this was the thesis of the previous chapters on the forgotten lessons of Hawthorne, that work satisfaction can be remarkably improved when participation is introduced, even though technology remains constant and the objective nature of work tasks remains unchanged. The next chapter will treat the rich and suggestive literature on participation which has emerged since the Mayo studies.

The participation solution to work alienation differs, then, from the others discussed here, for it does not abandon industrial work as a source of possible gratification, and it is grounded in the present rather than in the past or the distant future. In a sense, then, this answer is more 'optimistic', and—not overlooking the enormous political and economic obstacles—more 'practical' than the solutions outlined here.

Proposed Solutions to Work alienation / MOTIVATION

5. Alienation and Participation: A Review of the Literature

> To put the matter epigrammatically, we may say that the worker regards as his worst enemy, not the machine, but the boss. Among the causes of distaste for work, the social causes predominate over the technical; and among the social causes, the most important is the disciplinary subordination of the worker.—*Henri de Man*

What is 'participation'? Let us begin with the definition set down by J. R. P. French, Jr, who has been somewhat of a pioneer in the field. 'Participation', he writes,

> refers to a process in which two or more parties influence each other in making certain plans, policies, and decisions. It is restricted to decisions that have further effects on all those making the decision and on those represented by them.[1]

This definition has a number of virtues, of which the most important are that it conforms to our common sense understanding of the term and that it is compatible with a fairly wide range of power relations between two (or more) participating parties. Its major limitation is that its range is not quite broad enough for our purposes, and in order to extend this definition I should like to present a participation typology which had arisen out of the codetermination literature in West Germany.

As we move from the top to the bottom of this chart, the participation and power of workers increase at the expense of the prerogatives of management. In the initial type, management merely informs the workers of decisions which it has already made or will make on its own. At the other end of this scale, labour has exclusive control over decision-making and management is powerless or nearly so.

Crucial to French's definition of participation, however, is the process of *joint decision* between two or more parties; this would exclude the extremes of the participation scale above. In the first type, for example, where management merely supplies information to workers who passively receive it, this cannot properly be considered a process of *joint* decision-making or of mutual influence. It might be argued, though, that the mere act of giving information to workers

TYPES OF WORKERS' PARTICIPATION[2]

I. *Co-operation* (Workers influence decisions—except in No. 1 below where this is nominal—but are not responsible for these decisions.)

		Workers' role
1.	Workers have the right to receive information	passive
2.	Workers have the right to protest decisions	negative
3.	Workers have the right to make suggestions	positive
4.	Workers have the right of prior consultation but their decisions are not binding on management	positive

II. *Codetermination* (Workers control decisions and are responsible for them.)

1.	Workers have the right of veto	negative
	(*a*) Temporary, after which management	
	(i) may implement its decisions	passive
	(ii) must negotiate with workers	positive
	(*b*) Permanent	
2.	Workers have the right of co-decision	positive
3.	Workers have the right of decision	positive

---

demonstrates a certain influence on the latter's part, and I would tend to see this as a rudimentary form of participation.

At the other end of the participation typology, complete workers' control, French's definition is once more inadequate, for workers or their representatives completely dominate the field and again there is no joint decision-making. Yet I will call this type participation also, for what I am primarily concerned with is decision-making by workers, whether that decision-making is unilateral or not. If workers have exclusive jurisdiction in an area, this is of interest here, though it is not strictly speaking 'participation' as French defines it. Thus, without splitting too many hairs, I should like to broaden French's definition to include the entire spectrum of workers' power, from its most rudimentary form (receiving information from management) down to its opposite, complete worker determination.

Studies of workers' participation are rare, especially in American sociology, because of a simple but stubborn fact: the paucity of on-going systems of workers' participation within the economy.[3] Because it has been difficult for sociologists to enter and study at first hand factories in which meaningful workers' participation in decision-making exists, research on participation has taken the following substitute forms.

1. First, we have field experiments conducted upon groups which lie outside industrial organisations altogether, and which compare, for example, the effectiveness of various forms of participative and non-participative leadership. The ground breaking work of Lewin and his associates is probably the outstanding example here. I believe these studies represent a good starting point for a discussion of the effects of participation; and it seems quite evident that the findings of these studies have an immediate bearing and relevance upon an industrial milieu, despite the fact that they were not carried out with industrial problems in mind.

2. The second type of research which I have examined consists of those experiments which have been conducted within work organisations (factories, offices) or parts thereof (sections, divisions, departments) and into which *participation is introduced for purposes of the experiment*. The effects of participation are then compared with control groups in which participation was not introduced. Methodologically, these studies are among the best we have, for they build participation into the structure of the organisation. Participation in the experimental groups is likely to be thoroughgoing; it becomes a quality of the organisation, having official sanction, and is not an accidental result of an individual supervisor's personality.

3. We have next those accounts of incidents, probably quite common, in which workers have introduced innovations into their work *on their own initiative*, often spontaneously, with or without the knowledge of management. In these cases workers have taken over some of the decision-making power of management which in turn has led to changes in work satisfaction. Although these studies are interesting and worthy of note, their uniform defect is that we do not know whether the changes in work satisfaction derived from the changes in the content of the work itself or from the manner in which these changes were introduced.

4. Another type of study relevant to participation consists of survey research among workers in various industries. By means of interviews or questionnaires the researchers investigate the interrelationships among such things as morale, productivity, and supervision without, however, setting up any experimental situations. With this research, participation can be studied by examining the attitudes of those workers who are able to play some part in the decision-making process because of a supervisor's democratic leadership style with his workers. The workers under these types of supervisors are then compared to similar workers who are under more restrictive supervision. In this case participation arises, not out of the structure of the organisation, but from the personality traits of individual supervisors who, on their own, encourage various degrees of participation. Although this kind of research can be valuable in assessing the impact of participation upon satisfaction in work, they have definite limitations which will be treated at greater length later on and which are not characteristic of field experiments mentioned in type two above.

5. A final means of measuring the effects and importance of participation are the innumerable studies of job satisfaction in which workers are asked, in one way or another, about the aspects of their jobs, past and/or present, which are important to them. The importance of participation to workers, conceptualised in various ways, can then be assessed from these data. I mean to touch on the voluminous material on job satisfaction only peripherally in this chapter, as my major concern is a review of what might be termed the participation literature rather than the often-surveyed job satisfaction literature *per se*.

Experiments in participation have been wide-ranging. They have taken place in a great variety of organisational settings, including boys' clubs, women's organisations, college classrooms, factories of many different kinds, offices, stores, scientific laboratories, and so on. Similarly, they have been conducted upon a tremendous variety of persons differing in age, sex, education, income, occupation, and power. They have involved young boys, housewives, college students, manual workers at different levels of skill and in diverse types of factories, supervisors at different levels, clerical workers, salesmen, and scientists.

Throughout this survey of the literature I shall be concerned primarily with the effects of participation—of all kinds and at all points on the continuum—upon work alienation and upon its opposite, satisfaction and fufilment in work. Participation is, therefore, our independent variable; work satisfaction our dependent variable. In most of the studies I shall discuss, these two variables are present. But in some, other dependent variables are of central concern, such as the effects of participation upon efficiency or productivity, upon learning, upon changing habits and attitudes, or upon eliciting co-operation. While focusing primarily upon participation's effect on bringing about greater satisfaction in work, I shall occasionally mention these other effects also. I hope this will not be construed as an irrelevant digression but rather as a demonstration of the very broad powers of participation to affect many aspects of human behaviour.*

I

In the first group of studies, we have those field experiments which, though not conducted in work organisations, seem to have a direct bearing upon the question of the significance and effects of participation at work.

When discussing these early experiments one thinks almost at once of the deservedly classic studies carried out in the late 1930s under the direction of Kurt Lewin on the effects of different 'social climates' on the behaviour of groups of boys.[4] In one series of studies, small groups of eleven year old boys, members of after school clubs engaged primarily in various handicraft activities, were exposed to three types of leadership styles, termed democratic, authoritarian, and laissez-faire. In this summary, the first two types will be compared, as they are most relevant for the subject at hand.

In brief, in the authoritarian groups, the leaders were the sole determiners of policies, tasks, and activities, and a great part of the leader's interaction with the boys consisted of giving instructions and issuing direct or indirect orders. The group was not trained to solve its own problems or develop independence, but instructed to depend upon the leader for guidance and direction. The authoritarian leader maintained considerable social distance from the boys commensurate with his superior authority.

Under democratic leadership, policy was determined by group participation, discussion, and decision. The democratic leader supplied technical advice when necessary, he guided and structured the activities in a general way but always provided the group with alternatives from which it could choose, and he encouraged the development of group autonomy. In his personal relations to the boys, the democratic leader was intentionally egalitarian rather than distant and superior.

The differences in the boys' behaviour as a result of these diverse

* It should be made perfectly clear at the outset that no attempt is being made here to establish a relationship between morale and productivity. It is true, as we shall see, that participation often lifts both, but it has been established many times over that high morale and productivity do not always walk hand in hand. Of principal concern here is the means of attaining greater job satisfaction, not higher labour productivity. Especially in the 'over-developed' countries, as C. Wright Mills called them, the crucial need is the former, not the latter.

social climates was striking, and they can be conveniently summarised under three headings.

1. Efficiency. The authoritarian groups seemed superficially productive in terms of the proportion of time spent in actual work; as much or more work was done in the authoritarian groups than in the democratic groups. However, substantial evidence demonstrated that work in the authoritarian groups was done primarily in response to *external compulsion* (in the form of the authoritarian leader) rather than springing from any spontaneous and genuine work interest of the members themselves. This was discovered by a simple but ingenious device of having the leader leave the room for short periods, and then comparing the amount of work done in the leader's absence with the amount done in his presence. In one authoritarian group, the proportion of time spent at work dropped from 52 per cent to 16 per cent when the leader left the room; in another authoritarian group the drop was from 74 per cent to 29 per cent. In both cases the precipitous fall in work involvement when the supervisor left the room revealed that the motivation for work under authoritarian conditions was largely dictated from without.

In the democratic groups, on the other hand, the club members continued to work whether or not the leader was present. In one democratic group, for example, work involvement dropped only four percentage points, from 50 per cent to 46 per cent.

Are these findings not suggestive *vis-à-vis* the motivations to work under the prevail ng system of industrial authority, a model of authority which, for most workers, certainly lies closer to the authoritarian than to the democratic pole?

In still other comparisons between the efficiency of the groups, the experimenters found that those under democratic leadership had more self-generated work interest than those under authoritarian leadership. For example, members of democratic groups engaged in more work-minded conversation than members of authoritarian groups, and the experimenters also judged that under democracy there was more original and creative thinking.

2. Interpersonal Relations. The researchers found a much higher incidence of negative emotional reactions under authoritarian conditions than under democratic conditions. The authoritarian groups typically tended to respond in one of two ways, aggressively or submissively. In the aggressive authoritarian groups the observers noted far more expressions of hostility toward the leader and toward peers than in the democratic groups. There were also, in the aggressive authoritarian groups, high incidences of 'dominating ascendance', 'aggressive demands for attention', destruction of property, etc. Scapegoating was a conspicious feature of these authoritarian groups while hardly present at all under democratic conditions. In the submissive or dependent authoritarian group, reactions were different from the aggressive response but in most regards compared unfavourably with the democratic groups. For example, conversation was less varied and free in the submissive authoritarian groups than in the democratic groups, and there was a marked reduction of individual behaviour differences in the former as well.

3. Morale or Satisfaction. Overall satisfaction seemed far higher in the democratic than in the authoritarian groups, as suggested by a number of findings. First, all of the club dropouts occurred in the authoritarian groups, none in the democratic groups. Second, nineteen out of twenty boys who made comparisons preferred the democratic to the authoritarian leaders (boys in the clubs were exposed to different authority patterns consecutively). Third, discontented remarks voiced by members to each other were far more common in the authoritarian groups than in the democratic groups. Finally, the greater aggressiveness of some of the members of authoritarian groups suggested, in line with the frustration/aggression hypothesis, a greater degree of frustration or dissatisfaction with their conditions.

Three other studies conducted under Lewin's direction tend to confirm the power of participation discovered in the first experiments on boys' clubs.[5] The setting and the technique are entirely different, yet there is an underlying consistency with the earlier studies. These involved tests of the effectiveness of lectures (non-participative) versus group discussion and participation on changing and influencing habits and attitudes. Again, these studies are far removed from the industrial scene but they are relevant to it in terms of the wide-ranging implications of participation.

The first experiment concerned the attempt to encourage Red Cross home nursing volunteers during World War II to make use of such unpopular meats as hearts, sweetbreads, and kidneys. In both the lecture and discussion groups an equivalent amount of information was conveyed to the housewives. In the lecture situation the leaders did all or most of the talking with minimal participation from the members, while in the discussion technique group participation was used extensively by the discussion leader. The effectiveness of each technique was measured by computing the proportion of women who, after the meetings, did go on to use these meats. By this means it was found that women in the discussion groups were far more likely to buy and use these meats than those subject to lecture methods.

In a second experiment, housewives were urged to increase their home consumption of milk. Again, both lectures and discussion-participation methods were used on different groups of women and the effectiveness of the techniques was compared. Once again the participation method proved superior; a greater proportion of those in discussion groups increased their consumption of milk subsequent to the experiment.

In another study, the last of this type to be reported here, new mothers were informed of the benefits of feeding their infants cod liver oil and orange juice and encouraged to give these foods to their own babies. This time group discussion was not measured against lecture methods but against individual instruction to each mother from a nutritionist. It was thought that this method would prove more effective than lectures, and perhaps even than group discussions, as it involved giving personal and individual attention to each mother. However, once again the participation method clearly proved superior, measured by the proportion of mothers who decided to use these foods after the experiment.

When evaluating these and other studies which show the advantages of democratic over authoritarian leadership (or 'democratic' discussion over 'autocratic' lectures), it is important to bear in mind that these experiments have taken place in a larger social and cultural milieu in which democratic values are paramount. Perhaps in an authoritarian setting experiments such as these would turn out differently. As the psychologists Krech and Crutchfield observed:

> All of the experimental evidence . . . has been obtained by the study of so-called 'authoritarian' and 'democratic' leadership situations *in our democratic culture.* It is entirely possible that similar studies in other cultures might yield different results. The advantage for morale, the experiments find, seems to lie with the democratically led groups, but in an autocratic culture the reverse might possibly hold true.[6]

As suggestive as this hypothesis is, it should be noted that replications of the Lewin studies in immediate postwar Japan showed that despite the wide cultural differences between the United States and Japan and the authoritarian traditions of the latter, the similarities in the two groups of studies were greater than the differences.[7] In the Japanese as well as in the American experiments, democratic organisation usually evoked more friendliness, more work interest, generally higher morale, and high quality and quantities of work. But even granting the point that the advantages of participation might occasionally be weakened in an authoritarian setting, it is crucial not to lose sight of the major finding of the Lewin studies: the superiority and appeal of participation within a larger democratic cultural setting such as our own.

In reviewing the Lewinian experiments, E. B. Bennett noted that the group discussion method actually included four distinct elements or processes: *1*, group discussion; *2*, group decision; *3*, overtness or covertness of the commitment to the decision; *4*, strength of the consensus reached by the group in their decision.[8]

In order to discover which of these elements were most important and most effective in the group discussion method, she considered them separately in a study designed to test which of these elements tended to increase the willingness of introductory psychology students to volunteer for experiments. In brief, she found that group *decision*, rather than mere discussion of the problem, was crucial in raising the probability of action. Discussion *per se* was not nearly so effective as discussion plus decision.

II

We turn now to the second type of research considered here, field studies conducted in industrial settings. And it might be well to begin with an investigation carried out by Alex Bavelas that corroborates Bennett's study just mentioned.[9] This particular research took place at the Harwood Company, a garment factory located in Marion, Virginia, and the site of countless experiments in participation over a twenty-five year period. Bavelas compared the efficiency of two matched groups of sewing machine operators. One group was allowed to discuss *and decide upon* its own production goal; the other merely discussed effective teamwork but rendered no decisions and set no actual production goal. Bavelas found that the group which both discussed production *and made decisions* regarding it was clearly the more productive group.

This study has been criticised[10] on the grounds that the experimental group (discussion and decision) may have inadvertently been given more training than the control group (discussion only) and that the superiority of the former may have been attributable to its superior training rather than to the motivation derived from its decision-making power. Viteles noted also that the experimental group was given knowledge of production changes (charts, graphs), whereas workers in the control group were not, and he suggests that this may have had an effect.

In order to correct these possible sources of error, Lawrence and Smith replicated Bavelas' study.[11] Their experiment took place at a large mid-western garment factory employing about a thousand office and factory workers. Two experimental and two control groups were chosen of not more than six members in each; one experimental and control group consisted of office workers (on salary), while the other set consisted of factory workers (swatchers—on piece rates). Each experimental group and its corresponding control group were matched on a number of characteristics and they did not differ from each other with respect to conditions which might have affected productivity.

In both the experimental and control groups, discussions were set up and held once a week during the five week experimental period, an hour the first time and one half hour thereafter. In all groups, discussion focused on employee problems, social relations in the firm, company policy, rules, restrictions, employee benefits, and the like. Participation from all group members was encouraged. The experimental groups differed from the control groups in this respect: the experimental groups *discussed and set actual production goals*, in addition to discussing the other topics; the control groups, on the other hand, though they discussed the other topics, were not allowed to determine production goals.

The authors state that members of both the experimental and control groups reported an increase in morale as a result of the weekly discussions, but as the main concern was with output, little attention was paid here to matters of job satisfaction. The production of both groups rose during the experiment; however, the production increase of the control groups were of a very low order and not statistically significant. Each of the experimental groups, on the other hand, increased its efficiency over its original starting point to a degree significant at the 0·05 level and at the 0·01 level compared with changes in the control groups.

The study seems to confirm the results of Bavelas' experiment at Harwood and also Bennett's study mentioned above. What is crucial in participation is the ability and power of a group to arrive at a *decision*; this is more effective than when a group has less power and serves merely as a forum for discussion. Discussion and decision-making are both forms of participation but the latter is certainly the stronger form. If discussion and decision-making are seen on a scale of lesser and greater participation, then the tentative implications of the foregoing studies are that the greater the amount of participation, the more potent and effective an instrument it is for achieving a variety of ends.

This conclusion is also suggested by one of the most famous experiments in the participation literature carried out at the Harwood Company.[12] The experiments of Coch and French at Harwood are illustrative, I believe, of the potential of participation for increasing satisfaction in work within the factory setting although the essential nature of the work process and the technology of production remains unchanged.

At the time of this research in the mid-1940s, Harwood employed about six hundred workers, over 80 per cent of them women. The plant's labour force had an average age of twenty-three years and an average educational level of eight years. Payment in the factory was based on an incentive system with rates set by time study, which supplemented a basic minimum wage below which no worker could fall regardless of output.

Despite a generally liberal and enlightened labour policy, the company, like so many others, encountered severe worker resistance to any kind of change in methods of production or in job assignments. This resistance was partially due to the fact that transfers from one job to another usually meant lowered production for the transferred workers for a time until they had learned their new job. But management, through the use of a re-learning bonus, guaranteed that earnings would not drop during this period. Nevertheless, resistance to change was the rule, expressing itself in high turnover ($12\frac{1}{2}$ per cent per month for transferees as against $4\frac{1}{2}$ per cent for non-transferees), hostility toward management, feelings of pessimism, lowered aspirations, and output restriction. The latter was reflected in the fact that newly hired workers reached standard production on their jobs much faster than experienced operators who were transferred to these same jobs. The researchers, after investigation, concluded from the evidence that this difference in learning time was due solely to the transferred workers' lack of motivation. Moreover, 60 per cent of the transferred workers who had achieved standard production ratings on their previous jobs either became permanently substandard workers or quit work entirely after being changed to new jobs.

Part of the resistance to job changes was due to traditional workers' suspicion of the motives of any change introduced unilaterally by management. Some resistance was also due to the frustration of having to give up a task one has finally mastered (the old job) only to become an inexperienced novice once again. Another element, not stressed by the authors, was that each worker's performance was computed daily by the company, published, and posted for all to see, with the workers' names listed in order of productivity. Thus it was natural for workers to resist doing jobs which would result in initial lowered productivity during an extended re-learning period.

In this setting, then, Coch and French conducted two experiments designed to measure the effects of participation upon overcoming resistance to change. They selected four groups of workers and for each group introduced certain minor and roughly comparable changes in their jobs. The groups differed only in the manner in which the changes were made.

The first group was termed the 'no-participation' group, and changes here were effected in the manner customary in most enterprises. The production department studied the problem, altered the job, and set new piece rates. The group was called together, informed of the changes in the job and in the rate, questions were answered, and the meeting was adjourned.

In the second group a form of participation was adopted, participation through representatives, and job changes were made in the following way.

Before any changes took place, a group meeting was held with all the operators to be changed. The need for the change was presented as dramatically as possible, showing two identical garments produced in the factory; one was produced in 1946 and had sold for 100 per cent more than its fellow in 1947. The group was asked to identify the cheaper one and could not do it. The demonstration effectively shared with the group the entire problem of the necessity of cost reduction. A general agreement was reached that a savings could be effected by removing the 'frills' and 'fancy' work from the garment without affecting the folders' opportunities to achieve a high efficiency rating. Management then presented a plan to set the new job and piece rate [a plan which would be carried out by workers' representatives]: *1*, make a check study of the job as it was being done; *2*, eliminate all unnecessary work; *3*, train several operators in the correct method; *4*, set the piece rate by time studies on these specially trained operators; *5*, explain the new job and rate to all the operators; *6*, train all the operators in the new method so they can reach a high rate of production within a short time. The group approved this plan (though no formal group decision was reached), and chose the operators to be specially trained. A sub-meeting with the 'special' operators was held immediately following the meeting with the entire group.[13]

The researchers noted the 'co-operative' and 'interested' attitude of the elected workers and recorded that after the new job and piece rates were adopted, the operators referred to them as 'our job' and 'our rate'. At a later meeting of the entire group of workers, the new jobs and rates were introduced to all and the special operators took charge of training the others.

The third and fourth groups were 'total-participation' groups. Changes here were made in a manner similar to the representative groups except that the total-participation groups were smaller and, instead of delegating authority to some of the operators, all members participated in redesigning the job. The researchers remark significantly that in the meetings of the total-participation groups the workers' stream of suggestions was so heavy that 'the stenographer had great difficulty in recording them'.

The results of the experiment are extremely significant in terms of the guiding hypothesis of this chapter. Stated in the most general terms, the researchers found that 'success' in bringing about job changes—defined both in terms of productivity and worker satisfaction —was directly proportional to the amount of worker participation. In the no-participation group, for example, morale fell drastically right after the introduction of the changes and in the first forty days 17 per cent of the workers in that group had quit their jobs. Many of those who remained complained about the new job and some filed grievances regarding the new piece rate; paradoxically when the new rate was examined it was actually found to be on the lenient side. Hostility and lack of co-operation with supervisors and the methods engineer were very common. In addition, there was a marked and deliberate restriction of output; productivity fell precipitously from the pre-change level and showed little or no improvement during the forty days of the experiment (see Figure 1).

In the other groups where workers had participated through representatives in making the changes, the picture was entirely different. In the representative group, morale was quite high and there was no turnover at all in the first forty days after the change. Attitudes

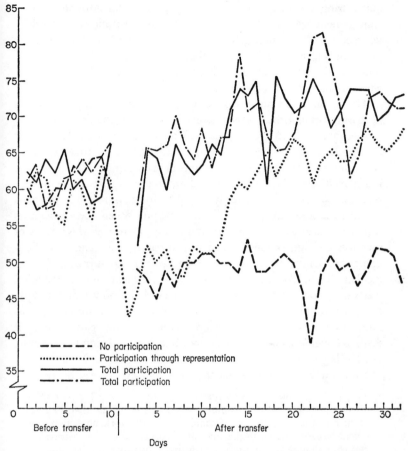

FIG. I. (Source: L. Coch and J. R. P. French, Jr., 'Overcoming Resistance to Change', *Human Relations*, I [1948], p. 522).

toward the methods engineer, training staff, and supervisor were co-operative throughout, with only one brief and minor incident of hostility directed against the supervisor. On the output side, the re-learning curve of the representative group was unusually high compared with the typical pattern and within two and a half weeks the group had reached and exceeded the level of production achieved before the change.

As successful as the representative group was, it paled before the performance of the total-participation groups. In these, not one worker quit during the forty days of the experiment and attitudes toward management were co-operative with no demonstrations of hostility whatsoever. Production gains were by far higher than for any other group as Figure 1 indicates; within just two days the groups had achieved their pre-change levels of production and they eventually went on and exceeded that level by 14 per cent.

The research did not end here. Following the first experiment the no-participation group was dissolved and its members distributed throughout the factory on new job assignments. Two and a half months later these same workers were brought back together again and given another assignment, but this time changes in their jobs were introduced using the method of total group participation. The group's reaction now was diametrically opposite from its reaction when its members lacked any power of participation. When these operators were organised as a no-participation group, there were high rates of turnover and aggression directed against management and lack of co-operation. Under total participation there was no turnover and no incidents in nearly three weeks of the experiment and co-operation was very good.* When these workers lacked any power of participation, their output declined and remained low as soon as the change was introduced; when the same group was allowed full participation, it easily recovered its previous efficiency and soon went on to exceed its old levels (see Figure 2).

Summarising these experiments, Coch and French say dryly:

> The first experiment showed that the rate of recovery [of output] is directly proportional to the amount of participation, and that the rates of turnover and aggression [manifestations of work alienation] are inversely proportional to the amount of participation. The second experiment demonstrated more conclusively that the results obtained depended on the experimental treatment rather than on personality factors like skill or aggressiveness, for identical individuals [not quite; some had quit] yielded markedly different results in the no-participation treatment as contrasted with the total-participation treatment. . . . Apparently total participation has the same effect as participation through representatives, but the former has a stronger influence.[14]

In short, the Harwood experiment was a striking confirmation of the participation hypothesis.

---

* One might argue that the workers who quit when they were first organised as a no-participation group purged the group of its most discontented and least productive members and that the later improvements were partially due to their absence. I doubt that this had more than a marginal effect. Morale and productivity stayed low until the very end of the first experiment, though the most discontented workers had already quit by then.

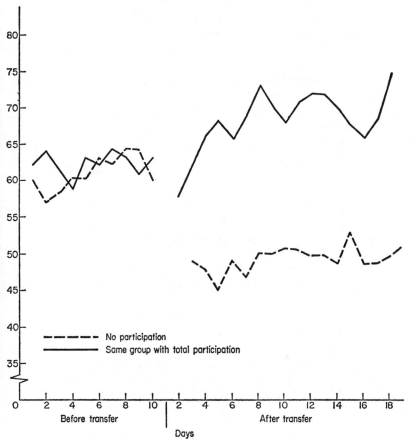

FIG. 2. (Source: L. Coch and J. R. P. French, Jr., 'Overcoming Resistance to Change', *Human Relations*, 1 [1948], p. 523).

Several years later the Harwood Company decided to modernise and completely overhaul its production methods.[15] These changes were much more thoroughgoing than those frequent modifications of jobs which Harwood workers had experienced previously. The new changes involved a complete re-engineering of production methods, the introduction of new equipment, and corresponding changes in jobs and piece rates. The company accomplished this conversion with remarkable success—in terms of work satisfaction and productivity levels—despite the fact that workers there had traditionally shown great resistance to, and suspicion of, any changes in production methods. Management overcame this resistance and suspicion and accomplished its modernisation smoothly and with little friction by bringing workers into the decision-making process. The company organised dozens of meetings with small groups of workers before and during the changeover, explaining the economic and technological necessity for the changes, encouraging discussion, and soliciting ideas and suggestions. Moreover, management encouraged workers to voice their grievances at these meetings on all issues, not merely those involving the conversion. Management noted and then acted upon these grievances. Beside group consultation, management also employed individual consultation with workers and occasionally senior operators interviewed their fellow workers. As far as material benefits, the company promised and put into effect a subsidy programme to compensate the workers for losses due to the extensive re-learning of new methods and new jobs.

As a direct consequence of this elaborate system of information and consultation, labour relations did not suffer during and after the changeover but, on the contrary, turnover and absenteeism declined while production increased. In this way radical changes and improvements were achieved with the workers' active co-operation instead of against their strenuous opposition.

But this is uncommon. It is almost axiomatic that whenever management introduces changes unilaterally, it arouses suspicion and resistance among its workers. As one writer described this difficulty:

> One of the most baffling and recalcitrant of the problems which business executives face is employee resistance to change. Such resistance may take a number of forms—persistent reduction in output, increase in the number of 'quits' and requests for transfer, chronic quarrels, sullen hostility, wildcat or slowdown strikes, and, of course, the expression of a lot of pesudo-logical reasons why the change will not work.[16]

Even more interesting, this resistance manifests itself just as strongly when the proposed changes are actually in the workers' objective interest. Fred Blum reports, for example, that when the Hormel Company attempted to introduce what was, in essence, a guaranteed annual wage for its workers in the 1930s, it was *fought* by workers and the union.[17] Part of the union's opposition, of course, stems from the fear of having its thunder stolen by the company, thus undermining its influence with the workers. But a good part of rank and file suspicion arises from the simple and logical conviction that a policy which is imposed solely on the company's initiative will be good for the company and not for the workers. Thus, we are not surprised at Elliott Jaques' report that when the firm he was studying (the British Glacier Metal Company) sought to establish joint consultation machinery for its workers, with shop committees, works committees, and a works council, the workers opposed it strongly and regarded it and management's motives with grave suspicion.[18]

In short, Harwood's record of successfully introducing major technological innovations stands in marked contrast to the experience of most other companies,* and tends to confirm Georges Friedmann's observation that 'until the worker has a voice in these constant technological changes, and in their control and re-adaptation, he will tend to believe that rationalisation is carried out for his employer's greater profit and only incidentally for his own'.[19]

At Harwood, Coch and French were primarily concerned with the effectiveness of participation in facilitating major or minor *changes* in company production methods. Neglected here was any treatment of the effects of participation, not upon changes, but upon the stable and everyday operation of the firm. It is to such an investigation that we now turn.

Some years ago Morse and Reimer carried out an ingenious piece of field research in one department of a large insurance company in the United States.[20] In the department there were four parallel divisions in which workers (typically young unmarried women) performed fairly routine and repetitive clerical work such as billing operations. The experiment involved *changing the level of decision-making* for the 500 workers in the four divisions. In two divisions worker participation in the decision-making process was systematically *increased*; in the other two divisions participation was systematically *decreased*. The operating hypothesis was that an increase in decision-making power among the workers would lead both to enhanced job satisfaction and higher productivity.

Morse and Reimer altered the nature and extent of participation in

* It might be added that in 1966, after more than two decades of experimentation with worker participation, Harwood's annual labour turnover rate had fallen under 6 per cent in an industry in which 25 per cent is considered excellent, it had the fastest rate of growth of any company in the industry and had become the largest pyjama manufacturer in the country, had the highest wage scale in the industry and was among the highest in productivity. (See the statement of its board chairman, psychologist Alfred J. Marrow in *Trans-action*, 3 (Sept.–Oct. 1966), pp. 36–7, 56).

the four divisions by creating new institutional arrangements to correspond with new levels of decision-making, and by training supervisors to ensure that their relations with their subordinates corresponded with the new structure of participation. The exact nature and extent of participation in the autonomous sections are described only in a general way by Morse and Riemer, but we infer that the workers enjoyed a substantial increase in power over what they had prior to the experiment. At group meetings their jurisdiction was expanded to include 'work methods and processes, and personnel matters, such as recess periods, the handling of tardiness, etc.'[21] In his account of the experiment, Daniel Katz, Morse and Reimer's colleague at Michigan's Survey Research Center, elaborates on the nature of the participation slightly:

> The rank-and-file employees took over the management of their sections. Hence, to implement their responsibility as a group, the workers had not only power formally vested in the supervisor but control over some of the decisions regarding personnel matters and work processes previously made fairly high in the supervisory line. They did not, however, have complete autonomy and were subject to some of the same rules and regulations as other employees.[22]

In the sections in which the amount of rank-and-file participation was *decreased*, the chief method of reducing control was by having staff officials develop rigid individual work standards for various jobs and in general through tightened control by upper staff and line officials. Thus, workers in these sections were subject to much greater *hierarchical control* than they had previously known.

The experiment continued for a year and a half and consisted of the following stages: pre-experimental measurement of productivity and satisfaction; training of supervisors for six months in the appropriate method of supervision; introduction of experimental conditions continuing for one year; and finally, re-measurement. Morse and Reimer's methods of measurement consisted of questionnaires administered to the workers, observations of the supervisory training programme, interviews with supervisory personnel and employees, and a study of relevant company records (on turnover, productivity, etc.).

Morse and Reimer conceived of satisfaction in work as having four dimensions. The first was the degree of 'self-actualisation' possible on the job, measured by asking the workers whether they felt their jobs were challenging, whether they were able to learn interesting things which might help them find a better job in the company, and whether they had a chance to try out new ideas or to do work in which they excelled. These questions were asked before and then after the participation experiment and the changes in response were naturally attributed to the experimental conditions. The workers responded using a scale running from one to five, with a rating of five expressing the greatest satisfaction; then, for each of the groups the members' scores were intercorrelated to form an index. The results on the 'self-actualisation' dimension are presented below.

TABLE I: WORKERS' PARTICIPATION AND PERCEIVED OPPORTUNITY FOR SELF-ACTUALISATION ON THE JOB[23]

	Mean Score Before Exp.	Mean Score After Exp.	Difference	N
Autonomous sections (average of both)	2·43	2·57	+0·14*	99
Hierarchically-controlled sections (average of both)	2·37	2·24	−0·13*	81

* significant at 5 per cent level, one tailed t test for paired data.

We see at once that the introduction of self-determination among the employees in the autonomous sections increased their sense of self-actualisation compared to the pre-experimental situation, while a decrease in the decision-making powers of the employees in the other sections resulted in a significant decline in their sense of self-actualisation.

The second component of job satisfaction related to the workers' attitudes toward their supervisors: the manager, the assistant manager, and the immediate supervisor. Morse and Reimer asked the employees how good these supervisors were at handling people, whether they could be counted on for good relations at all times, and how well the employees liked to work with them.

The third dimension was satisfaction with the company itself, derived from answers to the question: 'Taking things as a whole, how do you like working for —?'

To measure the final component of morale, Morse and Reimer constructed an index of intrinsic job satisfaction. They asked the employees whether their jobs were ever monotonous, how important they thought their jobs were compared with others at the company, and how they liked the kind of work they were doing.

With every measure of satisfaction, the results were similar to those shown above for self-actualisation. That is, in every case, employees whose decision-making powers were increased were likely to be *more* satisfied with their *supervisors* (at all levels), *more* satisfied with the *company*, and *more* satisfied with their *jobs* than before participation was introduced. By the same token, employees subject to hierarchical control were likely to be *less* satisfied with their *supervisors* (at all levels), *less* satisfied with the *company*, and *less* satisfied with their *jobs* than before hierarchical control was introduced. In only a few instances did all these changes fail to achieve statistical significance.

Other qualitative measures of satisfaction confirmed these statistical findings. Comments from workers in the autonomous groups differed markedly from comments of workers in the hierarchically-controlled groups. Those in the autonomous sections typically:

> wanted their programme to last indefinitely, did not like the other programme, felt that the clerks [i.e. they themselves] were one of the groups gaining the most from the programme and described both positive and negative changes in interpersonal relations among the girls. The clerks in the hierarchically-controlled programme, on the other hand, most frequently: wanted their programme to end immediately, liked the other programme and felt that the company gained the most from their progress. Not one single person in the hierarchically-controlled programme mentioned an improvement in interpersonal relations as a result of this programme. All of the noted changes were for the worse, with increases in friction and tension being most frequently mentioned.[24]

Comparative morale of the groups is also reflected in figures on turnover. Of nine employees in the experiment who left their jobs because of dissatisfaction, or in order to take other, better jobs, eight were from the hierarchically-controlled section, one was from the autonomous sections.

With respect to output, the researchers discovered that productivity in the autonomous sections increased by an average of 10 per cent over the experimental period, a striking success. Paradoxically, however, in the hierarchically-controlled sections, productivity increased also and in fact surpassed the production gains in the autonomous sections with an average increase of 14 per cent. One must interpret these comparative production figures with some care, however. The clerks in the four divisions had no control over the amount of work they did; this depended entirely on the flow of work to them from other parts of the firm. Thus, productivity could increase only by reducing the work staff while turning out the same amount of work. The greater productivity of the hierarchically-controlled divisions meant that their staff had been reduced to a greater extent than had the staff in the autonomous groups. In such a situation it seemed literally possible for workers to be capable of working themselves out of a job. Perhaps the autonomous group members were less likely to want to risk this—being closely attached to the participation programme that existed in their divisions—and thus held their production down below what it might have been if increases in output had been linked, not to reduction of the work force, but to the accomplishment of more work. The matter is speculative, however, since Morse and Reimer do not give enough information to test this hypothesis, but it is sufficiently plausible so that one cannot unequivocally say that the hierarchically-controlled groups were inherently more productive than their autonomous counterparts.

Rensis Likert, also of the Michigan Survey Research Center and one whose knowledge of the experiment goes beyond the published accounts, reports that work attitudes in the autonomous sections were vastly superior to those in the hierarchical sections.[25] In the participating groups, the employees' feeling of responsibility for getting work done increased (they continued working when supervisors were out); attitudes toward high producers improved; and, as reported here, attitudes toward supervisors at all levels improved. In the hierarchical sections, job attitudes moved in the opposite direction. Likert concludes that all these factors ultimately relate to productivity and he speculates that if the study had gone on, eventually the autonomous divisions would have surpassed the hierarchical divisions in production.

Whatever the ultimate effects on production, this field experiment, conducted among clerical workers, corroborates the Coch and French study at Harwood among manual workers. Daniel Katz has summarised the implication of Morse and Reimer's research in the following way:

> This field experiment demonstrates that work satisfaction can be increased if workers are given greater freedom, as a group, to make decisions and take responsibility for a task. The downward delegation of power did not wreck the organisation but actually raised the level of production 10 per cent at the same time that it increased morale. In short it may well be that worker satisfaction will increase to the extent that partnership in production becomes a social reality rather than a slogan.[26]

These remarks are equally applicable to the Harwood experiment; both studies demonstrated that work alienation is substantially reduced when workers acquire a substantial share of managerial decision-making power, even though the technological setting of their work and the intrinsic nature of their tasks remain unchanged.

So far we have been concerned with the participation hypothesis in general and have not specified more particularly the conditions under which participation is more effective and under what conditions it is less effective. French and his colleagues conducted an interesting experiment in a Norwegian shoe factory[27] which yielded suggestive evidence that the success of workers' participation in increasing job satisfaction depends in part upon whether participation in managerial decision-making is regarded as a *legitimate activity* for workers. If the idea of participation lacks legitimacy in the eyes of the worker, then it will be much less effective an instrument in increasing satisfaction in work than it otherwise would be.

The factory that French studied employed 1,600 workers. Much of the plant's production was carried out by four-man groups which autonomously decided on their own level of production and informed management of their decision. A piece rate system, set by time study, provided the incentive for these groups to produce as much as possible. Periodically these small work groups were retrained when a new product was to go into production.

During product changeover time, French selected nine of these four-man work groups (thirty-six workers in all); five of these groups were designated experimental groups, four were designated control groups. Both the experimental and the control groups continued their traditional function of setting their own rate of production and reporting to management. But the decision-making power of workers in the experimental groups was increased by allowing them to participate in meetings with management at which they determined the following issues: *1*, which work groups would be assigned what articles to assemble; *2*, whether and how much training was necessary for production on the new item; *3*, how the division of labour should be arranged within the work group; *4*, allotment of particular jobs to particular individuals within the group.* At the meetings the foreman acted as leader and technical information was supplied by various resource men. The workers made their decision after receiving the technical information and after discussion and debate had taken place.

The results of the study were interesting. The experimental groups

---

* Unfortunately, due to circumstances beyond the researchers' control, three of the five experimental groups were able to participate in decision-making only on the first problem listed above. The other two experimental groups did participate in all four of the areas.

showed no increase in productivity over the control groups. The researchers attributed this regularity to a widely accepted norm, similar to that in Mayo's Bank Wiring Room experiment, which established a standard for a fair day's work, a standard which arose primarily out of fear of a cut in piece rates if productivity advanced beyond that point.

On the question of morale, satisfaction with the company, and attitudes toward labour relations in the factory, however, French found that on fourteen questions in these areas, those in the experimental groups had more favourable attitudes on ten of them, three of which were statistically significant. This finding tends to corroborate the conclusions of the other research on participation which have been examined here.

French and his colleagues carried their research further by introducing an intervening variable which we might call the perceived legitimacy of workers' participation. The researchers asked these Norwegian workers how much influence and power it would be right and proper for workers to have, with responses ranging from 'management should make all decisions alone', to 'there should be joint decisions in which workers have the most say'. When French examined the responses of the workers in the experimental, decision-making groups, he found that workers who believed that participation was right and proper had more favourable attitudes toward job and company in ten out of fourteen questions, compared with those who questioned the legitimacy of participation.

There are a number of limitations to this study, however: *1*, the sample was rather small; *2*, there was some participation in the control groups (they continued to decide and set their production rates) while ideally there should have been no participation in the control groups; *3*, there was only limited participation in three of the five experimental groups. Because of the latter two factors there was not as much variation in the independent variable—participation—as one should like in an experiment of this kind.

Nevertheless, the study is suggestive and needs replication in different settings; in any case it points again to the possible importance of a favourable normative milieu if participation is to be as effective as other research has indicated that it potentially is.

Before we leave the area of field experiments on participation in the industrial setting, I should like to mention two more studies briefly which deal with the effects of participation, this time, on supervisory personnel. They show the broad spectrum power of participation, not only to enhance satisfaction in work and to increase production, but to change prejudices and facilitate learning.

The first was an early experiment at Harwood.[28] Management had noted a great resistance on the part of supervisors to hire older women for jobs in the factory, due to the prevalent belief that they are inefficient and slow workers, slow learners, are absent more, and have higher turnover rates than other workers. Management, in fact, had shared these beliefs until it discovered, by studying its own records, that these beliefs were erroneous. But just as management had refused to take the word of the consulting psychologist on this matter and had to find out the facts for themselves, so first line foremen refused to take the word of management and stuck tenaciously to their prejudices, regardless of the data handed down to them from above. As there was a rather serious labour shortage at the time (during World War II), it was imperative to take on additional older women workers, but this could not be done in the face of determined resistance by foremen.

Having found it futile merely to 'give the foremen the facts', management realised another method would have to be tried. Participation turned out to be the key to the problem.

> . . . the findings [on the efficiency of older women workers] were presented to groups of subleaders. Discussions followed, centring around the origin of the stereotype and the possible motivations for believing in it. In the course of these meetings, insights into the original bias gradually developed. What is more, group decisions were reached recommending that an experiment be made in the training of older workers. In this way the idea of hiring older women workers was gradually established. Only with this gradual shift in attitudes did the new policy become a reality.[29]

This experiment at Harwood demonstrated the effects of participation upon reducing prejudices or stereotypes among supervisory personnel. In another study, Levine and Butler also demonstrated the effects of participation upon supervisory personnel, this time in facilitating learning.[30] This study was conducted in a factory employing some 400 workers who ranged from unskilled to very highly skilled. Each worker was paid on the basis of 1, his level of skill and training; 2, the quality of his performance on the job as evaluated by one of twenty-nine supervisors.

What provided the stimulus for the experiment was management's observation that supervisors, in their ratings of the workers, tended to rate, not the performance of individual workers in their jobs, but the job itself. Thus, workers in highly skilled jobs were apt to get high ratings regardless of their performance on the job and unskilled workers tended to get low ratings for the same reason. In short, the halo effect of the job itself affected the supervisors' appraisal of the workers' performance on the job.

Levine and Butler arranged an experiment with these supervisors in order to ascertain which method—following Lewin's work—lecture or discussion and participation, would lead to greater correction of the error the supervisors were making. The researchers selected three groups of supervisors: a control group, a discussion group and a lecture group. In the discussion group, a leader launched the discussion by introducing the problem of biased rating and illustrating it by means of a graph. The leader played the role of a moderator, with discussion and suggestions for a solution to the problem left up to the participants. In the lecture group, the leader gave a thorough talk on the problem, its background, the reasons and sources of supervisory errors, and gave instructions on how to correct the errors. The control group was not exposed to any experimental treatment.

Following the experiment all groups again rated their workers and these ratings were compared with the pre-experimental ratings. The results clearly indicated that only those supervisors who had participated in discussions and had reached a group decision showed any significant change in their ratings toward elimination of the halo effect. The ratings of supervisors in both the control group and the lecture group remained essentially unchanged. In sum, the researchers' findings 'completely confirm[ed] those of Lewin in demonstrating the greater effectiveness of group decision over the lecture method of training'.[31]

III

Let us turn now to several studies in which participation was introduced, not 'artificially' for experimental purposes by researchers coming in from the outside, but rather naturally and spontaneously, from below on the initiation of the workers themselves, and in response to their own needs. In these studies both the setting and the characteristics of the workers differ greatly, yet the implications for participation are the same.

Babchuck and Goode studied a group of eighteen skilled, unionised men's clothing salesmen working in a large and successful Detroit department store.[32] Conditions in the salesmen's department were excellent, and theirs was one of the most desirable work areas in the store; advancement opportunities were plentiful and the pay was high. But despite these favourable conditions, morale among the workers was extremely low.

The commission system which management had inaugurated encouraged unscrupulous competition among the salesmen, and as a result there was constant quarrelling, conflict, antagonism, and sales grabbing. Moreover, the logic of the straight commission system led the salesmen to avoid all work which was not directly connected with making sales and earning commission. Thus, they ignored display and stock work, while high pressure selling was the rule, with much customer-stealing and other techniques such as trying to keep a customer in one's pocket, so to speak, while waiting on another. In spite of all this, however, productivity was quite high.

Nevertheless, conditions became so disagreeable that the men themselves took a measure of managerial power into their own hands and introduced an innovation referred to as 'pooling'. Pooling meant simply that the men shared all the work in the department, both selling and other duties, and shared all the commissions so that all received equal pay. In this way the men put a stop to their incessant rivalry. Confronted with a *fait accompli*, management agreed to accept the system and acquiesced in handling the necessary book-keeping and other details. Meanwhile the workers had taken over such managerial tasks as arranging the division of labour within the group, planning the work, and disciplining recalcitrant workers, etc. The system introduced by the men allowed them to pay more attention to all facets of their work, not merely to the selling; and in selling itself, there was no more need to try to monopolise customers or to engage in sharp practices. The men began to see their work as a group activity rather than an individual struggle with hostile forces working all around. The atmosphere in the department became more relaxed and easy-going but at the same time productivity actually increased. And there was unanimous expression of satisfaction among the men with the system that they had introduced. Intensive interviews later revealed that not one salesmen wanted the pooling system to be discontinued, and the success of the experiment led to its eventual adoption in other departments of the store.

In an entirely different setting George Strauss reports an interesting experiment in workers' participation that came along in the same way, i.e. on the initiative of the workers rather than as a controlled experiment instigated by researchers or by management.[33] The *dramatis personae* here were not male white collar workers but eight young female manual workers in a factory producing small toys. Their job was a relatively simple and repetitive one: to spray paint on wooden toys placed before them. The job had recently been re-engineered and, according to the new system, each girl would take a toy from a tray next to her, place it in a jig inside her painting cubicle, and spray paint on it. Then she would place the toy on one of the overhead hooks which moved by her at a constant speed on an endless belt, and the hook then carried the toy into an adjacent drying oven. Wages for the job, apart from basic pay, were calculated according to a group bonus plan, and, because the job was new, this was supplemented by a learning bonus which decreased month by month.

The job described here seemed simple and clear, and management expected no trouble. But there was trouble: the girls' productivity was very low and was not increasing at the rate management had hoped or expected. Many hooks on the belt went by empty. Morale among the girls was very bad: there were complaints, resistance, excessive absenteeism, and much turnover which only complicated and lengthened the learning process. Among the operators' most consistent complaints were, first, that the room was too hot due to the proximity of the drying oven and, secondly, that the speed of the belt, set by the engineers, was much too fast, and that it simply was impossible to keep up the pace.

In order to resolve these difficulties, management brought in a consultant and he advised the foreman, against the latter's better judgment, to confer with the operators. During a series of meetings which followed, the girls made a number of suggestions to the foreman. First, they requested that he install fans to ventilate the area. The engineer and the foreman were sceptical about the girls' complaint and didn't believe that the fans would appease them or cool their anger. Nevertheless, they agreed to try them, and when the fans were brought in the girls were delighted and took great pride in positioning and repositioning them until they found a satisfactory location for them. The experiment was a success and it was reflected in an immediate improvement in the relationship between the foreman and the workers.

At a subsequent meeting the focus of attention turned to the 'excess speed' of the belts, and here the operators made an heretical proposal: 'Let us adjust the speed of the belt faster or slower depending on how we feel'. The foreman was startled, the engineer aghast. But after lengthy discussion, arguments, and dire prophecies by the engineer, a control was installed at the group leader's booth which allowed her to adjust the speed of the belt slow, medium, or fast. After its installation, the girls immediately worked out an elaborate schedule of when during the day the belt would be operated slowly, when medium, and when fast. The results of this innovation were both ironic and significant. Although the girls' original complaint was that the belt moved impossibly fast, under *their own control* the average speed of the belt was actually *increased*. When the belt was running at a fixed speed determined by the engineer, it corresponded to low-medium on the operators' dial; under the girls' control, however, the average speed was up toward the high mark.

As a result of this surprising change, the girls' productivity increased between 30–50 per cent over expected levels; and, as their pay was tied to productivity, their earnings jumped enormously, for they were making basic pay, plus a learning bonus, plus a very high group bonus. Moreover, morale reached an all-time high and for the first time the girls seemed reasonably content with their work.

The story did not end happily here, however. These semi-skilled operators, their production at record levels, began to earn more than many of the highly skilled workers in the plant, and the latter complained vociferously. Furthermore, the extra production unbalanced the work of the other departments, leading to a vacuum behind and a pile-up in front of the girls' section. Equally disturbing, the impertinent success of the workers had undermined the prestige of the engineers by calling their competence into question, and had rudely challenged the whole system of managerial prerogatives.

The superintendent, engineer, and foreman were naturally very gravely disturbed over these developments. To resolve the 'problems' created by the success of the experiment, the superintendent unilaterally decided to return to the *status quo ante*. He had the girls' control dial removed and the belt adjusted to run at a constant speed as before. The general consequences of these acts are easily predictable for anyone remotely acquainted with the literature on participation. Production fell off immediately, and within a month six of the eight girls had left the company. Several months later the foreman also resigned for reasons which were related to the experiment and its ultimate débâcle.

In this entire situation we see a convergence of two kinds of workers' control which are crucial to job satisfaction. For simplicity's sake these two kinds might be roughly termed 'control over machinery' and 'control over authority'.[34] In this case control over machinery was satisfying to the workers because it allowed them to regulate their own work pace by alternately increasing and decreasing the speed of the belt. This variety alleviated somewhat the boredom and monotony of what was essentially a repetitive job, and the workers became autonomous masters of a machine instead of passive extensions of it.

Supplementing the workers' control over machinery here was their control over *authority* which was, as the participation literature amply demonstrates, a formidable factor in increasing their satisfaction with work. The fact that management consulted the workers on changes to be made, that their 'superiors' had accepted their suggestions, and that these changes had been successful—all this undoubtedly helped to account for the remarkably improved climate in the workers' room and for the ironic increase in production.

This case also demonstrates that the factory is an integrated social (and economic) system and that changes in one department are likely to have repercussions elsewhere. It was clearly evident that the workers' control could not survive here in isolation in one part of the factory: inherent instability demanded that it be either expanded or eliminated altogether. Or, as a dogmatic industrial democrat might say, a factory, like a nation, cannot exist half slave, half free.

A common defect of the two studies discussed above is that it is uncertain exactly what boosted the workers' morale. Was it the change itself or was it the way the change was introduced, i.e. by the workers themselves? Thus, we do not know what would have happened to morale in the toy factory if *management* had introduced the variable-speed belt on its own, or if *management* in the department store had introduced the pooling system. In essence, we lack control groups here which would have allowed a more accurate assessment of the effects of the changes themselves, on the one hand, and the manner in which the changes were introduced, on the other hand. Nevertheless, it is fair to assume, I think, that in both cases—the department store and the toy factory—the workers' gratification with the change *per se* was enhanced significantly by the knowledge that they had introduced it and in so doing had achieved success where management had been unable to do so.

This lack of a control group is corrected in two additional studies which Peter Drucker reports[35] and which I shall mention very briefly. In these two cases, as in the two preceding, participation arose spontaneously from below. In these instances, however, participation did not involve basic economic decisions of the firm, yet the findings are relevant nonetheless.

Drucker cites first the experience of a large electric power company with two plants in nearby cities, each with a life insurance programme for its employees. In the first plant, the insurance programme was very inefficient, giving inadequate coverage and charging high premiums. Nevertheless, the programme was extremely popular and had over 80 per cent of the work force enrolled. The insurance plan in the other plants was very efficient, having broader coverage and lower payments. Yet, less than 40 per cent of the workers in this plant belonged. The mystery is easily explained. The popularity of the first plan lay in its origin: it had been started by a group of workers in that company some twenty-five years earlier who had brought the programme in and drawn up the contract. Subsequently all the business was handled by fellow workers who were involved in insurance work in their spare time. It was thus a workers' project throughout. The comparatively meagre success of the insurance programme in the other plant is explained by the fact that it was a company project from beginning to end with no employee participation whatsoever.

Drucker also calls our attention to one aspect of General Motors' famous 'My Job' essay contest which 175,000 of their employees entered in 1947. Analysis of the data revealed that in plants where workers themselves had organised and operated the recreation programme, these programmes were 'among the major sources of job satisfaction—outranking even security, supervision or pay'.[36] On the other hand, in those plants where management organised and controlled the recreation programme and there was little or no worker participation in its management, workers were much less likely to comment upon the programme, and when they did, it was often as a source of dissatisfaction.

A final case, while lacking a control group, is nevertheless worth mentioning.[37] During World War II, in a large aircraft company which traditionally had very harmonious labour relations, the morale of the workers suddenly fell precipitously and production dropped off as well. The cause of the trouble was ultimately traced to management's decision to hire professionals to run the plant Red Cross, the Blood Bank, and the fund-raising drives. The workers themselves had organised and operated these activities from the beginning, and this sudden deprivation of their right to participate in these areas provoked a sudden crisis which did not subside until management restored control over these activities to the workers.

This incident reveals the disastrous consequences of *granting and then revoking* the rights of workers' participation. Another well-known study documents the difficulties which a firm created for itself by granting and revoking something akin to workers' participation, freedom from close hierarchical supervision and control. In his study of a mid-western gypsum plant, Alvin Gouldner discovered that work satisfaction and motivation to produce depended upon a so-called management 'indulgency pattern'.[38] This meant, in part, that the workers expected and demanded that management exercise a minimal amount of control and supervision consistent with getting the work done. The workers accepted production as a goal but refused to tolerate demands for obedience for its own sake, arbitrary assertions of authority, close supervision, invidious status distinctions, demands for deference, etc.; if these were insisted upon, the workers reacted with hostility towards their supervisors and with apathy towards their work.

Years ago the Belgian socialist, Henri de Man, saw this problem of the dual nature of authority as basic to modern capitalist industry and as a source of worker unrest and discontent.

> We always find that the ultimate cause of resentment against the disciplinary hierarchy . . . arises because it embodies, apart from the control technically necessary for the guidance of labour, also motives of private gain, on the one hand, and motives of social dominance, on the other.[39]

This was *precisely* the issue at the gypsum plant. The men refused to acknowledge the legitimacy of the authority system *per se*; authority could be invoked only when matters of production were involved. The workers thus expected and insisted upon leniency, that there be 'no constant check-up on you', no unnecessary 'pulling rank on a worker', no attempts by supervisors to 'throw their weight around'. This attitude came out in the workers' reaction to a working foreman. The union contract forbade foremen to engage in production work except in emergency situations. However, if a foreman attempted to do some work which the worker interpreted as trying to help out the worker, to lend a hand in a difficult job, there would be no objection to this informal infringement of the contract. If, on the other hand, the worker sensed that the purpose of the foreman's intervention was to intensify supervision, maintain a closer watch over the worker, or demonstrate his—the foreman's—superiority, the worker would almost certainly complain or file a grievance.[40]

In his book, Gouldner relates how a series of events in the plant over a period of years resulted in the gradual abrogation of the indulgency pattern and how the establishment of close and, for the men, oppressive supervision eventually culminated in a wildcat strike. Two conditions were primarily responsible for the strike, the introduction of new machinery and a series of shake-ups in the plant's managerial hierarchy. Regarding the machinery, management did not know the optimum speed and efficiency of the new equipment and so there were constant experiments with it. Because of this

> management was likely to stay *nearer* to the scene of operation. . . . It meant, also, that main office executives, or higher echelon supervisors who were unfamiliar to the workers, were on the scene more frequently than usual. Thus one of the . . . unnoticed by-products of technical change [was] a social change in the supervisory system.[41]

The changes in the managerial hierarchy, which were quite extensive, also led to a tightening of control over the workers. Insecure in their new positions, wanting to make a favourable impression upon higher-ups, lacking the immediate support of the workers, the new officials, from plant manager on down, exercised more formal, strict, and inflexible control over the men than they had ever been subject to before. The policy boomeranged, however, as the workers refused to tolerate any loss of their accustomed autonomy, and they reacted with reduced motivation to work. Their decreased output led to even greater pressure from management to work which, of course, merely aggravated the situation. This vicious circle ended finally in a wildcat strike. Autonomy was a precious possession not easily or willingly relinquished by the workers.

IV

The next series of studies I shall examine are not field experiments in the sense that experimental variables are manipulated. This group of studies consists of survey research which treats the relationship between 'styles' of supervision and job satisfaction. In most cases two types of supervision are compared: permissive or general supervision on the one hand, and restrictive or close supervision on the other. The concepts of general versus close supervision arose out of the University of Michigan Survey Research Center studies of productivity, morale, and supervision conducted in the late 1940s and early 1950s in a variety of industrial settings. General supervision came to mean in these studies that the supervisors set up

> certain general conditions for their employees and then [permit] their employees to work out the details of when and how the work will be handled. They [supervisors] do not seem to feel the need to get into the production process at every point to check on how things are going, to make changes, to reassign the work and, in other ways, to keep a close check on operations.[42]

This type of supervision seems to be related to a whole cluster of other traits, such as tendencies to delegate authority, not to impose pressure on subordinates, and to permit freedom of conduct to employees.[43]

On the other hand, supervisors who exercise close supervision tend to 'check up on their employees more frequently, to give them more detailed and more frequent work instructions, and in general to limit their freedom to do the work in their own way'.[44]

In the following discussion I have made the assumption that with general or permissive supervision the workers have some power of participation, however small, which they do not have under close or restrictive supervision. Under general supervision workers are freer to use their own initiative, to make more decisions concerning their job, and to implement these decisions. In thus comparing the effects of general versus close supervision, I shall implicitly be comparing the effects of participation versus non-participation. Of course, as stated earlier, in these studies participation arises because of the personality traits of individual supervisors rather than from the structure of the organisation, and this fact serves to put important limits on both the scope and the nature of participation and renders it somewhat artificial, alien, and anomalous. But although these studies are not as genuine measures of the effects of participation as the experiments discussed earlier—and I shall criticise them more fully later on—they nevertheless have a relevance which should not be overlooked.

I. R. Weschler and his associates conducted an interesting study of two divisions of a Naval Research Laboratory which employed physicists, engineers, scientific aids, and clerical workers.[45] Division A, consisting of twenty-eight members, was led by an outstanding young scientist who was quite restrictive in his leadership role. (Division leaders were classified as restrictive or permissive on the basis of specific incidents revealing the nature of their authority, as gathered from interviews and comments in sociometric questionnaires.) Division B, with thirty-eight workers, was led by an older man who was much more permissive toward his subordinates than the leader of Division A. When the job satisfaction of individuals in both groups was compared, the researchers found that only 39 per cent of the members of the restrictive group expressed definite satisfaction compared with 63 per cent of the members of the permissive group.[46] Employees were also asked to appraise the morale of their immediate work group, their division, and the entire lab. The results presented in Table 2 below

TABLE 2: PER CENT RATING MORALE AS HIGH OR VERY HIGH[47]

	Permissively-led section	Restrictively-led section
Own work group	82%	36%
Own division	82%	21%
Entire lab	37%	7%

reveal that workers in the permissive group perceived morale to be higher at every level of the organisation than did the workers in the restrictive group. It should also be noted that workers in the permissive group had higher morale in spite of the fact that only 15 per cent of the employees thought their leader was the best researcher in his division, whereas morale was lower in the restrictive leader's division although he was more generally acknowledged to be the best researcher in his division.

In another study of a research laboratory—this time devoted to medical research—Baumgartel studied twenty labs with a total staff of 310 scientists.[48] The work units were large enough so that they had substantial hierarchy and an elaborate division of labour. In these labs, Baumgartel singled out three types of authority patterns: *1*, laissez-faire, in which there was little contact between the director and his subordinates and little influence either way; *2*, participatory, in which there was frequent contact between the director and his subordinates while they had considerable influence upon him; with this type of leadership, joint discussion and joint decision-making were typical; *3*, directive, in which there was moderate contact between the director and his subordinates and in which the director had much influence over his subordinates and they very little over him. With this style of leadership the director typically made his own decisions. Although other qualities of leadership were investigated in this study, the focus here will be upon the relative effectiveness of the three types of authority mentioned above.

Baumgartel attempted to measure the morale and motivation of the research scientists in several ways. First, he tried to assess how motivated the scientists felt toward the research tasks and goals of the organisation. This was measured by their responses to three questions 'dealing with the importance they (the scientists) attached to the use of present abilities, freedom for originality, and making a contribution to basic science'.[49] (To the three questions in this group a fourth was added on whether the respondent felt he was able to set his own work pace.) Secondly, the scientists' motivation and morale were judged by the extent to which they believed their jobs provided for the three factors mentioned above. Finally, morale was assessed by enquiring into the scientists' attitudes toward their own directors.

The guiding hypothesis of the study—following Lewin's work— was that participatory leadership would be more effective in building morale and motivation than either laissez-faire or directive leadership. The extent to which this is born out can be seen in Table 3.[50] We see here that participatory leadership was superior to directive leadership in producing higher morale and motivation in fourteen out of fifteen items, and at magnitudes that ranged from suggestive to very highly probable. And in eleven out of fifteen cases, participatory leadership proved more effective than laissez-faire leadership, again with the same range of magnitudes.

In another study in which Baumgartel was involved, he and Floyd Mann discovered that the delegation of authority to supervisors increased their commitment to certain important goals of the organisation. In this study of a midwestern public utility company[51] Mann and Baumgartel focused on supervisory personnel and attempted to understand and explain the fact that while some supervisors were very concerned with costs and with keeping costs down, other supervisors were hardly concerned with this goal at all. The researchers discovered that supervisors who had authority delegated to them, who participated in deciding how the money budgeted to them would be spent, were more likely to be concerned with costs than those who had little or no responsibility in spending the money allotted to them. This was true among the supervisors in the field situation (overhead lines division) as well as in the office (accounting departments). In the office, for example, the researchers found that 'of the supervisors who say they have *almost complete say* or *quite a lot of say* in spending money

TABLE 3: MORALE AND MOTIVATION UNDER DIFFERENT LEADERSHIP STYLES

Task motivation	Participatory v. Laissez-faire leadership	Participatory v. Directive leadership
Importance of use of abilities	*	**
Importance of freedom for originality	*	***
Importance of contributing to basic science	—	—
Work pace set by respondent	*	*
Sense of Progress towards Scientific Goals		
Extent of use of present abilities	**	**
Extent of freedom for originality	*	***
Extent of contributing to basic science	*	**
Attitudes towards Leader		
Overall satisfaction with professional leadership	***	***
Enjoyment of director	*	**
Confidence in motives	—	*
Qualifications to help in professional area	***	*
General helpfulness	*	*
Professional leadership and stimulation	—	**
Accuracy in evaluation of work	—	***
Familiarity with scientists' work	***	***

* = predicted direction but not significant.
— = opposite direction but not significant.
** = significant at 0·10 to 0·05 levels. *** = significant beyond 0·05 level.

budgeted to them, 51 per cent say they are very concerned with costs' as compared to only 36 per cent of those who have some, little, or no say in spending the money budgeted to them.[52] Concluding their report, the researchers remark:

Financial decisions have traditionally been made close to the top of the organisation. But here, as in some of our research on industrial productivity, we find that a larger area of responsibility and more participation in decision-making apparently result in more efficient and productive activity. We cannot expect people to be concerned with costs or other organisational goals unless they have some meaningful part in the decision-making activities of the organisation.[53]

Another study of supervisors is especially interesting because it attempts to refine the participation hypothesis by specifying those psychological characteristics of individuals which aid the effectiveness of participation and those which inhibit it. We saw earlier, in French's study of a Norwegian factory, that an important intervening variable in the participation hypothesis is the normative milieu in which participation takes place or, more specifically, the norms of legitimacy or illegitimacy which attend it. We have also referred to Krech and Crutchfield's remark that democratic or participative leadership may not be effective under authoritarian political conditions. The present study attempts to assess the effects of participation, not in an authoritarian political setting, but among individuals who are characterised, to a greater or lesser degree, by what is commonly referred to as the authoritarian personality.

Victor Vroom studied the effects of participation upon supervisors in a large delivery service company which was responsible for delivering miscellaneous parcels from retail stores to customers' homes.[54] Of the thirteen branches which the company had in cities across the United States, Vroom chose two, in New York and Chicago, in which to carry out his research. He focused his attention on 108 first, second, and third line supervisors and by means of interviews investigated the relationship among several major variables. *1*. First, Vroom attempted to discover the degree of influence the supervisors believed they had with their own supervisors, to what extent they felt free to offer suggestions, how readily they thought they were consulted by higher-ups and, in short, how much *participation* in decision-making they believed they had. *2*. Vroom tried to measure by means of tests two personality characteristics of the supervisors, their personal independence needs and the extent to which they showed characteristics of the authoritarian personality (using the well-known F scale). *3*. Finally, Vroom assessed the degree of satisfaction each supervisor felt in his work. The relationship among these three variables is summarised below.

The conclusions one can draw from this table as well as from Vroom's entire study can best be summarised as follows. *1*. There is a positive and statistically significant correlation between perceived participation and job satisfaction among the entire group of supervisors. In other words, those who felt that they had more decision-making power on their jobs were more likely to derive satisfaction

TABLE 4: PERCEIVED AMOUNT OF PARTICIPATION IN DECISION-MAKING AND JOB SATISFACTION, BY PERSONALITY TYPE[55]

	r	N
Entire group	$+0.36$**	108
Supervisors with high independence needs	$+0.55$**	38
Supervisors with moderate independence needs	$+0.31$*	32
Supervisors with low independence needs	$+0.13$	38
Supervisors with high authoritarian personality scores	$+0.03$	34
Supervisors with moderate authoritarian personality scores	$+0.35$*	34
Supervisors with low authoritarian personality scores	$+0.53$**	39

** $= P < 0.01$.
* $= P < 0.05$.

from their jobs than those who felt they had less power ($r = +0.36$). Thus, the participation hypothesis is confirmed in yet another study. *2.* The relationship between participation and job satisfaction increases among those with high personal needs for independence and is reduced among those with low independence needs. It is important to note that participation does not have a *negative* effect on job satisfaction among those with low independence needs, but tends to have little or no effect at all. *3.* The relationship between participation and job satisfaction increases among those with egalitarian, non-authoritarian personalities, and is reduced among those with highly authoritarian personalities. Again, participation does not negatively affect job satisfaction among authoritarian types; rather participation is simply irrelevant to job satisfaction. It would not be proper to conclude from these data, therefore, that participation could lead to dissatisfaction with work among those with low independence needs and authoritarian personalities. However, it is likely to increase job satisfaction substantially among those with high independence needs and 'non-authoritarian' personalities. When these two traits are considered together, the relationship is extremely strong. For example, when the relationship between participation and job satisfaction is examined among those with *both* high independence needs *and* low authoritarian scores, the correlation is $+0.73$, which accounts for over 50 per cent of the variance.[56] The relationship is unchanged when age, education, and occupational level (supervisory level) are held constant.

To summarise, then, this study demonstrates the positive impact of participation once again, this time among supervisory personnel, and it also points to significant intervening psychological variables through which the effectiveness of participation is filtered.[57]

Although much recent research on participation has shifted in the direction of examining which kinds of individuals are more and which are less responsive to participation, I am not primarily concerned with that question here, for the structure of an organisation itself can alter values, expectations, norms, behaviour, and attitudes toward participation. For example, Tannenbaum, using the data from the Morse and Reimer study cited earlier, found that exposure to a participative environment for a period of one year tended to reduce some of the attitudes of dependency among the employees.[58] At the same time, working in the hierarchical sections tended to reduce some independent attitudes. The Lewinian studies also demonstrated that the same boys can react in completely different ways—passive, dependent and hostile, or active, independent and co-operative—according to the leadership climate (authoritarian or democratic) of the group. Personality traits in these studies were dependent variables, significantly altered by the organisation of the group into authoritarian, democratic, or laissez-faire structures. In other words, although it is true that participation does have different effects upon different individuals—depending upon their values, attitudes, expectations, personality needs, and the like—it is also true that a structure of participation *creates* appropriate values, attitudes, and expectations, and thus in the long run becomes more effective because of the eventual compatibility of personality with structure. In other words, the organisation that permits participation ultimately produces individuals who are responsible to participation.

In this section so far we have seen the effects of participation upon scientists and supervisory personnel. In the next two studies we shall move down the occupational ladder somewhat and examine the effects of participation upon lower white collar workers and skilled manual workers.

F. R. Wickert conducted a study of telephone operators and service representatives who were hired in several Michigan cities between January 1945 and February 1948.[59] He divided these workers into two categories: those who were still working for the company at the time of the study (designated 'on-force') and those who had quit the company (designated 'losses'). The two groups of girls were compared by means of questionnaires and interviews on a whole range of characteristics and attitudes. (Data on the girls who had quit were based on interviews with those whom Wickert managed to locate, which consisted of 50 per cent or more in most cities.) Wickert found a great similarity between both groups in their biographical data, their employment test scores which he examined at the company, their 'neurotic tendencies', etc. Surprisingly, also, there was little or no difference between the two groups on their attitudes toward the company's wages, hours, conditions, and the like. The girls who had quit did not seem significantly more dissatisfied with these things than those who remained on the job.

There was at least one variable, however, which did discriminate between the two groups and that variable was *participation*. Those girls who stayed with the company tended to believe that they were able to make decisions on the job; those who had left were far less likely to feel that they had this power, as Table 5 illustrates. Wickert found equally important differences between the on-force girls and the losses on the issue of how important they felt their contribution to the company is (or was). On-force girls were much more likely than the losses to believe that their work represented an important contribution to the telephone company.

TABLE 5: RESPONSE TO THE QUESTION: DO YOU (OR DID YOU) HAVE A CHANCE TO MAKE DECISIONS ON YOUR JOB AT BELL?[60]

OPERATORS	Yes, Very Often, Sometimes	Seldom or Never	N
Lansing, Mich.*			
On Force	78%	22%	88
Losses	42%	58%	43
Grand Rapids*			
On Force	74%	26%	125
Losses	45%	55%	40
Pontiac			
On Force	73%	27%	97
Losses	No data		
SERVICE REPS			
Lansing			
On Force	81%	19%	26
Losses	Insufficient number of cases		
Grand Rapids*			
On Force	86%	14%	36
Losses	38%	62%	26
Pontiac	No data		

* $P = < 0.01$.

Together, Wickert conceptualised these two variables, ability to make decisions and importance of the contribution of their job, as 'ego involvement' with the occupation, and he interpets his findings as follows.

> To the extent that turnover can be considered an index of morale, these results lend further support to the growing evidence that the psychology of *ego-involvement and participation* provides an important and valuable approach to the understanding of employee morale.[61]

'Here is a bit of empirical evidence,' Wickert concludes, 'in favour of industrial democracy.'

This study, however suggestive, has two methodological flaws. First, interviews with the losses took place long after these girls had quit, raising the possibility that the recollection of their jobs was distorted by the passage of time. Also, because Wickert was not able to locate all the girls who had left work, it is possible that the ones he did manage to contact differed in some, possibly significant, ways from those he was unable to find.

A study by Ross and Zander, also using turnover as an index of morale, was not subject to these potential errors.[62] Trying to assess important factors making for high rates of turnover, the researchers distributed questionnaires dealing with various job attitudes to 2,680 female skilled workers who were employed in a factory (not otherwise identified). The investigators then waited until four months had passed at which time 169 of the original respondents had resigned. The attitudes of these women, as recorded four months earlier when they were still employed at the company, were compared with a matched group of workers who remained on the job. Ross and Zander found that those who stayed on the job were more likely than those who had left to be satisfied with: *1*, the *autonomy* they felt they had on their jobs; *2*, the *recognition* they received on their jobs, especially how fully informed they felt about the quality of their work; *3*, their sense of *achievement*, the feeling that they were doing something important in their work. These were the major differences and all were significant at the $2\frac{1}{2}$ per cent level or greater. The first two items, autonomy and recognition, are related to the participation hypothesis, the first directly, the second indirectly, and both tend to confirm that hypothesis. And the findings as a whole tend to corroborate those of Wickert's study of telephone employees.

Another study pertinent to the participation hypothesis concerned the relationship between supervisory styles and work satisfaction.[63] In this research, work satisfaction was judged indirectly by examining both grievance rates and turnover rates among workers. The study was carried out in a major US truck manufacturing plant engaged in operations such as stamping, body assembly, painting, etc. The researchers selected fifty-seven production foremen and at least three workers from each foreman's department. The workers' turnover and grievance rates were computed for the eleven month period of the study and each foreman's supervisory style was evaluated.

The researchers focused on two types of leadership patterns among the foremen which were roughly similar to the concepts of general and close supervision employed in the Michigan studies: supervision characterised by 'consideration' and supervision characterised by 'structure'.

> *Consideration* includes behaviour indicating mutual trust, respect, and a certain warmth and rapport between the supervisors and his group. This does not mean that this dimension reflects a superficial 'pat on the back' kind of human relations behaviour. This dimension appears to emphasise a deeper concern for group members' needs and includes such behaviour as *allowing subordinates more participation in decision-making* and encouraging more two-way communication.

This mode is contrasted to 'structure' in which

> the supervisor organises and defines group activities and his relation to the group. Thus, *he defines the role he expects each member to assume, assigns tasks, plans ahead, establishes ways of getting things done* and pushes for production. This dimension seems to emphasise overt attempts to achieve organisational goals.[64]

The authors stress that these two modes of supervision are not entirely mutually exclusive, for supervisors may utilise elements of both.

The researchers discovered a striking relationship between these two supervisory styles and the indices of worker satisfaction (grievance and turnover rates). Figure 3 vividly demonstrates this. Although the relationship is not linear, the most significant finding is certainly that as foreman 'consideration' increases, the workers' grievance rate tends to decline. The correlation (eta) between the two is -0.51. On the other hand, as 'structure' increases, grievances rise, showing a positive correlation of 0.63. The pattern is virtually the same for the workers' turnover rate, strongly reduced by increases in foreman 'consideration' (yielding a correlation ratio of -0.61) and strongly increased by greater foreman 'structure' (a positive correlation of 0.63).

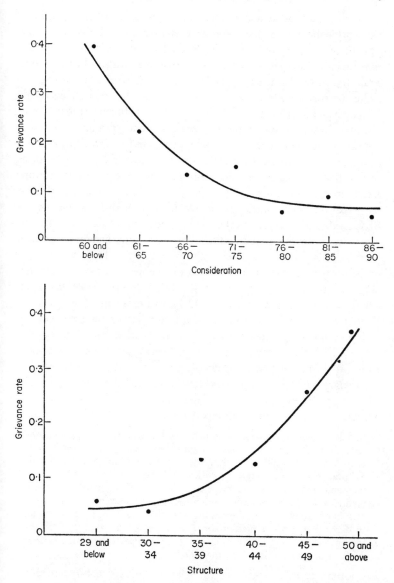

FIG. 3. (Source: redrawn from E. A. Fleishman and E. F. Harris, 'Patterns of Leadership Behavior Related to Employee Grievances', *Personnel Psychology*, 15 [Spring 1962], pp. 45–53, for R. Dubin *et al.*, *Leadership and Productivity* [Chandler Publishing Co., San Francisco, Calif., 1965], p. 32).

Bearing in mind that one important component of the 'consideration' style here is clearly worker participation and that one component of the 'structure' style is clearly lack of worker participation,
one may, I think, legitimately infer that this study illustrates once
again the positive impact of participation upon worker satisfaction.

Let us turn briefly now to the series of studies conducted by the
Survey Research Center of the University of Michigan in the late 1940s
and early 1950s. As mentioned earlier these studies dealt generally with
the interrelationships among morale, productivity, and supervision in
a variety of industrial settings: insurance companies, auto factories,
tractor factories, public utilities, railroad maintenance of way sections,
etc. Our interests in this chapter are limited to assessing the effects of
participation upon satisfaction in work. Within this framework, the
SRC studies lend weight to the participation hypothesis in the following way. *1.* In these studies those who have the benefit of general,
permissive supervision are generally more likely to have higher levels
of job satisfaction than those who are subject to close, restrictive
supervision. *2.* Although most workers do not make important
decisions on their jobs, most would like to make more and feel that
their decisions and suggestions would be valuable for the company.

For example, in their survey of 12,000 workers in an automobile
factory, the SRC focused attention on the relationship of the workers
to both foremen and union stewards and the resultant cross pressures
for loyalty to both. The researchers found that the men would give
loyalty to foreman or steward depending upon which one of them
allowed and encouraged participation.

> In departments in which the foreman called their men in to discuss prob-
> lems there was greater satisfaction with the foreman. Moreover, identi-
> fication with the union or with management tended to go with differen-
> tial practices by foremen or by stewards. Where foremen consulted the
> men and stewards did not, there was high identification with manage-
> ment. In departments where both foremen and stewards involved the
> men in decision-making, there was greater liking for the job as a whole.
> In departments where neither stewards nor foremen involved the men
> there was less liking for the company than in departments where either
> steward or foreman involved the men.[65]

In another report on the same study, Jacobson says that in general the
workers 'wanted the foremen to get their help in making decisions
because they know how the work should be done and are capable of
making suggestions that would add to the productive efficiency of the
job'.[66]

In another study of 5,700 workers in a heavy industry plant (not otherwise identified), 68 per cent of the men said that they had little or nothing to do with decisions on how their jobs should be executed.[67] However, slightly more than half said they *wanted* to have more to say about the way their work was done, and 65 per cent believed that if the men were consulted as to the design, setup, and layout of their jobs, the work would thereby be improved. When asked why the men didn't make more suggestions on improving work processes, 50 per cent said that the men wouldn't get credit for them, 28 per cent said that top management wouldn't use them, 23 per cent said that the foremen wouldn't use them, 11 per cent thought that other workers didn't think a man should make suggestions, and 10 per cent said that the men didn't know where to make suggestions. Only 7 per cent said that workers did not know what suggestions to make.[68] In the face of all these obstacles—perceived supervisory indifference at all levels to suggestions, perceived peer group norms against it, etc.—it is remarkable that over half the men did in fact want more decision-making power.

In a study of Detroit Edison, a large public utility company, the SRC found that among the white collar employees working in small groups those who were given the right of consultation with supervisors had greater job satisfaction overall than those lacking this right. Specifically, those with power of consultation viewed their supervisor more favourably, had greater work-group pride, enjoyed their work more, and were more prone to feel that the company recognised good work.[69] However, this relationship was not found among larger white collar groups and with manual workers in general. This negative finding became the stimulus for a significant theoretical development which will be discussed later.

In her study of several hundred clerical workers at a large Eastern insurance company, Nancy Morse found that 70 per cent of the employees, when asked, said that they would like to make more decisions on their jobs than they did at present.[70] In addition, those who reported that they did in fact frequently make decisions on their jobs were more likely to have higher job satisfaction than those who did not.

Of the two kinds of supervision, general and close, Morse found the former far more popular, and with general supervision went a belief in the supervisors' basic decency and competence. Thus, under general supervision, 32 per cent of the employees said that their supervisors' expectations were very reasonable as compared to only 18 per cent of those under close supervision. And 38 per cent of those under general supervision believed their supervisors' ability to handle people was very effective as compared to only 23 per cent of those who worked under close supervision.[71]

Morse found, in addition, that those under general supervision in the insurance company were much more likely to identify with the division in which they worked than those under close supervision. There were also tendencies for those under general supervision to have stronger identification with their section and to show greater in-group co-operativeness than those under close supervision.

Other findings were relevant for the participation hypothesis. For example, involvement with the company was related to how full and complete were the supervisors' explanations of job and method changes. On the codetermination continuum, we have seen that the right of full information and explanation represents a rudimentary form of participation, and so Morse's finding here is pertinent. Of those workers whose supervisors gave them full and complete explanations of job and method changes, 45 per cent had high company involvement as compared to 30 per cent of those employees whose supervisors gave them no explanations.[72] Also, company involvement was related to the frequency with which supervisors had discussions with their employees. Discussions in the company were not really a form of consultation at all, but merely a means for conveying information to the workers. But although the amount of participation here was merely nominal, it nevertheless had a strong influence upon morale, defined here as involvement with the company. Of those employees whose supervisors held regular or frequent discussions with them, 59 per cent were highly involved with the company, as compared with only 32 per cent of those whose supervisors never held discussions with them.[73] Most workers, however (404 out of 670), never had discussions with their supervisors.

We now come to some interesting negative evidence in this study. We have already cited the research at Detroit Edison where among blue collar workers and white collar employees working in larger groups, participation or general supervision had no particular effect upon job satisfaction. Morse found in the insurance company that clerical workers who worked under general supervision were slightly *less likely* to be satisfied with the intrinsic nature of their jobs, their chances for more pay and promotion, than those under close supervision.

Morse attempts to explain this phenomenon in terms of a discrepancy between aspirations and reality. She argues that general supervision, by giving the workers more freedom, responsibility and control, raised their aspiration level but the democratic supervisor *alone* did not have the power to satisfy these new aspirations and needs (for better salaries, promotions, better conditions of work, etc.). Thus, the discrepancy between heightened aspirations and the supervisor's inability to satisfy them led to dissastisfaction.[74]

Donald Pelz, in a follow-up to the study of workers and supervisors at Detroit Edison, elaborated and refined this hypothesis.[75] He found that job satisfaction among workers will tend to decline with democratic or general first line supervision if that supervisor has low influence with management, because employee expectations and aspirations, raised by their relative autonomy, will be thwarted and frustrated by the supervisor's relative impotence. Thus, a participative orientation of a first line supervisor may give rise to dissatisfaction among his subordinates if he has little power or influence above him. On the other hand, Pelz confirms the participation hypothesis, by demonstrating that when democratic supervisors are also influential and powerful, in other words, when participation is meaningful and when the first line supervisor can deliver on the aspirations he creates, then a democratic leadership style leads to increased job satisfaction among subordinates.

This finding reveals the dangers inherent in attempting to assess the participation hypothesis by focusing on the traits of individual supervisors rather than on the structure and norms of ongoing organisations. In the former case, participation is likely to be an oasis in an otherwise authoritarian desert. Participation is not throroughgoing: it is limited to interaction with one person (the first supervisor) who in turn has limited power. Morse says about the authority structure of the insurance company she studied:

> It would seem likely that the area of freedom for the supervisor is quite small. The basic structures of the job are decided by people other than the supervisor. Thus, the supervisor who wants to increase the decision-making of his employees in their jobs can do so only to a limited degree.[76]

Thus, the difference between general and close supervision—between participation and lack of it—is often not as great as one might desire in a test of the effectiveness of participation. For example, Morse found that even for employees under general supervision, only 13 per cent said they made fairly important decisions on their jobs (as compared to 8 per cent of those under close supervision).[77]

One major defect of many of the studies reported in this section, which try to assess participation by pointing to different personality traits of supervisors, is that the organisation really does not permit sufficient variations in participation. Moreover, because participation is not built into the structure of these organisations, does not have its official sanction but is rather a quality of individual supervisors, the workers may come to feel frustrated and sense that the participation is spurious and not genuine. For example, Arensberg and McGregor report on the poor morale among engineers in a plant where there was *nominally* a great deal of freedom from immediate supervision, but considerable subtle overall pressure and restrictions as part of company policy as a whole.[78]

If 'participation' is seen as pseudo-participation it is merely a short step from being perceived as manipulation which will almost certainly backfire. As one observer writes:

> In one plant we visited, an engineer confided to us ... that he was going to put across a proposed production layout change of his by inserting in it a rather obvious error, which others could then suggest should be corrected. We attended the meeting where this stunt was performed, and superficially it worked. Somebody caught the error, proposed that it be corrected, and our engineer immediately 'bought' the suggestion as a very worthwhile one and made the change. The group seemed to 'buy' his entire layout proposal. . . .
>
> It looked like an effective technique—oh, so easy—until later, when we became better acquainted with the people in the plant. Then we found out that many of the engineer's colleagues considered him a phony and did not trust him. The resistance they put up to his ideas was very subtle, yet was more real and difficult for management to deal with.[79]

It may be, then, that certain studies will show that general or permissive supervision is ineffective or even that it adversely affects satisfaction in work, and may be taken as evidence that participation itself is detrimental to job satisfaction. Such conclusions must be accepted only with the greatest reservation, for, as we have seen, studies of 'participation' which define participation solely in terms of a permissive supervisor ignore the larger non-democratic setting—including structure, values, and norms—of this supervisory relationship, its isolation, and the limitations on its power.

The work of the Survey Research Center as a whole, has generally substantiated the findings on participation which we have discovered throughout the literature. Summarising the main implications of their research *vis-à-vis* the participation question, Professors Kahn and Katz say that their results 'suggest that the full motivation of workers in a complex organisational system can be trapped only when some system of functional representation assures them of an element of control in the larger organisations as well as the primary group'.[80]

It was partially on the basis of this research that Rensis Likert, long associated with Michigan's Survey Research Center, wrote his widely praised *New Patterns of Management*, central to which is his Principle of Supportive Relationships:

> *The leadership and other processes of the organisation must be such as to ensure a maximum probability that in all interactions and all relationships with the organisation each member will, in the light of his background, values, and expectations, view the experience as supportive and one which builds and maintains his sense of personal worth and importance.*[81]

Suffice it to say that employee participation is a keystone of Likert's Principle and of his highly acclaimed new theory of management.

v

This brings us to our final section, the job satisfaction literature *per se*. I do not intend to discuss at any length this enormous literature which has been reviewed time and again.[82] But it is important to note that any survey of the literature reveals that far up on the list of factors making for satisfaction in work is the desire, among all groups, for autonomy, responsibility, control, and decision-making power on the job. For example, in his careful study of the job satisfaction material, Robert Blauner isolated four factors which, more than any others, accounted for satisfaction in work. They are: the status of the occupation, the presence of an integrated work group, the existence of occupational communities, and—*control*. Several dimensions of control are important here: control over 'the use of one's *time* and physical *movement* . . . control over the *environment*, both technical and social, and control as the *freedom* from *hierarchical authority*'.[83] It is the latter, control over or freedom from hierarchical authority, which concerns us here. In this regard, Blauner presents data showing that the job satisfaction of miners, truck drivers, and certain railroad workers is much higher than their prestige and other factors would otherwise suggest, and he tends to account for it in terms of these workers' general freedom from close hierarchical control. The evidence Blauner adduces leads him to conclude that '*the greater the degree of control that a worker has (either in a single dimension or as a total composite), the greater his job satisfaction.*[84] In assessing the importance of each of the elements mentioned above which are responsible for differences in job satisfaction, he states that 'variations in the degree of control over the conditions of work was the most important single factor accounting for these differences'.[85]

In a survey of 155 studies of job attitudes, Herzberg and his colleagues found that the nature and character of supervision were mentioned more often than any other factor except the intrinsic aspects of the jobs themselves.[86] These studies point to more than two dozen features of supervision which are important to workers as preconditions of job satisfaction. These numerous elements of desirable supervision which Herzberg lists seem to be divisible into three categories. In supervision, workers desire, first, what one may simply call *decency* which would include such items listed by Herzberg in his summary of the 155 surveys as consideration, fairness, courtesy, tact, recognition, praise, loyalty to workers, encouragement, sincerity, etc. Secondly, workers want *competence* in their supervisors including such traits as ability to handle people, consistency of orders, technical ability and aptitude. Finally, and most relevant for us, the 155 studies point to the fact that workers want *autonomy* from their supervisors, including such things as opportunities for decision-making, delegation of authority, permissiveness, availability of the supervisor for consultation, and the like.[87]

One study which called particular attention to the importance of participation and control on the job was conducted by Lloyd Reynolds and Joseph Shister shortly after World War II.[88] They interviewed some eight hundred manual workers in an Eastern city and found that of all the reasons the workers gave for being dissatisfied with their present jobs, the lack of independence and control was mentioned more frequently than any other factor. By independence and control was meant 'freedom from too close supervision and a chance to voice one's opinion on how the job should be done'.[89] Lack of these things was more important in creating dissatisfaction than numerous other characteristics mentioned by workers such as the physical features of the job, wages, job interest, relations with fellow workers, fairness of treatment, and fringe benefits. Moreover, when workers were asked why they were satisfied with their present job, again independence and control outranked the other factors. A sample of the workers' remarks adds meaning to the statements here.

> Yes, I expect to stay with my job indefinitely. I got a swell boss who gives me a list of jobs each day and turns them over to me to do as I please, so that actually I am my own boss most of the time (machinist).[90]

> I'm my own boss and nobody bothers me—it's a good job. Sometimes I don't see my boss for two or three days at a time. I sure like it that way (inspector).[91]

> I like my job very much. You see I'm my own boss. Nobody tells me what to do; I make all the decisions (school janitor).[92]

> The main difficulty with my present job is that they won't ask ideas from the workers; they rely entirely on hired engineers and technicians for suggestions and ideas. They don't want you to think, just follow directions. Now other firms are always ready for suggestions and the opinion of the worker's ideas. That's the way it should be (toolmaker).[93]

Finally, an assembler, who complained that the supervisors never listen to the workers' suggestions in improving the job and instead rely exclusively on upstart time study men, commented: 'Who do you think knows about the job more than the person who does it?'[94]

Before concluding my remarks here on the job satisfaction literature as it pertains to participation, I should like to say a word about the 'American Dream' and its relation to workers' management. The American worker's proverbial hopes and dreams of going into business for himself, discussed by Chinoy and many others, are an expression of the worker's desire to be his own boss, independent, and in control on the job. I think that in a very real way this can be interpreted as an individualised, depoliticised, and safely channelled and approved desire, partly unconscious, for what socialists have long called 'workers' control'.

Reynolds and Shister, in the study mentioned above, make essentially the same argument. They state that 'in response to a question on job aspirations, the workers who expressed a desire to go into business for themselves did not mention merely the profit potentialities of business. They mentioned also the possibility of having things *their* way if they were boss.'[95] And the workers they quote tend to substantiate this hypothesis.* A machinist told them, 'I'd like to have my

---

* Chinoy's auto workers echo these sentiments. 'The main thing [said a machine operator] is to be independent and give your own orders and not to have to take them from anybody else. That's the reason the fellows in the shop all want to start their own business.' See Ely Chinoy, *Automobile Workers and the American Dream* (The Beacon Press, Boston, Mass., 1955), p. 86.

own little business. I never had a high position like that, where I was in charge of a place. I'd be my own boss!'[96] And a dress operator said, 'I'd like to have the feeling that whatever I did was all right with no one to holler at me.'[97] And perhaps, in line with this thesis, it is significant that it is just that class which has the least control on the job (manual workers) which now more strongly retains the petty bourgeois dream of small business independence than any other class in America today.[98]

6. Alienation and Participation: Conclusions

We have now completed our survey of some of the most important research on participation conducted in the last two and a half decades. Table 1 summarises the conclusions of the major studies. In this participation literature we have seen tremendous diversity on all sides—diversity in the academic background and theoretical orientation of the researchers, diversity in the conception, design, and execution of the research, diversity in the settings in which this research has taken place, and diversity in the characteristics of the population studied. There is significance in this diversity. It is just this impressive diversity in the participation literature which makes the *consistency* of the findings, by contrast, even more profound, significant, and valid. *There is hardly a study in the entire literature which fails to demonstrate that satisfaction in work is enhanced or that other generally acknowledged beneficial consequences accrue from a genuine increase in workers' decision-making power. Such consistency of findings, I submit, is rare in social research.*

It is not really difficult to explain why participation 'works'; it is almost a matter of common sense that men will take greater pride and pleasure in their work if they are allowed to participate in shaping the policies and decisions which affect that work. But such common sense has long been ignored by sociologists. On the contrary, in fact, sociologists would much rather offer sophisticated empirical refutations of common sense beliefs than confirm such beliefs, despite the importance of the implications which might underlie them.[1] The participation literature, however, does not refute but confirms elementary common sense. Yet this literature which has potentially such far-reaching implications has until very recently all but been ignored in industrial sociology. And although every industrial sociologist has long been familiar with the Lewinian studies of democratic versus authoritarian leadership few of them, though their minds are trained to see and to make generalisations, saw any relevance of these and other studies to an industrial setting.

It is true that participation has lately become quite fashionable in

TABLE I: PARTIAL SUMMARY OF THE PARTICIPATION LITERATURE

Senior Author(s)*	Setting of Study	Subjects	Nature of Experiment or Survey	Major Conclusions
1. Lewin, Lippitt, White	Boys' clubs	Eleven-year old boys	Authoritarian, democratic, and laissez-faire leadership compared.	Democratic (participative) leadership most highly associated with high work motivation, harmonious interpersonal relations among group members, and overall satisfaction.
2. Bennett	Introductory psychology class	Psychology students	Examined components of participation: group discussion; group decision; overtness of commitment to decision; strength of group consensus; compared effectiveness of each in stimulating action (volunteering for experiment).	Group decision was more crucial in raising the probability of action than any other factor.
3. Bavelas	Garment factory	Sewing machine operators	Compared efficiency of workers who were allowed to discuss *and decide* upon production with those allowed to discuss only.	The discussion-and-decision group was clearly the more efficient.
4. Lawrence and Smith	Garment factory	Office workers and manual workers	Replication of above; compared efficiency of workers who were allowed to discuss and decide upon production with those allowed to discuss only.	The discussion-and-decision group increased its productivity to statistically significant levels over its own pre-experimental level and over that of the discussion-only group.

TABLE I: PARTIAL SUMMARY OF THE PARTICIPATION LITERATURE—*Continued*

*Senior Author(s)**	*Setting of Study*	*Subjects*	*Nature of Experiment or Survey*	*Major Conclusions*
5. Coch and French	Garment factory	Manual workers	Compared morale and efficiency of groups who were given different degrees of authority to participate in decisions relating to changes in work organisation.	Success in bringing about job changes—both in terms of productivity and worker satisfaction—was directly proportional to the amount of worker participation permitted. 'Total-participation' groups had highest productivity and morale; 'no-participation' groups, the lowest.
6. Morse and Reimer	Large insurance company	Office workers	In two sections of the company, workers' powers of decision-making were increased substantially; in two other sections, workers' powers of decision-making were decreased substantially.	Workers in the autonomous sections experienced these statistically significant changes from the pre-experimental situation: greater feelings of 'self-actualisation' on the job; greater satisfaction with supervisors at all levels; greater satisfaction with the company; greater intrinsic work satisfaction; workers in the hierachically-controlled sections experienced statistically significant decreases in all these areas.
7. French	Norwegian shoe factory	Production workers	Experimental groups given power of participation in certain areas of managerial	Experimental groups were not more productive than control groups but satisfaction with the company and

TABLE I: PARTIAL SUMMARY OF THE PARTICIPATION LITERATURE—*Continued*

Senior Author(s)*	Setting of Study	Subjects	Nature of Experiment or Survey	Major Conclusions
			decision-making with respect to the production process; compared with control groups.	attitudes toward labour relations tended to be higher; within the experimental groups, those whose attitudes had changed most tended also to believe that participation was a legitimate workers' right.
8. Levine and Butler	Factory	Supervisory personnel	Effectiveness of lecture and discussion methods compared with respect to correcting supervisors' error in evaluating workers.	Only supervisors in the discussion-participation groups showed any subsequent improvement in their ratings of workers.
9. Babchuk and Goode	Men's clothing department in large department store	Group of clothing salesmen	Workers spontaneously altered a management-imposed commission system which had created friction within the department; under workers' plan, all commissions were shared equally.	Friction eliminated, morale increased under workers' re-organisation.
10. Strauss	Toy factory	Female manual workers	Discontent of the workers convinced management to grant workers' request to allow them to regulate speed	Both productivity and morale increased greatly; however, when increased productivity 'unbalanced' the flow of work to and from other departments,

TABLE I: PARTIAL SUMMARY OF THE PARTICIPATION LITERATURE—*Continued*

Senior Author(s)*	Setting of Study	Subjects	Nature of Experiment or Survey	Major Conclusions
				of belt and other more minor conditions of work situation.	supervisors re-established control over speed of belt; productivity fell drastically and six of eight girls quit shortly thereafter.
11. Weschler	Naval research laboratory	Physicists, engineers, scientific aids, and clerical workers	Comparison of job satisfaction and morale of personnel in two divisions, one headed by scientist restrictive in leadership, one by scientist permissive in leadership.	Job satisfaction was more prevalent in division headed by permissive leader.
12. Baumgartel	Medical research	Medical scientists	Compared three leadership patterns in different labs: 1. laissez-faire; 2. participatory; 3. directive.	Participatory leadership was found to be more effective than the other two types in producing high work motivation, high morale and satisfaction with leadership.
13. Mann and Baumgartel	Public utility company	Field and office supervisors	Assessed the factors related to supervisory concern with costs.	Supervisors who were delegated authority and allowed to participate in decisions to allocate funds were more likely to be concerned with costs than those not participating.
14. Vroom	Delivery service	1st, 2nd, 3rd line	Examined job satisfaction in relation to amount of perceived	Positive correlation found between perceived participation and job

TABLE I: PARTIAL SUMMARY OF THE PARTICIPATION LITERATURE—*Continued*

Senior Author(s)*	Setting of Study	Subjects	Nature of Experiment or Survey	Major Conclusions
	company	supervisors	participation in decision-making of superiors and how this was affected by personal independence needs and/or authoritarian characteristics.	satisfaction; correlation increased among supervisors with high independence needs and few authoritarian tendencies.
15. Wickert	Telephone company	Telephone operators and service representatives	Compared girls who had resigned subsequently with those still on the job.	Girls who remained with the company were more likely to believe that they could make decisions on the job; those who left tended to feel they could not.
16. Ross and Zander	Factory	Female skilled workers	Comparison between characteristics of workers who resigned subsequently and those who remained on the job.	Those who stayed tended to be more satisfied with: *1.* their autonomy on the job; *2.* their recognition; and *3.* their sense of achievement.
17. Fleishman and Harris	US truck manufacturing plant	Foremen and production workers	Workers' grievances and turnover related to supervisory style of foremen.	Workers under foremen whose supervision was characterised by 'consideration' (including an element of participation) had far fewer grievances and far less turnover than workers under foremen whose mode of supervision was characterised by 'structure'.

* See footnotes or bibliography for sources.

management and business school thinking in the United States, having replaced the human relations approach which was considered too manipulative and thus self-defeating; and the new fad has given rise to concepts and approaches such as bottom up (!) authority styles, theory 'Y', T-Groups and an assorted alphabet soup of participative and pseudo-participative techniques.[2]

Our approach, of course, differs from all of these in that we do not see participation as a device to lower costs, to improve quality, to increase productivity, to undercut trade union or workers' demands, or to give workers the illusion of power without its actuality, the more easily to guarantee jealously guarded managerial prerogatives within the framework of private enterprise. We are interested in the question of participation as it bears on the larger sociological and philosophical issue of the alienation of labour, and we are prepared to follow wherever this research leads.

Now that participation is slowly beginning to catch on among behavioural scientists, one is still left with a question and a paradox. Despite the almost unanimous evidence on the favourable effects of participation in general and in industrial settings in particular, almost no one in any of the related fields has raised the question: to what extent does private ownership and control of modern industry place sharp limits upon the amount of participation that is structurally possible? Given the demonstrated beneficial effects of participation, to what degree is its application inherently limited by the framework of private ownership? Is it true, as T. B. Bottomore has said, that the full development of workers' participation is possible only on the basis of social ownership?

These questions are never raised. But what happens when staid social scientists conduct perfectly conventional research only to find their results telling them that perhaps the old advocates of 'workers' control' had something there? What happens is that they draw the narrowest possible conclusions which allow them to stay safely within the confines of the here and now. Participation is praised but no one asks any basic questions. Instead, the present system of ownership and control is merely assumed to be universal, despite the obvious fact that economic experiments are everywhere to be studied. But this is rarely done, and the current system is assumed to be given and then, within the accepted framework, minor adjustments (of supervisory techniques, for example) are urged.

We have said that common sense explains why participation is effective, and, as we have seen, research has confirmed these assumptions. Research since the days of the Mayo experiments indicates that satisfaction in work is just as dependent upon fulfilment of the employees' ego needs as upon satisfaction of their physical needs. Psychologists engaged in research on participation have argued that participation, power, and responsibility on the job tend to satisfy basic ego needs. Having the power of participation implies to workers that they are equal partners, collaborators in an enterprise, rather than passive, coerced, and unwilling subordinates. Participation strengthens the belief, or creates it, that they, the workers are worthy of being consulted, that they are intelligent and competent. When workers make the frequently bitter remark that 'they don't pay you to think around here', they are really saying that their opinions are not valued, that they are not regarded as competent collaborators, but merely living automatons, passive extensions of the machines they operate. Participation corrects this by gratifying basic human needs for respect, appreciation, responsibility, and autonomy. Is it any wonder, then, in the light of all the foregoing research, that Ralph White and Ronald Lippitt, pioneers, along with Kurt Lewin in group research, have concluded that: 'Of all the generalisations growing out of the experimental study of groups, one of the most broadly and firmly established is that the members of a group tend to be more satisfied if they have at least some feeling of participation in its decisions.'[3]

The participating worker is an involved worker, for his job becomes an extension of himself and by his decisions he is creating his work, modifying and regulating it. As he is more involved in his work, he becomes more committed to it, and, being more committed, he naturally derives more satisfaction from it.

A good case for participation can be made on other psychological grounds as well. It can be argued that the traditional forms of authority in economic enterprises, in which employees are allowed little or no rights of participation, directly contradict the psychological needs of mature adults. Borrowing from the work of contemporary psychologists, Chris Argyris has said that as a person develops from infancy to mature adulthood, he attempts to move: from passivity to *activity*; from a state of dependence to adult *independence* and *control* of his own behaviour; from having a short, here-and-now time perspective to a *longer perspective* which takes into account both past and future; from having a subordinate role in family and society to having an *equal* or *superordinate role*.[4]

But ironically, just as the mature individual strives for these goals, so they may actually be undermined by his day-to-day experience on the job. Without rights of participation, employees work under a system of authority, according to which they must, in exchange for a wage or salary, submit to conditions which subvert the creation and the sustenance of a mature adult personality. At work, an authority which is essentially not accountable to its subordinates controls, directs, co-ordinates, dispenses, orders, hires, fires, assigns, rewards, punishes, etc.

The main thrust of the autocratic organisation is to drive the mature adult back into childhood. The mature individual strives to take an active part in his world, but the chain of command at work renders him *passive*. He seeks to be independent and to control his own behaviour, but as an employee, he is rendered *dependent* and essentially lacking in control over his own behaviour. The mature individual strives for the long time perspective, but as he does not possess or have access to necessary information at work which would permit this, his *time perspective* is consequently *shortened*. He seeks to achieve relationships based on equality, but as a *subordinate*, he becomes just that, once again as in childhood. At every turn, the psychological needs of the mature individual are at odds with the demands of the autocratic organisation. The consequences, as Argyris has pointed out, are dysfunctional, both for the individual and for the organisation. The employee's principal reaction is frustration which may be expressed in any number of ways, most of which are detrimental all round: aggression, ambivalence, regression, apathy, restriction of output and otherwise subverting the goals of the organisation.

It can readily be inferred from the foregoing that while the autocratic organisation tends to undermine the employee's psychological maturity, the democratic organisation tends to strengthen maturity by stimulating the very traits associated with it: activity, independence, control, egalitarian relationships, and the like.

Having given so much attention to studies which confirm the participation hypothesis, we should at this point examine the negative evidence. This is rather easily done, for the contrary findings are sparse and often inaccurate.

It does seem true and reasonable, first of all, that participation is less useful in *crisis* situations such as in combat or in classrooms where examinations are imminent, to take two contrasting situations. Persons living under conditions of stress and crisis often feel that there is insufficient time and opportunity to indulge in the 'luxury' of participation and may prefer faster decisions made by designated leaders.[5] Valid as this is, it should be noted that these kinds of situations are not typical but, by their nature, extraordinary.

Robert Dubin, examining only a very small part of what we have called the participation literature, has argued that participation is effective only in certain types of technological settings—in unit or craft production. He claims, for example, that participation was important in Wickert's study of telephone employees only because 'these aspects of participation in work are mediated by the need for autonomy that comes from the technology employed'.[6] It should be obvious after our extensive treatment of the participation literature here, however, that its applicability greatly transcends the narrow technological band stipulated by Dubin.

The same author argues further that participation is useful only up to a point, beyond which greater participation may actually lead to a decline in work satisfaction. His view is based on the alleged fact that when participation increases beyond the expectations and abilities of workers, they may not be able to handle the added demands and responsibilities and may react negatively. Here Dubin leans heavily on a point made originally by Rensis Likert:

> Available research findings indicate . . . that when . . . the amount of participation used is less than or very much greater than expected, an unfavourable reaction is likely to be evoked. Substantially greater amounts of participation than expected appear to exceed the skill of the subordinate to cope with it and produce a negative reaction because of the threatening nature of the situation to the subordinate. The available theory and research findings suggest that the best results obtain when the amount of participation is somewhat greater than expected by the subordinate, but still within their capacity to respond to it effectively.[7]

Dubin concludes that this is a factor 'that is rarely given attention by those who urge participative management as the be-all and end-all of supervisory practice'.[8] But while Dubin has made use of Likert's premises here, he has systematically ignored Likert's own conclusions. If participation goes beyond the expectations and abilities of subordinates, Likert's solution is not to limit participation to some small but supposedly optimal amount, but to *increase* participation *gradually*, which will permit a steady expansion in the subordinates' expectations, abilities, feelings of legitimacy for the new system, and the like.

For the same reasons, Likert writes that when management goes immediately from very tight control from above to a system of participation, the short range reaction is often not appreciation at all, but resentment, hostility, and apathy. The reasons for this initial reaction: 'the need to release bottled-up animosity and the need to test the superior's sincerity'.[9] Thus, the initial negative reaction should not be taken as proof of the undesirability or unworkability of participation.

In conclusion, then, Dubin's hypothesis that there is a curvilinear relationship between participation and satisfaction is based really on a premise which sees the workers' expectations and abilities *vis-à-vis* participation as static and incapable of growing and expanding gradually as the quantity and quality of participation is increased.

It has often been argued that worker participation is undesirable and unnecessary primarily because of the apathy of the workers themselves. This argument requires two answers. First, if apathy were sufficient grounds for dismantling the democratic process, then we might have to dispense with political democracy altogether in the United States, for Americans are notoriously apathetic when it comes to political activity. In the presidential election of 1964 in the United States, despite the overwhelming political saturation of the mass media, less than two-thirds of the eligible voters cast their ballots for president (63 per cent), and less than 60 per cent voted for congressional candidates. In no off-year election from 1922 to 1962 have so much as 50 per cent of the electorate come to the polls, and in some years, the proportion fell below one-third. Local elections make these turnouts seem enormous. And an incredibly small number of citizens actually work for candidates, contribute to campaigns, or are thoroughly and intelligently aware of the major issues of the day.

Secondly, the charge of worker apathy to participation is an unfounded assumption, largely refuted by the research reviewed in Chapter 5 which indicates that workers are often eager to participate, if given the opportunity, and that job interest, commitment, and satisfaction are all generally heightened by the introduction of various forms of participation.

Further confirmation of this derives from an interesting study conducted among white and blue collar workers in Oslo, Norway.[10] Some 1,100 non-supervisory employees at eighteen establishments in Oslo were interviewed in 1962. Among the enterprises were ten factories employing between 100–400 workers each, seven insurance companies, and one large-scale industrial enterprise. Thirty to forty per cent of the employees were selected from each enterprise, yielding a sample of 628 blue collar workers, the remainder white collar workers. While the survey was originally designed to measure age and sex differences in job attitudes and behaviour, some pertinent data on attitudes towards participation were uncovered.

The researchers asked their respondents: 'Do you feel that the employees in general participate sufficiently in decisions that concern the management of the establishment as a whole?' Significantly, only 17 per cent of the blue collar workers answered affirmatively, while 78 per cent said that employees do not participate sufficiently. Of the white collar workers (employed primarily for the insurance companies), only 37 per cent said participation among employees were sufficient, 59 per cent said it was insufficient. The researchers also asked the workers: 'Do you feel that you personally participate sufficiently in decisions made at your place of work, or do you wish to participate more in them?' Only 22 per cent of the blue collar workers said that they had 'no special interest in more participation'. Over half (56 per cent) said that they 'would like to participate more in decisions that directly concern my own work and working conditions'. And an additional 16 per cent said that they wanted to go beyond that 'to participate more in decisions that concern the management of the whole enterprise'. The response of the white collar workers was comparable, with only 20 per cent expressing no special interest in participation, and the remainder desiring more participation, either at the job level (67 per cent) or at the enterprise level (11 per cent).

While no firm generalisations can be made from the attitudes of Norwegian workers to workers in other countries, this study nevertheless further calls into question the traditional view of workers as interested in only the narrowest and most personal satisfactions on the job and totally indifferent to larger issues of participation.

For Henri de Man, as well as for more contemporary scholars,[11] the crucial element in the definition of work is its *coercive* nature. One man may repair automobiles in a shop. This is work. Another man may repair his own automobile in his garage at home. This is a hobby, a pleasure. What distinguishes work from non-work is not always the nature of the task, but the elements of compulsion, necessity, regimentation, and unfreedom. Is it not reasonable to assume, then, that anything which gives the worker increased freedom and control over his work environment—which participation does—will make work seem less coercive, regimented, and unfree, less like the work he has always known, in short, less work-like?

Postscript

So successful is participation as a device that it has been used with some success among groups of persons who might be considered the *worst* possible risks and who might be regarded as the least likely to appreciate it, to benefit from it, to avail themselves of it, and to use its machinery properly. I am referring to imprisoned criminals.[12]

Experiments in prisoner self-government have had a long, chequered and controversial history in the United States, going back at least as far as 1793. There have been cases where inmate participation has worked spectacularly well, where prisons have been almost literally turned over to inmates via elected councils, but there have likewise been cases of spectacular failure. Of the notable early experiments, the movement beginning in 1895, which attempted to organise training schools for delinquents into self-governing 'Junior Republics', is worthy of mention.

Begun by William George, these Junior Republics spread to many privately run institutions in the United States within a few years. Thomas M. Osborne, whose name is now closely linked with the philosophy of inmate self-government, extended the idea to adult institutions at Auburn, New York (1914), and afterwards to Sing Sing and elsewhere.[13]

Inmate self-government was at that time far more thoroughgoing than it is today. According to Glaser: '. . . rules for inmates were established by an elected body of inmate representatives, internal surveillance was performed by inmate "police", and inmates who misbehaved were tried and punished by inmate courts'.[14]

Some of these early experiments were extremely successful in generating prisoner trustworthiness and reliability, and instances are occasionally cited wherein prisoners in a self-governing institution, having gone on field trips, returned to the prison virtually unchaperoned. And an early observer reported that inmate participation led to fewer escapes, fewer riots, fewer fights among prisoners, less recidivism, and higher productivity among working inmates.[15]

Nevertheless, these successful experiments tended to break down after a short period. Baker attributes their failure to: *1*, the adverse effects of giving to prisoners power to discipline their fellow inmates, and 2, the dependence of the experiment upon single crusaders who did not have staff support and who fell victim to adverse publicity and the outrages of a public that was aghast at the idea of giving extensive powers to hardened criminals.

To this day the issue of inmate self-government generates considerable emotion and many prison officials condemn it in the most vehement terms, while others defend it and claim that it has been unjustly maligned. A few of those officials opposed to inmate participation have had bad experiences with them personally; more of them have heard bad things of them from others; and probably most share a *Weltanschauung* with administrative and managerial personnel in all walks of life whose very status and role incline them against systems of participation from below, whether 'below' means factory workers, university students, or prison inmates. Nevertheless, as many experiments in inmate self-government have clearly failed, there are legitimate grounds for opposing them and these include the following: the inmate council may become dominated by 'model prisoners' and others who do not have the respect of the informal inmate leaders; on the other hand, the council machinery may be seized by aggressive criminals who may exploit the system for their own ends; cliques, ward politics, and privileges for members of the inmate council may develop; there may be bullying of prisoners and excessive punishment where inmate councils control discipline; the council may facilitate inmate unity and provide them with an instrument for prison disorders; or the inmate councils may degenerate into so-called 'gimme groups', fault-finding bodies which make excessive and unreasonable demands of the prison staff.

Nevertheless, many wardens and prison officials remain convinced that inmate self-government, properly organised, can be of great value to the institution, the staff and the inmates themselves. A recent survey indicated that, in one form or another, inmate councils exist in eight out of thirty-two US federal prisons and in thirteen of forty-four state penitentiaries. Their powers are quite circumscribed compared with earlier, more radical experiments. Of the councils existing in state penitentiaries, most operate under a formal constitution and by-laws, are usually staff-sponsored, are elected by democratic ballot (subject to administrative approval), prepare their own agendas, and meet on the average of once a month. Many of the previous abuses have been corrected. Nowhere are prisoners allowed to discipline their fellows and membership on the councils is usually restricted to those with good conduct records, in order to keep them out of the hands of those who would corrupt them and turn them to their own personal advantage.

In a survey of the activities of councils in the state penitentiaries, Baker found them most often involved in matters of recreation and entertainment (talent shows, deciding on TV, radio, and movie programmes, planning holiday events), organising blood bank and eye bank campaigns, taking charge of postage funds, charity drives, sanitation drives, and self-improvement programmes.

The inmate council systems at the Terre Haute (Indiana) and Leavenworth (Kansas) prisons have gone beyond the kinds of activities sketched above. Officials at Terre Haute began a bold experiment in 1960, based on the premise that inmates were to be considered part of the prison staff itself, responsible, along with the regular staff, for the administration of the prison. This new concept is symbolised by the inclusion of inmates in the contests for federal prison employees. Inmates' suggestions are considered along with those of actual employees, and prisoners are equally eligible for prizes.

Prison officials at Terre Haute provide the elected inmate council with financial information concerning the operation of the prison, plus other pertinent, non-personal administrative data. The warden has written that integrating the council into prison management is instrumental in creating a harmonious dialogue between staff and inmates. In typical prisons, for example, inmates often feel that the amount of funds administered by the staff is unlimited and when food and facilities are less than what the inmates feel is adequate, they tend to believe that funds are somehow being wasted, misused, or diverted to the personal enrichment of the staff. At Terre Haute, according to the testimony of the warden, the council knows the details of budget allocation and realises that the food and facilities are commensurate with the funds available. The council is free to make suggestions as to a different allocation of monies, if they think improvements might result. There is, as a result, less discontent, less bitterness, less suspicion than there otherwise might be. Furthermore, knowing the financial situation, the prisoners more readily appreciate that waste and malicious damage hurt only their own welfare and this tends to create among them genuine group responsibility, manifested in spontaneous campaigns to cut down waste and damage. Having access to financial information, the prisoners are made aware that their own misbehaviour may produce public reaction with adverse effects on funds for the prison.

Agendas for the monthly council meetings at Terre Haute are

generally open, and are set by what the staff and inmates wish to discuss. In recent years, the inmate council has been divided into several separate committees composed of both inmate and staff members, and these committees are the sole prison bodies for their particular area of competence. There are committees for sports, entertainment, food, sanitation, laundry, safety, and one designed to oversee and improve relations among inmates and between inmates and staff.

As compared to the single inmate council system which exists in many prisons, the Leavenworth experiment has broadened participation considerably among inmates by having some forty separate committees, each of which has a special jurisdiction. This system of involving as many persons as possible in participatory groups recalls the recent Yugoslav innovation which has divided the factory (or enterprise) work force into small, self-governing economic units.

In general, those in the field of corrections who continue to favour the idea of inmate self-government tend to believe it worthwhile for the following reasons: *1*, it is often a good barometer by which to measure inmate morale; *2*, it not only reflects morale but tends to raise it as well, undoubtedly for the same reasons that participation lifts morale in the factory, the office, and the laboratory; *3*, it instills in the inmates a sense of responsibility; *4*, it calls into existence machinery for communication in both directions, and especially permits inmates to gain direct insight into aspects of prison administration; *5*, it creates a situation where staff and inmates are conceived as part of a co-operative unit in operating the institution; *6*, and finally, it tends to encourage inmate identification with anti-criminal persons, a basic element in the rehabilitative effort.

7. The Case against Workers' Management: Hugh Clegg's World of Industrial Democracy

The recent discussions of industrial democracy by Hugh Clegg—one of Britain's leading industrial relations experts—are extremely important for the entire subject of workers' management. In essence, Clegg's views represent the culmination of an ideological and political retreat from the idea of workers' control, an idea which reached the peak of its influence in Britain in the period between 1910 and 1922 with the influence of syndicalism in British unions, the rise of guild socialism, and the development of the shop stewards' movement. What Clegg offers is the latest, most contemporary, and most sociologically sophisticated refutation of workers' management, a refutation which has been embraced by the Centre and Right of the British Labour party and used as a justification for opposing any extension of workers' management in the nationalised sector.[1] Clegg directs his theses both at and beyond the British industrial scene and stresses that his arguments against workers' management have near-universal applicability. It is therefore crucial to assess these arguments here.

Before offering a critical appraisal of Clegg's theory of industrial democracy, I should like to sketch out his argument as it has developed in two books which he has written since 1951. The theories I shall discuss here were developed in his *Industrial Democracy and Nationalisation* (1951)[2] and were later repeated and elaborated in *A New Approach to Industrial Democracy* (1960)[3]

Underpinning this new view of *industrial* democracy, according to Clegg, is a changed definition of *political* democracy, especially among socialists. Clegg argues that the conception of political democracy held by nineteenth-century social democrats was both naïve and fallacious. For the most part they believed that socialism would abolish not only class conflict but political conflict as well. Once the opportunity for economic exploitation was removed, then political exploitation arising out of the class struggle would also disappear. In the new society checks on political power would be unnecessary because a workers' government would naturally rule in the interests of the workers.

However, under the impact of twentieth-century totalitarian socialism, democratic socialists have had to revise their previous views drastically. Now it is recognised that it is indeed possible for political exploitation to be superimposed upon a socialist economic base, as in the Communist world. Democratic socialists, according to Clegg, have come to realise that political pluralism, meaning the existence of an opposition to the government, organised and ready to replace it by peaceful means, is the *sine quo non* of democracy today, under capitalism or socialism. As Clegg says:

> Democracy is not only a matter of choosing who shall govern, it is a matter of making that choice more than formal by allowing opposition between parties, so that the electorate may choose between men and parties. . . . We now believe that the dangers of power are so great that even when a socialist government is in office every opportunity must be given to its opponents to bring about its defeat—so long as they use democratic methods.[4]

Standing at the root of his argument, then, is the assertion that opposition is a necessary condition of political democracy as we know it and that opposition is as vital in a socialist as in a capitalist framework to prevent abuses of political power which will otherwise inevitably arise.

Now, from this premise, Clegg goes on to make a direct analogy from politics to industry. He claims that just as political democracy is based on the existence of an opposition, so therefore industrial democracy is also contingent upon the existence of an opposition within the industry to the prevailing power of management or ownership. What constitutes an effective industrial opposition for Clegg is a strong trade union organisation. The trade union within the factory is to management what the opposition political party is to the government in power. According to Clegg, 'the most important function of a trade union is to represent and defend the interests of its members. Trade unions owe their existence to the need felt by the workers for an organisation to oppose managers and employers on their behalf.'[5]

As political or—in this case—industrial pluralism tends to be his prime criterion for democracy in any system, Clegg's definition of industrial democracy tends, therefore, to be quite modest and bland, especially when compared to the ambitious dreams of socialists of a previous generation who viewed industrial democracy as a system of complete workers' management, administered either by trade unions or by other forms of elected workers' representatives. Not so for Clegg, however. In fact, armed with his new theory of democracy, Clegg believes that the key elements in any system of industrial democracy are merely: *1*, the existence of a trade union strong enough to oppose management; and *2*, a management which accepts trade unionism as a 'loyal opposition' and is willing to compromise and come to terms with it in the interests of industrial harmony and unity. As Clegg says:

> ... industrial democracy consists, in part, of the opposition of the trade unions to the employer, and, in part, of the attempt of the employer to build his employees into a team working together towards a common purpose. ...[6]

Now, it is not clear in this early work, *Industrial Democracy and Nationalisation*, whether Clegg believes that industrial democracy is attainable in private as well as in publicly-owned industry. Indeed, logically it should be, for if industrial democracy consists of no more than trade union opposition and a management which accepts this opposition, then certainly this kind of 'industrial democracy' has been attained and is compatible with private ownership of industry. However, in this work, Clegg, a prominent Fabian, does not go quite this far; he refers occasionally to 'capitalist authoritarianism' and it is clear that he still retains a sentimental, if not a logical, attachment to socialism. Indeed, perhaps it was sentiment that caused Clegg to delay for nine years what seemed an obvious logical jump, i.e. to realise that if industrial democracy consists primarily of the existence of trade union opposition, then capitalism offers this as well as does socialism; and, if this is so, then nationalisation is actually unnecessary because the dream of industrial democracy—Clegg's version of it anyway—is already fulfilled under capitalism. Clegg, in fact, does ultimately reach this conclusion in a later work, *A New Approach to Industrial Democracy*, and we shall examine its major hypothesis later.

Having established to his own satisfaction the argument that the major purpose of trade unions is to act as an industrial opposition, he goes on to argue that for several reasons trade unions should never attempt to share the job of management with management itself. First of all, Clegg disputes the technical ability of trade unions to administer industry, and believes that they could not do so even if they chose. 'To take a serious part in the planning of large-scale industry', he argues, 'requires a high degree of technical knowledge, or briefing by technical experts. Hardly any of those who represent the workers have either of these advantages.'[7] Elsewhere he asserts that 'trade unions have not the technical, administrative, and commercial experience to run a large-scale industry'.[8]

A second argument against extending trade union power into the management of industry pertains to the question of democracy within the trade unions. Clegg argues that as a fighting organisation, a trade union must be granted a certain amount of indulgence for its frequent violations of democratic procedure, but one should be fully aware that penetration by unions into the realm of managerial responsibility means that these undemocratic practices are sure to accompany the unions as their power spreads. Clegg argues that an undemocratic voluntary organisation (such as a trade union) is far more tolerable in a free society than one which is not voluntary as trade unions would be if they assumed total responsibility for industrial management.[9]

Finally, we come to Clegg's primary reason for opposing trade union encroachment into management and it is a reason which stems from his initial discussion of the nature of industrial democracy. If, as Clegg asserts, industrial democracy is defined in terms of the existence of organised and autonomous trade unions, then any act or policy which would jeopardise the independence of trade unions from management or which would deflect union policy from its proper role as opposition, would to that degree undermine industrial democracy. As Clegg says:

> The trade union cannot . . . become the organ of industrial management; there would be no one to oppose the management, and no hope of democracy. Nor can the union enter into an unholy alliance for the joint management of industry, for its opposition functions would then become subordinate and finally stifled.[10]

If the trade unions were to participate in management, they would inevitably be drawn into an organisational role conflict, with the workers as the ultimate losers, for the workers' primary need is to have a force behind them which is in every respect free and independent of management, which bears no responsibility for management's decisions, and which is not in any way obliged to defend management policy. For this reason, according to Clegg, 'the conception of trade union leaders getting together with the board of a nationalised industry round a table which has no sides in order to solve together all the problems of industry, is both false and dangerous'.[11]

In addition, unions in a managerial role would inevitably begin to share the managerial *Weltanschauung* and would take on new concerns for productivity, profit margins, and the like. Clegg argues, for example, that the acceptance of wage restraint by British unions during Labour's first post-war government 'led them to use arguments about inflation, about prices and profits which they would have scorned even so recently as during the last war. . . .'[12]

Clegg also discusses and dismisses quickly the proposal that another group of workers' representatives, outside of the trade unions, should assume managerial authority. In such a case, Clegg asserts (in a vastly oversimplified way) that there would be a struggle to the death between the two organisations as both would claim to represent the workers. Confronted by this threat to its power as the sole voice of the workers within the plant, the trade union would undoubtedly attempt to capture control of the workers' management organs by getting its nominees placed. If this were successful there would be a reversion to trade union management and all the disadvantages mentioned above. If unions were unsuccessful in capturing workers' management bodies, then, according to Clegg, union power would be smashed and there would, again, be no effective workers' opposition to management.

Clegg argues, therefore, that any attempt by modern-day 'industrial democrats' or enthusiasts of workers' control to extend the influence of workers or their unions or other workers' representatives into the realm of management threatens to destroy the very basis of industrial democracy as it exists today, the autonomous trade unions. Advocates of workers' control would create an industrial despotism, not an industrial democracy because they would destroy independent trade unions which are the bulwark of industrial pluralism which in turn is the essential component of industrial democracy. Clegg believes that the kinds of complete workers' control envisaged by those firm believers in total industrial self-government is possible only 'if industry is operated by small independent groups of free associates'.[13] Unfortunately, however, such workers' control is incompatible with the irreversible large-scale organisation of industry today. But this should not be a cause of concern. Rather, Clegg advises that, like Molière's *bourgeois gentilhomme* who never realised he had been speaking prose all his life, those contemporary worshippers of workers' control should realise that industrial democracy need not be a remote aspiration, but rather is an accomplished fact, and lies in the existence of a free trade union movement whose activities are accepted by modern management.

If industrial democracy operates imperfectly in the public sector today in England, then Clegg's remedy is not to scrap the entire machinery of the public corporation in favour of thoroughgoing workers' participation, but rather a few very modest proposals to improve its operations such as methods to improve selection of industrial leaders, reform of promotion, hiring, and educational policies and improvement in the joint consultation machinery.

> We place our hope . . . in the eagerness of boards to build up good relations, in the wide use of their powers of appointment and promotion, in the democratisation of promotion and training systems, and in the extension and improvement of schemes for educating managers in new methods for democratic leadership.[14]

I find Clegg's arguments both logically and empirically weak, and thus desperately in need of correction. First of all, his definition of democracy is simplistic and inadequate, for he tends to believe that the mere existence of an opposition has certain magical properties which guarantees democracy wherever it is found. The truth of the matter, however, is that opposition, though one means of achieving democracy, is neither a necessary nor a sufficient condition of democracy. For example, there are historically many circumstances where opposition has existed but where political democracy was completely absent. Medieval society saw conflicts between rival royal and aristocratic élites for power and was thus partially pluralistic, but certainly not democratic in any meaningful sense. In England before the second Reform Act which extended the suffrage widely, there was political opposition, political rivalry between Whigs and Tories, but little democracy as far as the vast majority of the population was concerned.[15]

On the other hand, there are numerous examples of democracy, mainly on a small scale, which have flourished without any organised opposition—the town meeting, the dissenting chapel, the trade union lodge, the consumers' co-operative.[16] And modern Mexico has achieved a measure of political democracy without the presence of a meaningful opposition political party.

I believe, therefore, that to define democracy exclusively in terms of opposition is a mistake; democracy is much more appropriately defined as the *accountability* of leadership to an electorate which has the power to remove that leadership. In this sense, the role of opposition is to make accountability effective by facilitating the selection of alternate sets of leaders. It should be made clear, however, that the mere existence of political opposition, without accountability, does not assure democracy.

Clegg himself realises the importance of accountability to democracy when he discusses nationalised industry, and he argues correctly that industries must, if they are to be democratically organised at all, be accountable in some fashion to the public. With respect to the socially owned sector, he argues that '. . . we must have some means of public accountability and control'.[17]

Now, if we are correct in arguing that democracy is best defined in terms of accountability, rather than in terms of opposition, then surely one must conclude that there is very little democracy—industrial or otherwise—in the ordinary trade union-organised factory as Clegg claims there is. For although the trade unions do constitute an opposition, nevertheless the employer is only minimally accountable to the union or the workers for decisions which lie outside the immediate job area. Thus, trade union opposition in itself does not constitute a sufficient condition for genuine industrial democracy.

But suppose we grant Clegg's definition of democracy as being synonymous with the existence of organised opposition. Even if we do so, his argument fails and the analogy he has made from politics to industry will not stand. Remember that Clegg has argued that in government the 'essence' of democracy is organised opposition and that in industry the same is true, so that the existence of trade union opposition is sufficient to guarantee industrial democracy. However, the crucial condition of any true multi-party system, or any system where political opposition exists, is that one or more parties is always ready and able to *replace* the party in power. An 'opposition' whose role is confined to protesting, making suggestions or criticising, but which can never itself *assume power*, is not an effective or a genuine opposition at all.

Now, it is obvious that British trade unions, in the public as well as the private sector, can never 'replace' their employer and become the ruling power in industry as, for example, the Labour party may replace the Conservative party in government. Clegg himself is quite aware of this, for as he admits parenthetically, 'The trade union is thus industry's opposition—*an opposition which can never become a government.*'[18] Further on, he states the idea again, but this time more explicitly.

> The aim of a parliamentary opposition is to defeat and replace the government. A trade union can never hope to become the government

of industry, unless the syndicalist dream is fulfilled [which Clegg believes is impossible].[19]

What Clegg does not seem to realise is that with this admission his analogy between political and industrial democracy completely breaks down and his entire argument lies in ruins. If trade unions have no power to replace the present government of industry but are merely able to challenge management in a carefully delineated sphere of its activity—the job area—then in terms of Clegg's own definition, there is no pluralism, no choice, no alternative, and no opposition—in short, no democracy. Nowhere does Clegg meet this issue.

In summary: *1*. Clegg's definition of democracy is faulty. He defines it in terms of the formal existence of an opposition rather than in terms of the accountability of leadership to the led. As employers are not accountable to their employees or to trade unions for the vast majority of their decisions, industrial democracy cannot be said to exist in the ordinary trade union-organised enterprise. *2*. Even if we accept Clegg's definition of democracy as synonymous with the existence of opposition, industrial democracy is still absent in public and private enterprise, for the trade union does not constitute a genuine opposition in the full sense of the word, i.e. one that is ready and able to assume power and replace the present leadership. If this is true, then industrial democracy is something still to be attained and not, as Clegg argues, something to be cherished as an accomplished fact.

Nine years after *Industrial Democracy and Nationalisation* appeared, Clegg published his *New Approach to Industrial Democracy* which contains an extension and elaboration of the arguments set forth in the earlier volume. In the years which intervened between the publication of these two volumes, Clegg's views on industrial democracy changed basically in two ways. First, he no longer looks to joint consultation in Great Britain, whether voluntary (as in private industry) or compulsory (as in the nationalised sector) as a fruitful means of enlarging industrial democracy. He claims that in recent years joint consultation has proved itself a failure on all counts—increasing productivity, raising the standards of labour relations, interesting the workers in the decision-making process, or improving the wages and conditions of workers.[20] In short, Clegg has now turned against joint consultation, claiming that it 'can be written off as an effective instrument of industrial democracy'.[21]

More important than this, however, is Clegg's new position on the role of socialised industry in creating the pre-conditions for industrial democracy. Clegg's view in this later volume, which provides further ammunition for the Right wing of the Labour party, is that the owner-ship of property is now *irrelevant* to industrial democracy, that indus-trial democracy can be achieved just as readily with private as well as public ownership of the means of production.

As we mentioned earlier, this shift from his 1951 work was not par-ticularly unexpected as it follows from all the premises of his previous discussion of industrial democracy. Nevertheless, it took Clegg nearly a decade to make the short logical hop from his earlier position to this later one. In the earlier work, as we have said, he talked of industrial democracy almost solely in terms of opposition, but he still stressed the importance, or at least the desirability, of public ownership. In the later work, however, he 'realised' that if trade union opposition is all that really matters, then the locus of ownership has nothing to do with industrial democracy, in which case it is sentimental foolishness to continue arguing for public ownership. This rather obvious logical jump is finally taken early in his *New Approach*:

> Public ownership may have profound effects on the management of in-dustry, but if the essence of democracy is *opposition*, then changes in *management* cannot be of primary importance to industrial democracy.[22]

This argument, which we shall discuss later, is part of a codification of principles of industrial democracy which Clegg sets forth early in the volume. These principles are as follows:

> The first is that trade unions must be independent both of the state and of management. The second is that only the unions can represent the industrial interests of workers. The third is that the ownership of indus-try is irrelevant to good industrial relations.[23]

These principles he spells out in a chapter entitled 'Return to Tradition' which, for Clegg, is a euphemism for a retreat from socialism into the waiting arms of the *status quo* and political liberalism. As Clegg him-self admits, these principles assume 'that the political and industrial institutions of the stable democracies already approach the best that can be realised. They return to traditions of liberal thought which preceded the rise of socialism.'[24]

Of these three principles, the first, trade union independence from management, is a clear carry over from the earlier volume, while the second and third are inferences readily made from the arguments pre-sented in that book. All three are so clearly based upon his theory of industrial-democracy-as-opposition which we have already described that they need no further explication here; however, further criticism is definitely in order.

Clegg argues that these principles, which constitute the basis for his new approach, have been applied successfully in many western countries including Britain, the United States, Scandinavia, Holland, Switzerland, Canada, Australia, and New Zealand, and he proceeds to examine the industrial relations systems of other countries (West Germany, France, Israel, and Yugoslavia) in order to test and validate the principles he sets forth initially. The book is interesting methodologically, for it is really a deviant case analysis of several countries whose industrial relations systems do not adhere to Clegg's three principles. But unlike most successful deviant case analyses which, as the textbooks say, suggest new lines of inquiry, qualify and enrich the original hypothesis, etc., this deviant case analysis drives his original hypotheses into a full-scale retreat and in the end we have nothing or nearly nothing. The deviant cases prove so formidable and contradict his initial hypotheses so blatantly that Clegg immediately begins to hedge, retreat, qualify, modify, offer *ad hoc* excuses and explanations, so that by the time his analysis of the deviant cases is completed, his original principles lie in shambles and, in his attempt to salvage them, they become so watered down as to be meaningless.

Clegg's approach, as we have said, is to state his principles boldly and then turn and run from them as the contradictory evidence pours in. His first principle, for example, is that trade unions must always remain independent of both the state and of management if they are not to compromise their essential freedom to oppose which would jeopardise industrial democracy. 'This principle', according to the author, 'seems to prevent unions from sending direct representatives to serve on the boards of nationalised industries. That would compromise their independence.'[25] But then Clegg examines at some length the West German experiment in codetermination in which labour representatives are accorded one half of the seats on the Supervisory Boards* in the steel and coal industries and one third of the seats on the Supervisory Boards in most other German industries. In the steel and coal industries both the union federation (DGB) and the appropriate industrial union (Metal Workers or Mine Workers Union) directly

---

* The German Supervisory Boards are roughly comparable to American corporate boards of directors.

select many of the labour members of the Supervisory Boards. In addition union officers are very frequently selected to sit on these boards. Data collected in the 1950s from thirty-five mining and twelve steel enterprises revealed that sixty-three of the 252 labour representatives on the supervisory boards were union functionaries, from locals, industrial unions, and the federation. An additional 105 were plant workers, of which 99 were representatives of the plants' works council, a workers' defence organisation with collective bargaining functions. Undoubtedly most of the 105 plant worker representatives were also trade unionists.[26]

In all probability, the proportion of trade unionists on supervisory boards has *increased* since this data were collected, for in the early days of codetermination there was a great shortage of qualified union personnel due to the Nazi decimation of trade union leadership and the initial lack of training and preparation of trade unionists for board positions.[27] The unions also play a large role in the selection of the Labour Director in each coal and steel company who is one of three members of top management. These labour directors are very frequently old trade unionists.[28]

Now, reasoning *a priori* from Clegg's first principle, one would conclude that such an arrangement would deal a death blow to German trade union independence and thus to 'industrial democracy' in that country. But is this the case? According to Clegg himself, this is emphatically *not* the case and he readily admits that '. . . it cannot be shown that the German unions have lost their independence under codetermination'.[29] He adds that:

> Above all, no widespread unofficial movement has been called into being to protect the workers against representatives who can no longer represent them because they have 'gone over to the other side'.[30]

This is true 'despite the considerable salaries, fees, and other perquisites which go with membership on the boards [and to an even greater extent to the labour directors in top management, Clegg might have added] and the responsible way in which the workers' representatives have exercised their managerial authority'.[31]

If codetermination has not weakened trade union independence and industrial democracy among German unions as a whole, then perhaps it has done so in the Metal Workers and Mine Workers Unions which play a larger role in codetermination than unions in other industries. But Clegg concedes that this also is not the case.

There is certainly no evidence that codetermination has weakened the
metal workers and mine workers in comparison to other unions in the
Deutsche Gewerkschaftsbund. On the contrary, they are two of the
strongest links in its armour.[32]

Forced to admit that worker and trade union representation on
supervisory boards and in positions of top management 'appears to
contravene the rule enjoining trade union independence',[33] and that
in general 'it is difficult to reconcile codetermination with the three
principles'[34] stated early in the book, he casts around for an explanation of why codetermination has 'done no obvious harm'. He asks
rhetorically:

> Why has it not undermined the independence of the German unions?
> If British unions with their greater strength, longer traditions and more
> continuous progress fear that the acceptance of joint responsibility with
> management for the running of industry would undermine their in-
> dependence and destroy their value as unions, then surely the weaker
> and less stable unions of West Germany ought to have suffered badly
> from codetermination. But they have not.[35]

Trying to turn a rout into a strategic withdrawal, Clegg attempts to
explain the anomaly. In brief, his explanation is that codetermination
gives unions only a *partial* share in management; a larger share would
certainly be dangerous. According to this explanation, however, we
would expect the German Metal Workers and Mine Workers Unions
which have a greater voice in management than other German unions
to be less independent than other unions, but we have seen that this is
not the case.

A more convincing rebuttal to Clegg's argument is apparent when
we turn from the experience of West Germany to that of Israel where
trade union participation in management is not partial at all but *total*.
But even here, according to Clegg himself, the Histadrut 'appears to
have maintained its independence',[36] even though it is inextricably tied
into ownership and management. Histadrut, again in Clegg's words,
'has not realised the fears of those [i.e. Clegg himself!] who think
trade unions cannot avoid corruption if they lose independence from
management'.[37]

In need of another patch to mend his badly tattered hypothesis,
Clegg tries one that he hopes will do the job. He begins tentatively by
allowing himself to hope that 'perhaps this state of affairs [successful
Histadrut management combined with maintenance of its autonomous
trade union functions] cannot continue'. He goes on:

Israel's experience as an industrial country is very brief. [But Histadrut has managed and owned enterprises for forty years or more.] It is very difficult to believe it [trade union independence] could continue if Histadrut's share in industrial ownership expanded to include the great majority of industrial undertakings. [But he does not explain why he believes this is so, and it is certainly not self-evident.] But for the moment it is so, and an explanation must be found.[38]

Clegg eventually 'finds' an explanation for Histadrut's success, but it is, to this writer at any rate, *ad hoc*, vague, and unsatisfactory.

Although Israel's own trade union movement is relatively young, many of the men and women who built it had long experience of the working and tradition of labour movements in other countries. Some of them had been amongst the most capable, the most trustworthy, and the most independent-minded in those labour movements. Consequently, far greater strength and self-reliance were implanted into the Israeli trade unions than could have developed if they had been a purely indigenous growth. It is this which has enabled them to bear the strain of a power and responsibility which otherwise would have broken them.[39]

So, although this principle of industrial democracy was initially based upon rigid and inflexible structural imperatives, now we see that it can be easily contravened by trade unionists who are 'experienced', 'capable', 'trustworthy', and 'independent-minded', and thus able to build up a strong trade union movement which can weather the storm of managerial responsibility. But if this can be done in Israel, then why not elsewhere, and if it is possible elsewhere, then why the need for strict trade union independence from management? And in that case, what has become of Clegg's cardinal principle of industrial democracy?

Not quite satisfied with this explanation of Histadrut's success in Israel, Clegg invokes an alternate hypothesis.

. . . in the past the Histadrut has left the boards of its own concerns to run their own firms, and has been able to do so because the Israeli movement threw up a number of dynamic entrepreneurs eager for industrial expansion and very ready to accept responsibility. Consequently left-wing circles attacked the Histadrut industry on the grounds that it was no better than private industry—not that the Histadrut management had the Histadrut unions and shop stewards in their pockets.[40]

It is indeed true that trade union enterprises in Israel traditionally have had considerable autonomy from the Histadrut. Clegg, in pointing to this independence, treats it as a curiosity or a quirk; he does not realise that in managerial autonomy lies the key to the successful trade union management of industry. Clegg has correctly pointed out that in trade union management there is a great danger of the development of conflicting loyalties and of a general undermining of the traditional role of the trade union as a workers' defence organisation. Any trade union, then, which seeks active participation in management, must carefully *isolate* its trade union functions from its managerial functions, and in this way the autonomy of each can be protected. The Histadrut did just this long ago by creating the *Hevrat Ovdim,* the separate holding company for Histadrut enterprises, and in giving considerable managerial autonomy to the boards of the enterprises and to their directors. With this done, the trade union as a defence organisation is not endangered and meaningful collective bargaining between the 'two halves' of the organisation remains possible.

Trade union management has been ridiculed and caricatured by those opposed to it by reference to the story of the trade union secretary who demands a wage increase and then goes round to the other side of the table and, as manager, denies it. However, it is inconceivable that any trade union which also possesses managerial responsibility would not recognise the necessity for a rigid organisational segregation of trade union functions from managerial functions. Arguing from the point of view of the feasibility and not necessarily the desirability of trade union management, what is obviously needed to ensure trade union independence and to prevent the development of conflicting loyalties, are two hierarchies, independent from one another, but both responsive and accountable to the rank and file.

Actually, the Israeli experience totally refutes almost all of Clegg's arguments.[41] Although there is little space here for an elaborate discussion of the Histadrut as a test of Clegg's major arguments, the following points should be made.

I

Granted that the Histadrut has had a rather unique history, nevertheless, the assertion that trade unions are somehow by their very nature intrinsically incompetent and unable to organise and operate modern industry will not stand in the light of the record of this trade union organisation, as Clegg himself has had to admit. It is hardly a matter of dispute that the Histadrut, since its founding in 1920, has not only managed to organise 90 per cent of the working population, but has proved its technical and managerial ability in running modern industry.

Histadrut's major industrial holdings (in the so-called *Koor* group) employed some 9,000 workers in the mid-1960s and comprised a vital share of Israeli basic industry (iron and steel, building materials of all kinds, glass, rubber, electrical equipment, and much more). The labour economy, in short, is in the vanguard of the industrialisation of the country, accounting for about 25 per cent of total GNP and employment.[42] In addition to its industrial holdings, the Histadrut is directly or indirectly involved in agriculture (via the collective settlements of various kinds), construction (through the large and venerable *Solel Boneh* construction firm, one of the first and most influential of all Histadrut enterprises), transportation (the wide network of transport co-operatives), plus diverse fields of commerce, finance and services.

The Histadrut has had no difficulty holding its own with the private sector of the economy and its strength has never been greater. It is well known that many important Histadrut enterprises today were originally purchased from private investors who were ready to close down operations or move them out of the country because of their inability to make them profitable. Such Histadrut hallmarks as *Phoenicia* (glass) and *Vulcan* (foundries) were purchased from private capitalists, not originally with the idea of making a profit, but of maintaining and expanding employment for settlers. And although Histadrut acquired these firms at the low ebb of their fortunes, the labour organisation eventually went on to make them thoroughly solvent and prospering organisations.

Finally, as for the productivity of its workers, the Histadrut has proved itself an able competitor of private industry. In mining and manufacturing, construction, and transportation and communication, the productivity of workers in the Histadrut sector exceeds that of workers in the private sector.[43]

II

Clegg fears that trade union management would lead to a new form of industrial despotism, not to industrial democracy, because, by taking responsibility for management, the unions would be unable to protect their workers' interests. This has also been contradicted by the Histadrut experience. First, workers in Histadrut firms are organised into an autonomous National Organisation of Workers in Histadrut Enterprises, and at the plant level, relations between management and the workers' committee are characterised by a genuine 'two sided bargaining approach'.[44] In brief, a healthy conflict of interest exists between the two groups. Second, there is regular grievance machinery in *Koor* firms to settle differences which arise between the union and management. It is significant that most of the levels through which grievances pass are weighted in favour of the trade union, and Derber found that *Koor* personnel managers thought that this grievance procedure was unfair to management. But workers had their complaints, too, and believed that management usually came out on top. Third, at least one study has shown that Histadrut managers tend to think like managers in the private sector, and, more important, trade union leaders representing workers in the Histadrut sector tend to think like trade union representatives in private enterprise, i.e. they have worker-oriented attitudes and have not been co-opted by management in any sense.[45]

Fourth, the trade unions in Histadrut plants have *more* power and influence over management than they do in private establishments. Especially regarding discipline, transfers, promotions and the like, the Histadrut management regularly consults the workers' representatives, and to a degree unknown in the private sector.[46] Fifth, wages and conditions in *Koor* plants are generally superior to those in private industry and are recognised as such by the workers who regard an appointment in a *Koor* factory as a privilege: job security is much greater, wages are as high or higher, and fringe benefits are 10–20 per cent better.[47]

Finally, management's authority in Histadrut enterprises does not take the form of despotic, arbitrary, and unchecked rule over groups of docile workers who have been abandoned by their trade union, as suggested by Clegg's thesis, but, on the contrary, management tends to be weak and timid, from the level of the foreman upwards.[48]

III

It may be charged that the widespread revolt of professional and white collar workers within the Histadrut in recent years, their clamour for greater income differentials between themselves and the working class, the spread of unauthorised strikes of clerks, teachers, physicians, engineers and others, sometimes against the Histadrut itself, the development of white collar secession movements within the labour movement—all suggest ominously that the Histadrut, as employer, cannot consistently represent the interests of its white collar union members.

My own view is that this conflict arises not out of the Histadrut's role as employer, but out of other qualities and values of the organisation, namely: *a*, that as a Socialist organisation, Histadrut has historically pursued an egalitarian wage policy and has resisted the widening of income differentials; *b*, this Socialist egalitarianism was reinforced by the unique 'religion of (manual) labour' that inspired the early Zionist settlers in Palestine; *c*, finally, the Histadrut has traditionally been, not only a *class* organisation but a *nationalist* (Zionist) organisation as well, and has always taken special responsibility for the stability of the national economy and opposed inflationary pressures to which the country is constantly exposed. In these factors, then, and not in its role as entrepreneur, lies the recurring conflict of the Histadrut with its white collar membership.

IV

However one may define industrial democracy, one cannot claim that there is less of it in the sector in which the trade union movement is owner and manager. And yet, there has been disappointment with the Histadrut economy, not because there is less industrial democracy than in the private sector, but because there is not significantly more. While satisfaction with the strictly economic performance of the Histadrut is common and a source of pride, there has been, in recent years, disillusionment with its social achievements. There has been disappointment with the Histadrut because the attitudes of the workers toward their jobs and toward the Histadrut companies is not appreciably different from the attitudes of workers in the private sector, thus illustrating the principle mentioned in Chapter 1, that the locus of ownership at the highest level has little effect on the attitudes of rank and file workers in the factory. Alienation and depersonalisation continue, according to the Histadrut leaders themselves, and the workers show no greater tendency to identify with and feel responsibility toward 'their own' Histadrut enterprises than toward industries in the private sector.[49] And in this sense, the Histadrut General Secretary admitted in 1957, 'there is no difference between Histadrut and privately owned enterprises'.

For this and other reasons, during the late 1950s the Histadrut embarked upon an experiment in joint consultation in about thirty of its enterprises which was meant to lay the groundwork for eventual joint management of these firms. Although we cannot discuss these in any detail here,[50] the initial results were less than successful: managers were suspicious, and the workers—perhaps because the councils had little power (the meetings were often called mere 'tea parties)—the workers were largely apathetic. Nevertheless, given the continuing ideological sentiment, by the leadership as well as the Left wing, in favour of direct workers' participation, it seems only a matter of time until the Histadrut undertakes bolder experiments.[51]

Let us now examine Clegg's explanation for the success of the German trade unions in maintaining their independence while sharing in industrial management. Here he hits upon a distinction between strong and weak trade unions. Retreating once again to what he believes is a more secure position, Clegg admits finally that his first principle of industrial democracy, the necessity for strict trade union independence from managerial responsibility, applies 'only to weak trade unions, to trade unions which lack strength to bear responsibility.'[52]

True, this *is* a more secure position; it is as secure as tautologies always are: what he is saying is that unions which are strong enough to bear responsibility for management are *in fact* able to bear responsibility. But a much more important point is that with this admission, that his principle does *not* apply to strong trade union movements, he has clearly exempted the British and the American trade union movements (among others) from his entire discussion. The obvious, indeed the natural, inference from his own argument is that strong trade union movements, such as those in Britain and the United States, *can* bear considerable managerial responsibility without eroding or jeopardising their traditional functions. This point cannot be stressed too strongly. And now Clegg, who has argued for a book and a half that trade union independence is a delicate mechanism likely to be upset and destroyed by the slightest tampering with its traditional functions by assuming managerial power, now tells us that the mechanism is much sturdier than he heretofore led us to believe.

Now we are informed that 'the fragility of trade union independence can be exaggerated',[53] and that it would be a mistake to believe 'that the independence of British or American or Scandinavian unions would be destroyed by a dose of codetermination'.[54] We have now come a long way from the original statement of his first principle which at the outset stressed that it is essential 'to prevent unions from sending direct representatives to serve on the boards of nationalised industries. That would compromise their independence'.[55]

At the end of the volume, Clegg offers a 'restatement' of his principles of industrial democracy in the light of empirical data from Germany, France, Israel, and Yugoslavia. But the term 'restatement' which he uses is actually a misnomer, for it is more a retraction of these principles than a restatement or revision or reformulation of them.

Regarding his first principle, which we have discussed here, the necessity for absolute trade union independence from management, he introduces the following modifications. He states first of all that trade unions cannot be *so* independent from management that they refuse even to sign a contract with it, or so independent from government as to eschew bringing political pressure for favourable labour legislation. This restatement is an obvious and correct and minor one and does not constitute a serious revision of his first principle. But what follows certainly does:

> On the other hand, they [trade unions] must not become so dependent on management, a party or the state as to be directed from outside, for then they would be used for some other purposes than the protection of their members' rights and interests. Between these two extremes there is a wide scope for different trade union movements to take up their own positions, and they can offer little guidance to the trade union movement which seeks to increase its responsibilities without coming too close to losing its independence.[56]

After such a statement, exactly what remains of Clegg's first principle of industrial democracy? What he seems to be saying here—when he argues that trade unions must not become so dependent on other institutions as to be directed from outside—is *merely* that industrial democracy is incompatible with: 1, company unionism, or 2, with totalitarian state control of trade unions. If this is all he is saying, and I believe it is, then Clegg, in these two volumes, has badly let us down and left us with, at most, a theoretical truism of the most elementary kind. There is, it must be emphatically stated, no new approach to industrial democracy here.

But what of Clegg's second and third principles of industrial democracy. Perhaps they remain standing where the first has fallen. Unfortunately they do not. Clegg's second principle, the reader may remember, is that the trade unions and only the trade unions, not any other body of workers' representatives, are able to represent the 'industrial interests' of the workers themselves.

We have already seen Clegg's methodological approach: it is to state a hypothesis boldly at the outset and then chip it away with the relentless knife of deviant cases until nothing or almost nothing remains. In the light of deviant cases, theory is not refined but abandoned. Clegg's second principle of industrial democracy is treated just this way, as was the first. The instrument of his undoing here are the non-union works councils in West Germany which were established by law following World War II and resembled in their form and function the councils of the Weimar period. These councils bear major responsibility for collective bargaining and grievance handling at the plant level in West Germany. Among its major functions, the works council: *1*, 'concludes agreements on piece rates, wage systems',[57] etc. in the absence of union-management contracts or as a supplement to it; *2*, 'negotiates the work rules (beginning and ending of work periods, pauses, time and place of wage payments, timing of vacations, inservice training' and so forth); *3*, possesses the right of consultation on matters of hiring and firing and in some cases has veto power; *4*, 'negotiates with the employer on changes in the plant (restriction of activity, transfer of departments, merger, introduction of new work methods)'; *5*, 'supervises the enforcement of the applicable labour laws and of the collective agreement'; *6*, aids in handling grievances; *7*, 'administers the social welfare agencies of the plant'.

It is evident that the works council is extremely important at the plant level and has powers which are normally in the hands of trade unions, with the exception that they are not allowed to call a strike. The unusual powers of the councils stem partly from their legal status and partly from the traditional weakness of German unions at the plant level. Normally the local union organisation, comprising workers from several plants, is the smallest administrative unit of German trade unions.[58] And although unions often try to establish shop committees, these attempts are not always successful and even if they are, their power is almost always subordinate to the legally recognised and empowered works councils.

Also, the nature of collective bargaining between national unions and employers' associations strengthens the works council. The agreements, regional or national, usually do not specify the actual terms of employment but instead set minimum rates and conditions which are then used as a starting point in the negotiations between works council and management.[59]

Such a dual structure of worker representation is bound to engender conflict from time to time. Occasionally management strives to set council and union against each other in an attempt to weaken the union which is usually the less conciliatory organisation. And from time to time, the councils themselves, jealous of their power and their support from the workers, will try to undercut union power and policy. But though works councils in certain cases have undermined the power of unions, it must also be remembered that the local union plays a large role in the nomination of workers to the works council, and that, according to Clegg himself, the near-universality of works councils in German industry has led to union penetration of firms which would otherwise have been closed to the trade unions.[60] There are other links between works council and union as well. Most of the members of works councils are also trade unionists whose loyalty to the union is heightened by the knowledge that the works councils have achieved their legally recognised status in German industry by virtue of the economic and political pressure brought to bear by the trade union movement.[61] This indebtedness is not likely to be forgotten.

The major issue here, though, is that in spite of the occasional conflicts between works council and union—and they should not be underrated—it is difficult to see any significant limitation or abridgement of *industrial democracy per se* because of it. This will be elaborated below.

In the face of these facts, therefore, Clegg is forced to back down once again. 'The authority given to [West German] Works Councils comes close to breaking the rule of sole representation [by trade unions]',[62] Clegg admits midway through the volume. And finally, in his 'restatement' at the end, he abandons all qualification and concedes that 'the principle of sole representation can no longer stand by itself',[63] as he recognises the successful operation of works councils in German industry alongside the trade unions.

Actually, Clegg's principle that 'only unions can represent the industrial interests of the workers' contains two propositions which he never separates and which remain confused throughout his work. Clegg is saying first of all that no other body but trade unions can represent the specifically trade union interests of the workers. This would presumably include plant committees, works councils, and all other types of bargaining councils which are independent of the unions. But he is also saying something else, namely that workers have no other industrial interests *except* trade union interests (i.e. interests as employees), and no body, such as workers' managerial councils, should attempt to represent other than these trade union interests of workers.

With respect to the first argument which we have already discussed above, Clegg is partially right but mainly wrong. He is correct in the sense that the creation of bargaining councils parallel to trade unions, serving the same function as trade unions but independent or semi-independent of them, does create a dual structure, with its attendant rivalry and competition for worker loyalty and the possible weakening of the union position within the factory. This is not a new discovery, however; it was recognised long ago by German trade unionists, for example, who after World War I saw the new factory works councils, their revolutionary potential exhausted, as a threat to the trade unions and to the solidarity of the workers. As early as 1919, Karl Legien, the leading spokesman of German trade unionism at that time, said:

> The works councils are not an effective organisation; they split the unity of the trade . . . All existing laws of solidarity cease to exist for them. . . .[64]

And there is no doubt that the councils today, which play such a key role in plant collective bargaining, have driven a wedge between the workers and the unions and have deprived the unions of considerable power and influence at the grass roots. Some unions, recognising that the works councils undercut their influence, have reacted to it by attempting to capture some power and influence from the councils.

> The establishment of union groups in the plants, attempts to inject these groups into the process of grievance handling, efforts to subject the councils to union control, the slogan of 'collective bargaining close to the plant'—all these are symptoms of a growing realisation that the councils deprive the unions of a vital sphere of action.[65]

It is, after all, an elementary observation that potential for conflict exists in situations in which two or more groups seek to represent the identical interests of workers in a plant, or any group of people anywhere. But however unpleasant this is, and however adversely it may affect some trade unions, one cannot thereby conclude that industrial democracy is inevitably weakened by it. Furthermore—and this is an important point—in insisting upon the trade union principle of sole representation, Clegg is overlooking the *positive* and *necessary functions* which non-union bargaining councils have played historically and continue to play. In both France and Germany, for example, the trade union movements have traditionally been split due to differences in political and/or religious allegiances. This fragmentation has been aggravated by the rigid social class divisions between blue collar and white collar workers and the additional distinctions within the latter group. Lacking a unified trade union organisation the workers necessarily felt the need 'for a representative organ of all the workers in the plant which could rise above the level of union divisions. As a result, workers' plant representatives must to some extent be independent of the unions'.[66] In thus demanding that the trade unions be the workers' sole representatives in industry, Clegg is considering only the relatively homogeneous trade union movements of Britain and the United States; he is ignoring the *unifying* functions which these extra-union bargaining councils have traditionally served in countries where there are fundamental cleavages in the trade union movement.

Now let us turn to the second proposition clearly suggested by Clegg, that workers have no other industrial interests but trade union interests and no organ such as workers' managerial councils should attempt to represent other than these trade union interests of the workers.

First of all, it is an *a priori* and unwarranted assumption to claim that the 'industrial interests of workers' are limited solely to wages, hours, and working conditions, as Clegg clearly implies. Of course the whole matter is a question of definition, but the fact that over 90 per cent of German steel and coal workers voted in the early 1950s to take strike action unless codetermination could be saved or won,[67] suggests that one might just as easily suppose that the 'industrial interests of workers' involve, not only their interests as employees, but their interests as producers as well. And if this is true, then it certainly justifies the creation of other bodies, e.g. managerial councils, besides trade unions, to represent industrial interests of the workers hitherto unrepresented.

This idea goes back to the Guild Socialist theory of functional (or multiple) representation and it seems as theoretically applicable today as a half century ago when it was proposed. Men are connected to society by a complex of associations and in these associations they play many different roles. As men's lives are thus multi-faceted, it is impossible for a man to be 'represented' in all his different capacities by means of one or two elected representatives sitting in Parliament. Many roles encompass many vital interests, according to Guild Socialists, and each deserves representation. It is accordingly impossible for a man 'to choose someone to represent him as a man or as a citizen in all aspects of citizenship'.[68] In such a situation, 'the person elected for an indefinitely large number of disparate purposes ceases to have any real representative relation to him'.[69] Instead of this, it is necessary in a thoroughgoing democratic society '. . . only to choose someone to represent his [the citizen's] point of view in relation to some particular purpose or group of purposes, in other words, some particular *function*'.[70] Cole elaborates on this argument:

> It follows that there must be, in the Society, as many separately elected groups of representatives as there are distinct essential groups of functions to be performed. Smith cannot represent Brown, Jones and Robinson as human beings; for a human being, as an individual, is fundamentally incapable of being represented. He can only represent the common point of view which Brown, Jones, and Robinson hold in relation to some definite social purpose, or group of connected purposes. Brown, Jones and Robinson must therefore have, not one vote each, but as many different functional votes as there are different questions calling for associate action in which they are interested.[71]

In short, the Guild Socialist argues, 'man should have as many distinct, and separately exercised votes, as he has distinct social purposes or interests'.[72]

It can be argued then, along these lines, that workers might need one set of representatives to speak for their interests as employees or wage earners, desiring good wages and working conditions, and another set of representatives to speak for their interests as producers, as economic citizens desiring the efficient operation of their firm and the adequate provision of goods and services for the community. Is it not then an arbitrary and unnecessarily restricted view to define the 'industrial interests of workers' in such a one-dimensional manner as Clegg has done?

The argument is often made that for two reasons it is an absurdity to have both trade unions and workers' managerial councils existing within the same enterprise: *1*, that as the workers' council would already represent the workers, the trade union would be redundant and unnecessary; *2*, that 'union-management negotiations' would amount to workers talking to themselves, as both groups would be representing the workers, and thus 'negotiations' would be meaningless.

Both of these arguments are faulty. First of all, the trade union is not superfluous in a factory with a system of workers' management because the two bodies, though both representing the worker, represent different functions and different interests of the workers. The function of the trade union is to protect the worker as employee; the function of the council is to promote the interests of the worker as producer. Insofar as these functions are distinct, two organisations are justified and neither is redundant; insofar as these functions conflict with one another—as they must at times—there is room for negotiations, for 'labour management negotiations'.

For those who believe that it would be a peculiar spectacle indeed for one set of workers' representatives (the trade union) to sit down at a bargaining table with another set of workers' representatives (a workers' council), it would be instructive to turn for a moment from this economic setting to a political setting. In the election of a school board and a city council, we do not think it at all odd for citizens to elect two different sets of representatives for different purposes, and for these representatives to discuss, bargain, and occasionally even clash.[73] In such a case we do not wonder how it is possible for citizens to 'disagree with themselves' and think the idea absurd, but realise that it is the natural outcome of the exercise of different functions, activities, assignments, and interests in the community. When Congress and the President clash, both in essence popularly elected, we do not wonder how it is that the voters can disagree with themselves. There is no reason why this analogy cannot carry over into an industrial setting and why it is any more ludicrous to think of workers 'bargaining with themselves' than for citizens to do the same.

Furthermore, it can be very cogently argued—on Clegg's own ground at that—that real industrial pluralism exists when workers acquire a rich diversity of organisations to represent their industrial interests, and not when they have but one, a trade union which may be so heavily bureaucratised as to clog the expression of genuine worker interest. Thus, Herbert Spiro argues that the elaborate apparatus of codetermination in German industry offers workers a

> multiplicity of channels through which they may influence central decisions [and] also tends to increase the range of alternatives among which they can choose. This is so because it often happens that works council, union local, industrial union, union federation, and labour manager—to mention only some of these channels—pursue different policies. The workers can choose which policy they want to support.[74]

A *re*-definition of industrial democracy, beginning with Clegg's own premise that pluralism is vital to industrial as well as political democracy, would stress the necessity of numerous organisations within the framework of industry representing the various industrial interests of workers. This kind of industrial pluralism—characterised by multiple associations—much more readily fits the analogy of political pluralism than the one described and advocated by Clegg which provides for only a single workers' organisation.

Summarising my criticism of Clegg's second principle, that trade unions only can represent the industrial interests of workers, I would argue as follows:

1. He is correct in a very limited sense, viz. that the creation of bodies parallel to trade unions in the plant which have the same functions as trade unions is likely to provoke conflict between the rival organisations as the power and position of the union is challenged;

2. However, this does not necessarily mean that 'industrial democracy' inevitably suffers because of it, as the elected non-union plant committees may be as effective a spokesman for the workers as the union;

3. A dogmatic insistence on the principle of trade union exclusiveness in the plant overlooks the important unifying functions non-union committees have played in countries where the union movement is seriously divided;

4. Clegg's definition of the industrial interests of workers is artificially restricted and one-dimensional. A definition of workers' industrial interests of broader scope is equally, if not more, convincing, and would justify other kinds of worker representation (managerial) which might very well enlarge rather than restrict industrial democracy.

Of the three principles which constitute Clegg's 'new approach' to industrial democracy, two have fallen, partially by his own reluctant admission, and only one remains. But on this last principle he remains firm and refuses to yield. 'There is no particular reason for the established democracies to reject the principle that public ownership is irrelevant to industrial democracy.'[75] In other words, for Clegg, industrial democracy is compatible with private ownership of the means of production. This argument stems from his belief that, as the essence of industrial democracy lies primarily in the existence of a strong trade union organisation which acts as industry's opposition, the nature of ownership or management is consequently irrelevant. Trade union opposition can flourish in the private as well as the public sector. However, as we have suggested earlier (pp. 145–6), this argument is logically defective and based on a fallacious analogy to political democracy. For as we have said, if we grant Clegg's premise that industrial as well as political democracy depends on the existence of an opposition, then surely we have the right to expect that it be a genuine opposition, i.e. one which is able to replace the party (or the management) in power. And if industrial democracy now be defined in terms of the existence of a *genuine* opposition—trade union or worker-based—which is ready to assume managerial power, then how can this possibly be compatible with a system of private ownership? The very definition of private ownership would seem to preclude it.

No, according to the logic of Clegg's own premises, private ownership is no more compatible with industrial democracy than unlimited monarchy is compatible with political democracy: in neither case is opposition permitted to come to power. Of course, in the modern private corporation, rival groups of stockholders may constitute an opposition and may at times seize control of the organisation. However, this has as little to do with industrial democracy as a palace revolution has to do with political democracy. It is interesting to note that proponents of codetermination in Germany make the identical analogy between the monarchical state and the owner-or-management-controlled private corporation. In both institutions there has been an evolution. These Absolutist societies,

> just as these corporations, were once ruled by single sovereigns, accountable only to God or history, and possessed of sole responsibility for all that transpired in their realms. Their responsibility, too, was gradually . . . restrained and then divided and subdivided among ever more of those people who were affected by the consequences of decisions centrally made, until finally all citizens came to share in it.[76]

It is questionable, however, to what extent private ownership as we know it, embodying the right of control, is compatible with industrial democracy defined either as accountability or in terms of effective opposition. According to the natural inferences from Clegg's definition, public ownership seems a necessary (but not a sufficient) condition for industrial democracy, as only public ownership permits (but does not assure) the possibility of a true industrial opposition and genuine accountability of economic leadership.

Postscript: Clegg's Principles and Stable National Democracy

Clegg argues that the trade union movement in countries which are the world's stable democracies—viz. Britain, the United States,

Scandinavia, Holland, Switzerland, Canada, Australia, and New Zealand—have all accepted his three principles, and that a relationship can 'be discovered between these three principles of industrial democracy and the central principles of political democracy. . . .'[77]

This argument, like so many of his others, is extremely weak. First, he does not make entirely clear the direction of causality, i.e. it is difficult to decide whether Clegg is arguing that stable political democracy gives rise to trade union adherence to his three principles, or whether trade union adherence to his principles promotes stable democracy. But as he subscribes to the pluralistic conception of democracy, he generally seems to imply that trade union adherence to the three principles contributes to stable political democracy, presumably because trade unions constitute an independent source of power within the society and prevent undue concentration of power at the top. But certainly, even trade unions which do not subscribe to his three principles may discharge these same pluralistic functions.

Furthermore, Clegg does not make it clear whether he believes that stable democracy is possible in countries whose trade union movements do not accept his three principles (West Germany, France, Israel) nor, more important, does he explain how codetermination in Germany, tripartism in France, and Histadrut industry in Israel (all of which violate Clegg's principles) actually undermine political democracy in those countries. It is obvious why Clegg has not attempted such an explanation, for there is at best only the most tenuous relation between political democracy and trade union acceptance of Clegg's three principles.

Certainly free trade union movements exist in stable democracies and they play a role in maintaining democracy, but they play this role whether or not they seek to participate in managerial decisions, whether or not they are the workers' sole representatives, and whether or not they urge nationalisation of basic industries.

The case of Germany illustrates the spuriousness of the alleged relationship between trade union adherence to Clegg's principles and the existence of a stable political democracy. On the one hand, Clegg tends to argue that the autonomy of trade unions from management contributes somehow to the maintenance of stable national political democracy. The German trade union movement, on the other hand, in their proposals for complete and full trade union codetermination on every level of the economy, argues that union *involvement*, not union abstention from management, is the only way to assure stable political democracy in that country. Believing that it was the uncontrolled and enormous economic power of industrial monopolies and oligopolies which helped Hitler to power, the trade unions argue that *only by labour co-management* will this force potentially destructive to democratic values be controlled and held in check. A cardinal principle of the German Trade Union Federation (DGB) is that: 'The struggle for the full right of codetermination in social, personnel, and economic questions represents above all *a problem of the existence or non-existence of democracy*.'[78] This intimate connection between codetermination and political democracy exists, according to Victor Agartz of the DGB Economic Institute because full codetermination, with union penetration of economic institutions at all levels, will

> make impossible once and for all the political significance and influence on national policy . . . exerted in the past by representatives of the great economic complexes . . . by assuring that both the political and social power of the great economic complexes is neutralised.[79]

Furthermore, the trade union movement believes that the participation of labour in economic planning bodies at enterprise and supra-enterprise levels will help to guarantee full employment, a redistribution of income, greater productivity, rationalisation of industry not detrimental to workers or the society as a whole, and, in short, will be able to prevent a recurrence of the economic and social conditions which laid the groundwork for Nazi strength. As Erich Ollenhauer, the late chief of the Social Democratic Party, said in an address in 1953:

> . . . as things are in Germany, we will not be able to make democracy a basis for our national life which is, in the long run, panic-proof and stable if we do not succeed in extending the principles of democracy beyond political life into the economy through the realisation of codetermination.[80]

So, for the German trade union movement, what will ensure political democracy in their country is the *maximum* of trade union penetration of economic management and not, as Clegg urges, a complete withdrawal into merely a collective bargaining position. It was the latter, it is firmly believed today, that helped lead to the defeat of the trade unions in the 1930s and to the defeat of the democratic republic as well.

8. On the Origins of Workers' Management in Yugoslavia

To understand the ideology of Yugoslav Communism, one would do well to bear in mind this sociological dictum of Karl Marx. One should not, he said, 'set out from what men say, imagine, or conceive'; rather, one should begin with 'real, active men, and on the basis of their real life process demonstrate the development of the ideological reflexes and echoes of this life process'. This method is indispensable when discussing Titoism, for the ideology is not really intelligible unless one understands the 'real life process' which accounted for its development. Titosim, as an ideology, was not immaculately conceived and nurtured in isolation. Eloquently as the Yugoslavs deny it, Titoism was born and developed as a direct result of their expulsion from the Cominform in 1948 and the subsequent attempt of the USSR and Eastern Europe to destroy the régime.

Prior to 1948, Tito was an excellent Stalinist. This is not to say, however, that there were no strains, suspicions, or points of conflict between Yugoslavia and the Soviet Union. There were, but none of these was in any way related to the ideology of workers' management which only emerged much later. The major issues which eventually led to the split, some of which laid the basic groundwork and others which were of more immediate importance, included the following: *1*, the Soviet Union's timid, meagre, belated and disappointing help for the partisans both politically and militarily during World War II,[1] a partial consequence of Stalin's fear of antagonising the Allies, plus the Soviet's insufficient support of Yugoslavia on Trieste in 1945; *2*, the fact that the partisans had liberated their country and made the revolution virtually without the help of the Red Army, which inclined the Yugoslavs eventually to pride in their accomplishments and to *relative* independence; *3*, the alleged misbehaviour of Russian troops on Yugoslav soil in 1944 which shocked the Partisans who had always idealised the Red Army which now showed itself capable of the atrocities of any other army, such as assault, rape, murder, and widespread looting;[2] *4*, certain personal conflicts and antagonisms which developed between Stalin and the Yugoslav leaders;[3] 5, the post-war attempt of the USSR to dominate, control, and exploit the Yugoslav economy by means of the so-called joint-stock companies which were also imposed on other Eastern European countries,[4] plus other infringements on Yugoslav sovereignty; 6, the alleged harassment of Soviet civilian and military advisors in Yugoslavia following the war.[5]

We might say that the Yugoslavs were initially 'guilty' of a most rudimentary form of nationalism which outraged Stalin. Unused to the slightest expression of independence from foreign parties, he arrogantly demanded complete and abject capitulation which the Yugoslavs, conciliatory and compromising though they were throughout, were unwilling to grant.

But despite the Soviet grievances which were blown way up out of all reasonable proportion, Tito and Stalin were, on the most important issues, in almost identical agreement and always had been. Many things illustrate their essential fraternity. During the great purges of the 1930s, Tito not only managed to keep his head while all about him were losing theirs, but in 1937 he was selected by the Comintern for the top post in the Yugoslav Communist party. If there had been the slightest blemish on Tito's record, the slightest anti-Stalinist taint, he would never have achieved such a position at such a time. Indeed, Tito might have gone the way of many other foreign Communists of the day; he might have gone the way of his own predecessor in the Yugoslav Party, Milan Gorkic, who was summoned to Moscow in 1937, arrested, and liquidated.

During the war the Yugoslavs demonstrated their loyalty to Stalin and the Soviet Union. It would be no exaggeration to say that the Yugoslav Communist Partisans, fighting desperately to liberate their country, were also somewhat gratified by the enemy's presence; for a prevailing frame of mind among the Partisans at that time was that 'every bullet the Germans fire at us is one less bullet fired at the Red Army'. Partisan songs during the war reflected, not only devotion to Tito, but to Stalin as well. Montenegran partisans in 1942, with a burst of revolutionary enthusiasm, declared Montenegro annexed to the Soviet Union. During this period, the Yugoslavs bestowed eulogies upon Stalin which were fit for no one of lesser stature than a Messiah. The newspaper, *Borba*, organ of the Yugoslav Communist party, spoke of Stalin in the following fashion in 1942:

> Stalin has become the dearest symbol of our villages and towns . . . our heroes are dying with his name on their lips. . . . The sun itself would

lose its brightness without Stalin. . . . Stalin is the greatest enemy of everything inhuman, the most careful, and wisest educator of human gentleness.[6]

After the war, Yugoslavia developed more quickly along orthodox Stalinist lines than any other Communist state in Eastern Europe. For example, Tito's first five year plan was initiated at least two years before the plans of any other East European country (1947). Following the Stalinist model, the plan emphasised heavy industry, transportation, and a very high rate of investment made possible by low personal consumption. The goals of the plan were gigantic. Despite the tremendous human and material losses of the war—ten per cent of the population had been killed—the Yugoslav plan envisioned that by 1951, industrial production would be triple the 1939 level. To fulfil this plan, the economy was organised in the centralised, Soviet fashion. The state plan was all-inclusive, specifying overall production quotas for the entire economy as well as quotas for individual enterprises. Investment plans were centrally determined. Prices of all commodities were set by federal pricing offices. Wages and salaries were determined by a centrally devised scale of work norms. And, in the Soviet manner, directors of each enterprise were appointed from above by the appropriate state body and were not responsible to their work force.

In other respects, Tito's Yugoslavia before 1948 was a model Stalinist state and became one faster than the other countries of Eastern Europe. Hugh Seton-Watson has noted that the political evolution of Eastern Europe between 1945 and 1950 can be divided into three stages: *i*, the first period was one of genuine coalition where the Communists shared control of the government with other, non-Communist parties, though the former almost always controlled such decisive 'levers of power' as the police and the army; at this stage, freedom of speech and press were, in the main, permitted; *ii*, second was a stage of 'bogus coalition'; non-Communist parties were represented in the government but they had little power and their representatives were usually chosen by the Communists because of their co-operative spirit; freedom of speech and press at this stage became increasingly difficult to exercise; *iii*, in the third and last period, Communists gained a monopoly of political power; all non-Communist parties were either outlawed or, in the case of the social democratic parties, 'fused' with the Communists. Every East European country reached this third stage sooner or later, but Yugoslavia was one of the first, preceding other countries by two to three years. As early as the

autumn of 1945, all non-Communist representatives had left the Yugoslav government for good and the Communists thereupon established
a monolithic régime.

Another manifestation of Tito's close ideological ties with Stalin
in the early years was the structure of the Yugoslav government as
established by the 1946 Constitution. This document is a very close
copy indeed of the Stalin Constitution of a decade earlier. So similar
are the two constitutions that, in looking for differences, one is forced
to mention such trivialities as that in Yugoslavia the component republics were called 'People's Republics', not 'Socialist Republics' as
in the USSR.

Just as Stalin pursued an aggressive policy in Eastern Europe after
World War II, so Tito also followed an expansionist course. Tito
successfully expanded Yugoslavia's frontiers at the expense of Italy
by means of military occupation of Venezia Giulia (the area surround-
ing Trieste). He attempted by the same method to annex parts of
Austrian Carinthia and Styria, though this was unsuccessful. Over
Albania, Yugoslavia exercised considerable domination and that small
country was frequently referred to before 1948 as 'a satellite's satellite'.
The Yugoslavs had helped to create the Albanian Communist party in
1941 and had played an important role in the partisan struggle in that
country during the war. After the war the Yugoslavs exercised considerable control over the Albanian economy. In 1946 the economic
plans and currency of the two countries were co-ordinated, and so-
called Yugoslav-Albanian 'mixed companies' were set up in Albania,
giving the Yugoslavs a strong voice in the development of the Albanian
economy. These were similar to the mixed companies set up by the
Soviet Union in Eastern Europe to which Yugoslavia later objected so
strenuously, calling them instruments of foreign domination.

Tito's expansionism took one other form. He hoped eventually to
create a Balkan Federation, which would have incorporated all of
Bulgaria into Yugoslavia as a seventh Yugoslav Republic. Negotiations
with Bulgarian Communists on this plan were started as early as 1944,
but as a result of the events of 1948, they came to nought.

In their foreign policy, naturally, the Yugoslavs linked arms with
the Soviet Union. As Tito correctly stated in 1948: 'Our faithfulness
to, and solidarity with, the Soviet Union and other countries of people's
democracy on questions of foreign policy consisted not only of words
but of deeds.'[7] Add to this the fact that in 1946 the Yugoslav air force
shot down two American planes, plus maintaining a steady barrage of

anti-Western propaganda, and one can see why Yugoslavia's relations with the West were worse than those of any other Soviet bloc country except, perhaps, Albania.

After the Cominform resolution, a bitter joke circulated in Yugoslavia on the subject of that country's poor relations with the West. 'We Yugoslavs,' the joke went, 'have discovered a new proof that the earth is round. For five years we hurled mud at the West, now it comes flying back at us from the East.'[8]

Finally, Tito's allegiance to Stalin and Stalinism is demonstrated by his behaviour after Yugoslavia had been expelled from the Cominform. Instead of denouncing the USSR, the immediate response of the Yugoslavs was to plead their innocence. They protested that all along they had been loyal to the principles held dear by the Soviet government. They claimed that there had been some misunderstanding and they urged the Cominform to send an investigating committee to see for themselves. This hope for a reconciliation with Stalinism is well expressed by Tito's address to the Fifth Congress of the Yugoslav Communist party which was held about a month after the Cominform Resolution. Tito promised:

> We shall work with all our might to mend the relations between our Party and the CPSU(B). We hope that the comrades, leaders of the CPSU(B), will give us an opportunity to show them here, on the spot, everything that is inaccurate in the [Cominform] Resolution. (All rise amid hails of 'Stalin—Tito!')[9]

There was to be no reconciliation, however. At least not in Stalin's day. And for years after 28th June 1948, when the Cominform Resolution expelling Yugoslavia was passed unanimously, the USSR and Eastern Europe engaged in a concerted effort to bring Tito down, by every means short of direct military intervention. A watertight economic blockade was imposed almost immediately; this had the same disastrous effect on Yugoslavia as did the American blockade against Cuba. And although fully half of Yugoslavia's trade had been with the Soviet bloc, by 1950 and for years afterward, not a pin passed the Yugoslav-Cominform borders. Despite the ironclad blockade, however, one item did manage to get through. Bullets passed the borders regularly, but these were not transported across, they were fired across. Hundreds of border incidents, provoked by Hungary, Bulgaria, Albania, and Roumania, kept the Yugoslavs fearful of imminent invasion. Radio broadcasts from the USSR and adjoining East European countries called on 'loyal' elements of the Yugoslav party to overthrow the 'Tito group'. And the Soviet Union attempted to recruit officers in the Yugoslav army to assist the process. Court trials in Eastern Europe, reminiscent of Russia in the 1930s, 'unmasked' fantastic Titoist plots and had as their *dramatis personae* such prominent Communists as Gomulka, Rajk, Kostov, Xoxe.

The Yugoslavs did not realise immediately that there could be no accommodation with Stalin, that Stalin would recognise only capitulation. Gradually, however, as the aggression from the Soviet bloc did not abate but became actually more intense, the Yugoslavs began to be re-educated. And toward the end of 1949 a new set of ideas began to appear in the Yugoslav press. Instead of merely defending themselves against the Soviet charges, instead of just declaring their innocence and their undaunted desire to prove it, the Yugoslavs began to counterattack. In other words, they began to develop some theoretical justification for their dispute with the USSR. But this theoretical justification—this ideology known as Titoism—whatever 'independence' it has since gained, was originally rooted in historical necessity and historical development. That is, Tito's rejection of Stalinism was a matter of necessity, not a matter of choice.

The Yugoslav Communists are well aware that this view of the origin of Titoism prevails in the West. And of course they reject it. The Yugoslavs vociferously proclaim it a myth that 'in both ideology and political form . . . Yugoslavia until 1948 adhered to the Stalinist Soviet System'. It is likewise a myth, Edvard Kardelj claims, that 'only in reaction to Soviet pressure in 1948 [was] Yugoslavia . . . driven' to develop a distinctive ideology. And against these myths, the Yugoslavs resolutely argue that '. . . the clash with the Soviet Union was not the *cause* but the effect of dissimilarity in tendencies of the internal developments of the systems of Yugoslavia and the Soviet Union'. The Yugoslavs can assert these things but they cannot prove them by reference to concrete example, for as I have tried to show above, until 1948 Yugoslav Communism was a slavish imitation of the Soviet model.

Furthermore, there was nothing in the strictly internal development of the country between 1944 and 1948 which dictated an ideological turn; there was nothing in Yugoslavia's relations with the West which necessitated a change; and there was nothing in the thinking of the leading Yugoslav Communists at that time which suggested or foreshadowed any ideological innovation. It is true, however, that there was a conflict between Stalin and Tito before 1948. But this was not an ideological struggle; it was a power struggle plain and simple and only later became—as all power struggles eventually become—ideologically embellished.

With this ideology, the small group of Yugoslav Communist leaders tried to reinterpret and refashion their shattered world. But certainly this was not the only, nor the most important, need the ideology served: it furnished the Yugoslav Communists with a weapon in their struggle for survival; it helped to mobilise and consolidate support for the régime at home; and it served to appease some of the democratic aspirations of the Yugoslav people. Eventually, however—and this I shall argue later—the ideology began to show signs of going beyond the original intentions of those who formulated it.

To most people, Titoism is associated with the theory of 'national Communism' which holds that although there is only one Socialism, there are many roads leading to it, and that each nation must pursue its particular path according to its own social, economic, political and historical peculiarities. However, this is not all of Titoism nor is it the most interesting aspect. Such a theory of 'national Communism', after all, is no more than an assertion of independence from Moscow, a commonplace today. More interesting than the mere claim that there are many roads to Socialism is the question of exactly what road the Yugoslav Communists have chosen and what the major landmarks along that road are.

One of the most important elements in the ideology of the Yugoslav Communists has been the thesis—developed in the course of their struggle with the USSR—that the abolition of private property does not *in itself* guarantee the end of exploitation. The Yugoslavs share this belief with a whole potpourri of twentieth-century socialists, from Trotskyists to Social Democrats.* This socialist belief grew directly out of the experience of the Russian Revolution; the theory was a description of something which history had already demonstrated.

There were those who came before, however, who did not need an historical example to prove that exploitation could continue even after private property had been abolished. The original idea is not, as Daniel Bell claims, a product of 'recent years'.

---

* Conservatives have said all along, of course, that the abolition of private property would mean despotism and exploitation. Socialists differed from this view in their belief that the abolition of private property *could* end exploitation.

Anarchist and Syndicalist theory from the beginning rested on the premise that the state is an exploitative institution regardless of the forms of property relations which may co-exist with it. And if the state is permitted to remain under Socialism, they warned, then Socialism, too, will be an exploitative society. Bakunin, especially, developed this idea. What do we find throughout history with regard to the state, he asks. 'The state,' he replies, 'has always been the patrimony of some privileged class or other: a priestly class, an aristocratic class, a bourgeois class, and finally a bureaucratic class. . . .'[10] And in a prescient passage, he describes the Marxist state of the future as he envisaged it.

> . . . there will be a government, and, note this well, an extremely complex government, which will not content itself with governing and administering the masses politically, as all governments do today, but which will also administer them economically, concentrating in its own hands the production and the just division of wealth, the cultivation of land, the establishment and development of factories, the organisation and direction of commerce, [etc.]. . . . [Such a state will see] the reign of *scientific intelligence*, the most aristocratic, despotic, arrogant and contemptuous of all régimes. There will be a new class, a new hierarchy of real and pretended scientists and scholars. . . .[11]

Bakunin felt that a state such as this, combining political and economic power, would result in unprecedented regimentation of the proletariat: it would be 'a barrack régime where the standardised mass of men and women would wake, sleep, work and live to the beat of the drum. . . .'[12] Bakunin so feared a new ruling class rising on the back of a successful revolution that he advocated the suicide or the prompt disappearance of the revolutionary leaders following the event.[13] Though an extreme and unrealistic solution, it shows, nevertheless, that Bakunin perceptively saw the situation which might arise.

What did Marx have to say about Bakunin's ominous predictions? We have the marginal notes which Marx made on an important text of Bakunin and in these notes Marx ridiculed and dismissed Bakunin's ideas completely.[14] At the very least one must say that Marx did not give sufficient attention to the problem of the new forms of exploitation to which the dictatorship of the proletariat could give rise.

True, in their discussion of the Paris Commune, both Marx and Engels stressed the importance of certain measures which would allow the working class to 'safeguard itself against its own representatives and officials' [Engels]. These measures were: 1, the election of all officials; 2, the provision that these officials were removable at all times; 3, the reduction of officials' salaries to the level of working men's wages. And Lenin, in *State and Revolution*, affirmed the importance of these devices and re-emphasised that official positions must be stripped of every semblance of privilege.

Nevertheless, considering their works as a whole, Marx, Engels and Lenin gave only fleeting attention to problems which later were to assume such enormous proportions. To put it another way: these problems have occupied a much more important place *historically* than Marx, Engels or Lenin accorded them *theoretically*. They recognised these problems, yes, but really only in passing. They vastly oversimplified the problems of administering the state and they underestimated the autonomous power which the state could wield over society.

Perhaps the reason they did not consider these problems at greater length was their belief that economic power is basic and determining and political power only derived, only part of the superstructure; and once the economy was socialised, the state would not, could not, pose any problems of its own. Daniel Bell explains clearly this chain of reasoning:

> When critics asserted that Socialism itself might become an exploitative society, the Marxist had a ready answer: the source of power was economic, and political office was only an administrative extension of economic power; once economic power was socialised, there could be no basis for man to exploit man. Q.E.D.[15]

Thus, Marx reprimanded the authors of the Gotha programme for merely advocating the 'elimination of all social and political inequality'. Instead, Marx argued, they should have realised that 'with the abolition of class distinctions, all social and political inequality arising from them would disappear *of itself*.'[16] In other words, with the abolition of class distinctions (i.e. the abolition of private ownership of the means of production), all social and political inequality vanishes automatically. This belief would naturally lead one to underplay or even ignore the possibility of a new exploitative society arising on Socialist economic foundations.

The ideology of the Yugoslav Communists which emerged and took shape during the early 1950s lays new stress on this area which Marxists have passed over too quickly and which Stalinists have ignored completely. The basic Yugoslav ideology has never altered since its inception, although its specific anti-Soviet elements have received fluctuating emphasis with changes in Soviet-Yugoslav relations. The most bitter attacks on the Soviet Union—the period of 'high Titoism'—came during the early and mid-1950s; since that time, with the gradual improvement in relations with the USSR, the pointed and explicit anti-Soviet aspects of the ideology have faded. The recent culmination of the new soft line toward the USSR was the arrest and conviction of the young Yugoslav writer, Milajlo Mihajlov, for having published in a Belgrade monthly accounts of Soviet concentration camp life, his first of a string of troubles with the government. Our discussion of Titoism here, however, pertains to the ideology in its 'purest' form as it emerged during the early 1950s when the Yugoslavs were not concerned with the Soviet reaction and did not temper their analysis of the Soviet régime for reasons of state.

The ideas expressed by the Yugoslavs are not particularly new, but they take on an added significance because they are advanced by representatives of a genuine Communist state, not by an isolated theoretician or a small and impotent party.

After the revolution, the Yugoslavs say, Socialism is endangered on *two* fronts, not just one. Communists have too often believed that the danger to socialism is represented *solely* by a threat of a restoration of capitalism. This is not true. The dictatorship of the proletariat must guard against *both* a capitalist restoration *and* monopolistic tendencies which result from the total power which the state exercises. To battle the first threat while ignoring the second can be fatal to Socialism. An uncontrolled Socialist state can easily transform itself into a master of society instead of its servant, and become a fetter on the development of Socialist Democracy, just as capitalism became a fetter on the further development of the productive forces.

When a centralised Socialist state is allowed to concentrate in its hands enormous and unrivalled strength in society, a new stratum of bureaucrats emerges at its helm which in all respects resembles the capitalist class of old. While claiming to rule in the name of the working class, this group actually transforms itself into 'a privileged caste which lives at the expense of society as a whole'.[17] The process is symbolised by tremendous wage and salary differentials, as wide or wider than in capitalist societies. If the state insists upon controlling the means of production centrally, then the position of the workers remains identical to that which they held under capitalism. State management of the economy perpetuates the alienation of the worker from the means of production, for he has no more control over them than he ever did. Furthermore, the traditional forms of antagonism continue between those who work at the means of production and those who control it. Thus, the Yugoslavs agree with the thesis suggested by Berle and Means, developed by Burnham[18] and then Djilas,[19] that the crucial element of ownership is *control*; and he who controls the means of production—regardless of where nominal ownership lies—is the effective owner. Under 'state capitalism',[20] as the Yugoslavs call this form, state-appointed administrators control—and thus own—the economy, and therefore the position of the working class *vis-à-vis* the means of production is in all ways similar to that under capitalism.

The Yugoslav view that antagonisms continue under centralised state management of the economy is, of course, in direct contradiction to the official Soviet position. In the USSR, such harmony prevails between workers and administrators that both belong to the same trade union. This is justified by the claim that:

> . . . there do not exist and cannot exist any class antagonisms between workers and economic administrators . . . the parties to any collective agreement are representatives of the same class and pursue the common objective of developing Socialist production. . . .[21]

The Yugoslavs dispute this claim. They dispute also the Stalinist notion that surplus value has no meaning under a socialised economy. The concept of surplus value continues to be applicable under socialism, the Yugoslavs argue. And the relevant question under Socialism as under capitalism continues to be: who appropriates the surplus value? Under a system of state management of the economy, the state appropriates all surplus value and thus merely substitutes itself for the capitalist class which it replaced.

An unchecked growth of the Socialist state can thus produce extremely harmful effects upon the economy. Worse yet, such a state can poison the entire society. The Yugoslavs pointed to the Soviet case, showing exactly what can happen when the state becomes omnipotent: exploitation of the working class; development of a cult of the leader; an expansionism and exploitation of foreign countries—a kind of state capitalist imperialism; development of great Russian nationalism and chauvinism; an underestimation of the role of the masses in creating a Socialist society; etc.[22] Such a system also takes its toll on the development of Marxist thought, too. The attempt is made to establish ideological domination and monopoly, which reduces Marxism to an inflexible dogma, a set of abstract verities, instead of a creative tool.[23]

In 1956, the Yugoslavs turned to the Hungarian events and

interpreted them along the lines which have been suggested above. It is too simple, Tito said, to blame the unrest merely on a cult of the individual, some accidental aberration under Socialism. 'From the very beginning,' Tito said, 'we have been saying that we are not faced here only with a question of the cult of personality, but with a system which has made the emergence of such a cult possible, that it is there that the roots of evil lie.'[24] And Edvard Kardelj, chief theoretician of the party, spoke of a 'bureaucratic despotism' in Hungary which had so systematically operated against the working class that armed resistance was the only way that class could express its will. He went on to warn of the dangers of permitting the state to monopolise the entire social and economic life.

> The thing we Marxists must never forget is that bureaucracy grows, and economic technocracy . . . inevitably drives society back toward a bureaucratic political system. And when such a process becomes powerful, unless inner political forces stand up against it, it starts to give birth not only to Stalinism but also to the Hungarian events.[25]

What is the Yugoslav answer to this peculiarly insidious threat to socialism which arises from within the socialist state bureaucracy itself? A crucial element is their insistence that the state must begin to *wither away immediately* once the foundations have been laid for Socialist development. 'A state is not really Socialist,' Kardelj wrote, 'until it begins to wither away'. Compare this with Stalin's formulation of the year 1930 which is still considered to be one of his most important contributions to Marxism.

> We are for the withering away of the state. But at the same time we can stand for a strengthening of the proletarian dictatorship. . . . The highest development of governmental power for the purpose of preparing the conditions *for* the withering away of governmental power, this is the Marxian formula. Is this 'contradictory'? Yes it is. But this contradiction is life, and it reflects completely the Marxian dialectic.[26]

The Yugoslavs claim, in contrast to this, that the state is really a temporary and 'necessary evil', but in any event can play only a very limited role in the building of socialism. In the case of a slow evolution to Socialism in the advanced, democratic countries, the state plays a role insofar as it is the repository for the gradual nationalisation of the means of production. In the case of the establishment of Socialism by revolutionary means, the role of the state is limited to the 'forcible destruction of the old social relationships' insuring against bourgeois restoration, and the securing of the basic political and economic conditions for the development of Socialism. This, however, is *all*. The state must do no more than establish the basic conditions for the development of Socialism, after which it must vacate the historical stage. If it persists, if it tries to act 'in the name of the working class', attempts to 'be the chief prime mover in building socialist relationships', if it attempts to 'act infallibly as a personified Socialist consciousness' —then the state will inevitably become a force above society and prevent the very realisation of Socialism which it was originally created to achieve.[27]

What is meant here by the immediate withering away of the state? Orthodox Marxism held that withering away meant primarily an attenuation of the coercive arm of the state, made possible by the reduction or elimination of class conflicts in society. To the Yugoslavs, however, withering away of the state does not primarily mean a relaxation of its coercive role. It is true that the powers of the secret police (UDB) have been drastically reduced since 1945. On the other hand, the Yugoslavs readily admit that as a proportion of national income, their military budget in the recent past has been one of the highest in the world. No, what is meant by the withering away of the state to the Yugoslavs is something else: the all-pervasive role of the state in the economic and social affairs of the community must be diminished, and these functions turned over instead to 'the people as a whole'. Power must be *decentralised* and the state must accordingly cede to 'society' the management of the economy, plus the administration of other institutions such as universities, hospitals, schools, the social insurance system, scientific institutes, apartment houses, etc. Society must be permeated, in other words, with a network of self-governing units, loosely federated and served by a centralised, but responsible body of experts. The result of all this is a new kind of pluralism, Socialist pluralism.

The Yugoslavs are thus trying to re-introduce into Socialist thought some of the decentralist ideas that have for so long been drowned in the sea of centralism and giantism. For their model, they have returned to Marx's discussion of the Paris Commune and the sketch which the Communards drew up for the administration of France. And drawing upon this plan, they have described their ideal Communist state.

> At the top, a small apparatus, highly qualified and subordinate to the central *representative* organs, with its rights and duties strictly defined.
> At the bottom, in the sense of the 'commune' of Marx, the real basis of social activity, the social organs of the districts, localities, factories

institutions, etc., and as the centre of gravity of all of these a qualified apparatus of professionals responsible to the social organs and fulfilling its tasks within the framework of strictly determined rights and duties.[28]

The cornerstone of Titoism is, of course, the decentralisation of the economy and the introduction of an elaborate system of workers' management. One Yugoslav Communist has said this about the original 1950 law which inaugurated the system of workers' management: 'With the adoption of this law, Yugoslavia, having severed its political connection with the Soviet Union in 1948 . . . now also severed its ideological connections with Stalin's theories on Socialism, and set out upon a new path of Socialist development.'[29] When workers themselves manage the economy, we pass from *state* ownership, which is 'the lowest form of Socialist ownership', to a new and higher form of *social* ownership. 'Wages'—a term which is applicable to exploitative economic systems such as capitalism or state capitalism—'wages' are now replaced by 'personal income', which the workers themselves have a powerful voice in determining. The alienation of man from his work begins to disappear because for the first time in history, 'those who create material and spiritual values also dispose of them. . . .'[30]

What can we say about such a magnificently democratic ideology which, paradoxically, emanates from a society which we must regard as essentially undemocratic? I said at the outset that to understand Titoism, one should follow Marx in setting out from 'real, active men' and not from what those men 'say, imagine or conceive'. I think it would be a mistake, however, to draw the traditional Marxist conclusion that the ideology cannot retain any 'semblance of independence'; that it can have 'no history' or 'no development' apar from the material conditions which brought it about.

The psychologist, Gordon Allport, in his theory of 'functional autonomy', demonstrated that certain activities which once served a basic, biological drive, can become independent from that original drive, and develop a life of their own. Thus, a pre-occupation with fine clothes, say, may *originally* serve the interests of sex. But this instrumental activity may eventually develop complete autonomy and continue on for a lifetime, long after the sex drive has disappeared or been satisfied. In exactly the same way one must look at Titoism, an ideology which developed out of material necessity, but an ideology which, nevertheless, goes its own way and has power to influence the development of the society, even *against* the wishes of those men who originally expounded it. Like the sorcerer's apprentice who conjured up a force which he was unable to control, so the Yugoslav Communists have created an ideological force which they cannot contain and which, in the long run, will act against them.

The intellectual development of a man like Djilas illustrates the unintended consequences of Titoism. All of Djilas' democratic ideas since he broke with the party spring directly from, and are logical extensions of, the ideology of the Yugoslav Communists themselves.

For example, when the Djilas heresy first exploded early in 1954, his one defender, Vladimir Dedijer, appealed to the other members of the Central Committee by saying that there seemed to be no essential difference between what Djilas had said and what Tito and Kardelj had been saying in speeches and articles during the previous three years.[31] In his series of articles written at the end of 1953 which became a *cause célèbre*, Djilas argued, among other things, that in the interests of democracy, the party had to play less and less a role in the direction of Yugoslav society. He stressed that it was foolish and dangerous to believe that Communists alone had a monopoly on 'Socialist consciousness'. But this was not an original idea: Tito and Kardelj had been speaking for two years about the eventual withering away of the party as a necessary concomitant of the withering away of the state. In fact this idea took on a kind of institutional reality in 1952 when the party was officially transformed into a 'league' and its announced purposes changed. From an organisation depending upon coercion and direct rule, the new League of Communists was now supposed to step somewhat aside and use devices of education and persuasion.

But it is in *The New Class* that one sees most clearly the debt which Djilas owes his adversaries. For what is *The New Class* after all but the extension of the Yugoslav analysis to all Communist society, Yugoslavia included?

It was the ideology of Titoism itself that drove Djilas to certain conclusions regarding Communist society; and so in similar fashion may this ideology ultimately affect Yugoslav society as a whole. Djilas' political metamorphosis, from a doctrinaire Stalinist—which he was—to a democratic Socialist, represents a *personification* of the development which one day may characterise all of Yugoslav society.

Marx saw social change as resulting from the clash and struggle of antagonistic social classes. But there are other contradictions in society besides class contradictions which can set off tremendous social change. Gunnar Myrdal in *An American Dilemma* studied one potent set of contradictions: the clash between the racist reality in the South, and the democratic and egalitarian ideology of American society. This contradiction between the reality and the ideology, the 'deed' and the 'creed' was, in Myrdal's opinion, a dynamic force for social change. And indeed, the tremendous changes which have occurred in the South, just since the publication of Myrdal's book in the 1940s, do testify to the essential correctness of his theory.

But the contradictions between the American ideology and reality pale before the same contradictions in Yugoslavia, and, to a somewhat lesser extent in other Communist states as well. Like so much else in Yugoslavia, the elections demonstrate the clash between the monolithic reality and the democratic ideology. One astute observer of the Yugoslav scene in the 1950s has described the overall problem which elections posed for the régime: '. . . the chief problem in running the new elections . . . [was] to make them as free and democratic as possible, while at the same time insuring that the "right" results were obtained'.[32]

Is this hypocrisy? Yes, certainly. But is that all it amounts to? No, certainly not. Leszek Kolakowski, the Polish political philosopher, has cautioned: 'Let us not disregard the positive role of hypocrisy.' What is this positive role?

> When a social system based on lawlessness, oppression, and misery masks itself with humanistic verbiage, it does not, contrary to appearances, make itself more effective in the long run. At a certain stage its façade turns against it because it was always alien to it and was imposed only under the pressure of historical circumstances. . . . The façade takes on a life of its own and, when this is incompatible with the system, breeds and nurtures the seeds of its destruction.[33]

Adam Wazyk's famous 'Poem for Adults' expresses well the clash between Communist ideology and reality and the potential this contradiction holds for social change.

> Fourier, the dreamer, charmingly foretold
> that lemonade would flow in seas [under socialism].
> Does it flow?
> They drink sea water,
> crying:
> 'lemonade!'
> returning home secretly
> to vomit.

And later in the poem:

They came and cried:
'Under socialism
a hurt finger does not hurt.'
They hurt their fingers.
They felt the pain.
They began to doubt.[34]

One must react with more than the word 'hypocrisy!' when observing the mammoth discrepancy between Communist ideology and practice. One must see that here we have a unique historical circumstance: *a ruling class whose own ideology actually undermines its rule.* Djilas himself, though now anti-Communist, believes that one cannot overlook the contradiction between the democratic ideology and the undemocratic reality.

> This contradiction, when intensified, holds prospects of real change in the Communist system, whether the ruling class is in favour of the change or not. The fact that this contradiction is so obvious has been the reason for the changes made by the new class especially in so-called liberalisation and decentralisation.[35]

In fact, political evolution in Yugoslavia seems to be responding to this dynamic. Western observers note the increasingly active role of elected assemblies in the mid-1960s and that elections to these assemblies are contested more often than previously. Fred Warner Neal, one of America's keenest observers of the Yugoslav scene, has written:

> The importance of the new Federal Assembly goes beyond its growing role as a formulator of legislation. Over the past few years, its legislative committes have taken the initiative in developing policy, have worked out compromises between federal and local interests, between government planners and segments of industry and even individual enterprises ... and have assumed the responsibility of supervising the administration. Elections to that body have been contested more frequently, debate in the various chambers has been sharp, and independent legislative proposals have begun to emerge from the legislature itself.[36]

In Slovenia in the mid-1960s, an unprecedented conflict developed between the elected assembly and its executive over a tax proposal. The Slovene premier, along with his cabinet, resigned and was not reinstated until he agreed to modify his legislative proposal.[37]

But going beyond this, one can see that this contradiction between ideology and practice has revolutionary, not only reformist, potential. The Hungarian Revolution itself can be seen as an explosive attempt to bring Communist practice into line with its democratic ideology. As one authoritative source on that revolution put it, the aim of the Hungarian revolutionaries 'was not to criticise the principles of Communism as such. Rather, as Marxists, they were anxious to show that the system of government obtaining in Hungary was a perversion of what they held to be true Marxism'.[38] Djilas in fact claims that all the demands for freedom in Communist lands amount to nothing more than demands for bringing reality into line with what the law provides.

The ideology of Soviet Communism is less democratic than that of the Yugoslavs; nevertheless there is a strong contradiction between that ideology and Soviet practice, so strong, in fact, that some have said that a 'theme' of hypocrisy runs through much of Soviet life. A few years ago a literary controversy arose, associated with the name of Pomerantsev, over the issue of whether a work of art could be judged aesthetically in terms of the *sincerity* of the artist who created it. Such a theory in the West would undoubtedly be confined to art critics alone. In the Soviet Union, however, the issue created somewhat of a sensation, especially among the youth of Moscow universities who 'swamped the desk of the editor of *Komsomolskaya Pravda* with letters ardently supporting Pomerantsev's "thesis".'[39]

Students, constantly exposed in their books and lectures to the purest expression of the society's ideals, are especially likely to see the discrepancy between Communist ideals and current practice. One Russian student who observed the unrest which disturbed Soviet universities in 1956 described the strong 'neo-Bolshevik' group which saw in present Communist society a failure to create the egalitarian conditions which Lenin described in *State and Revolution*. 'Lenin's programme of 1917 is well known,' this observer remarked, 'and no extraordinary perspicacity is necessary to see that Soviet reality does not conform to his definition of socialism'.[40]

The decade and a half since Stalin's death has been a period of political, intellectual and cultural ferment in the Soviet Union, and, taking what was perhaps the most important upheaval of the period, the entire de-Stalinisation campaign, it might not be too far amiss to say that what ultimately underlay it was the crying need to square Soviet practice with some of the sorely neglected Soviet ideals. Meanwhile, writers, artists, students and intellectuals are in the forefront of a continuing movement which perhaps also can best be understood as an attempt to bring repressive Soviet reality into greater harmony with its own democratic ideals. Whether in Yugoslavia or in the Soviet Union, the dynamics for discontent and for liberalisation seem to be rooted in the internal contradictions of the Communist system itself.

Most recently in the Soviet Union, for example, Pavel Litvinov, grandson of the former Foreign Minister, has sent to the West a partial transcript of the trial of the writer Vladimir Bukovsky who was arrested in 1967 for participating in a Moscow street demonstration in support of the arrested editors of an underground literary magazine. At his trial, young Bukovsky boldly quoted parts of the Soviet constitution to the judge, especially those sections proclaiming the citizens' rights of freedom of speech, press, assembly, and peaceful protest. 'Isn't the Constitution the basic law of our country?' he asked the judge.

Interpreting these events, *The New York Times* editorialised:

> In the Soviet Union, for decades, tens of millions have known that the boasts about Socialist legality and workers' democracy were shams behind which was the reality of Communist party dictatorship. Now young people of the Litvinov-Bukovsky generation are with truly remarkable courage demanding an end to this hypocrisy and a beginning to the kind of freedom that has been theoretically assured the Soviet people for so many years. . . .
>
> Behind their call for genuine legality is the demand for return to the original ideals of the Bolshevik Revolution, ideals of freedom and justice far removed from the harsh reality of the past half-century.[41]

The subsequent conviction of other writers has led to a protest among Soviet intellectuals unprecedented in its boldness.

Deutscher has observed the same paradox operating within the working class. The political thoughts of the workers, he believed, are concerned more and more with:

> the contradictions between their nominal and their actual position in society. Nominally, the workers are the ruling power in the nation. In the course of forty years this idea has been ceaselessly and persistently instilled into their minds. . . . They cannot help feeling that they should, that they ought, and that they must be the ruling power. Yet everyday experience tells them that the ruling power is the bureaucracy, not they.[42]

The young Russian poet, Yevtushenko, has written much on the original Communist ideals. 'The great', he says, 'cannot be a deception,/ But it can be deceived by men'. And he concludes with this entreaty: 'Comrades!/Give back to the word/Its original meaning!' Whether the 'comrades' Yevtushenko mentions will restore to the word its original meaning is doubtful; but there is no doubt that the word itself will be a force for its own realisation.

Just as the original Soviet idea has led to liberalisation of the régime since Stalin's death—liberalisation whose course is, to be sure, slow, uncertain, and subject to reverses—so with the Yugoslav idea. Workers' management was perhaps at first an ideological device fashioned for the purpose of distinguishing Yugoslav society from the Soviet antagonist, used also to rally public support for Yugoslavia in its battle with the Cominform. But, having been created to serve a specific political purpose, it has now taken on a life all its own and has become a firmly rooted institution in Yugoslav society, and almost every modification in its structure since its creation in 1950 has been in the direction of broadening its powers, extending its scope, and more decisively establishing its legitimacy.

9. The Yugoslav Experience

Introduction

'Workers' control.' Although the phrase itself is Guild Socialist and thus of fairly recent origin,[1] the idea behind the phrase has roots that go deep into nineteenth-century Socialism. Without stretching the meaning of the term too far, one may say that some form or other of workers' control has been the call of many Utopian Socialists, Anarchists, Syndicalists, non-Communist Marxists, left wing Social Democrats, radical trade unionists, and many others. The idea of workers' control has inspired revolutionaries for decades, and workers' councils of one type or another have sprung up spontaneously but with predictable regularity during some of the most important upheavals of modern times: Paris, 1871; Russia, 1905 and 1917; Bavaria, 1919; Barcelona, 1936; Poland and Hungary, 1956. Less dramatically, limited forms of workers' advisory councils have been accepted in many lands, in addition to isolated pockets of workers' management in the form of producers' co-operatives and so-called 'communities of work'.

The Yugoslav experiment in one respect represents the culmination of all that has come before, but, in other respects, represents a complete break with the past. In one or more of the following ways, workers' management is unique in Yugoslavia. *1*. The system originated 'from above'. That is, workers' management was devised and put into operation by the ruling group in society; it did not originate as a demand from the mass of the population, 'from below'. *2*. Workers' management took form and shape and was put into practice during a period of relative social peace. True, Yugoslav Communism in 1950 was in crisis as a result of the break with the USSR two years earlier and the ensuing blockade. However, there was no revolutionary movement within the society; the threat was external, not internal. *3*. Never before had any form of workers' management been completely national in scope nor such an integral part of a national economy. *4*. Finally, workers' management in Yugoslavia shows every sign of becoming a permanent institution—not a fleeting hope as in so many of the revolutionary situations of the past. With Yugoslavia's ideological demolition of the system of central planning during the 1950s, the thoroughgoing transformation of its economic and political institutions, and the incorporation of the right of social management and workers' management as central pillars of the 1963 constitution, it would be almost impossible to revert to the earlier form. The most recent events in Yugoslavia, summarised at the end of this chapter, suggest that the prospects for the continued development of workers' management in Yugoslavia are favourable.

Let us return for a moment to the idea of workers' control and its tenaciousness within the body of all political thinking that one may broadly label as socialist. How can its persistence be explained? Edvard Kardelj argues that workers' management inevitably arises in every society which is tending towards Socialism. Showing his Marxist credentials, he claims that it is somehow the development of society's 'productive forces' which demands a turn toward workers' management.

This is a dubious assumption, at best. Nevertheless, Kardelj is probably correct in predicting the persistence of the idea and the form, but we must look to the *ideology* of Socialism itself, not to the productive forces in society, for an understanding of why workers' control has had a long history in the Socialist movement and why it may have a bright future. And here we return to an argument mentioned in Chapter 1.

Socialists have always aimed at abolishing classes, at establishing the classless society, but, as we know, classes are not merely groups which differ in income, or style of life, or placement with respect to ownership of the means of production. Classes are also groups which possess different amounts of *power* within society. And as recent history has amply demonstrated, abolishing private property is not alone sufficient for the elimination of classes. For in the administration and control of the economy, power differences—and thus class differences—can persist even though property is socially owned. Socialists, therefore, committed as they are to the abolition of class, status and power differences, have naturally turned to some forms of democratic control of the economy by the workers. Workers' control remains a watchword because it is seen as a means of levelling inequalities of power, just as nationalisation is seen as a means of levelling inequalities of property. Thus, it is not the development of the productive forces, but the logic of the Socialist idea which explains the tenaciousness of workers' control in the history of Socialism and may assure it a promising future.[2]

To whom do the Yugoslavs give credit for the inspiration of their system of workers' management? The question need not be asked. They give credit to those three who have always been given credit by Communists, no matter what the deed: Marx, Engels and Lenin. One repeatedly reads in the Yugoslav literature, for example, of

> *the Marxist* theory of socialisation of the means of production according to which the producers themselves must govern these means thereby bringing about democratic and Socialist relations in production.[3]

Paradoxically, however, the only thing inspiring about these three men on the question of workers' control is their silence. On the part of Marx and Engels this vacuum is primarily attributable to their reluctance to spell out the nature of the coming Communist social order. As we know, Communism for Marx was not so much a society of the future as it was a political movement of the present. In Marx's words:

> Communism is for us not a stable state which is to be established, an *ideal* to which reality will have to adjust itself. We call Communiism the *real* movement which abolishes the present state of things.[4]

And later on, in his *Civil War in France*, he attributes his own ideas to the fighting Paris working men.

> The working class did not expect miracles from the Commune. They have no ready-made utopias to introduce *par secret du peuple.* . . . They have no ideals but to set free the elements of the new society with which old collapsing bourgeois society itself is pregnant.[5]

Because Marx, and Engels, too, refused to discuss the future, we have nothing direct from either of them on workers' control. Nevertheless, taking their work as a whole, it is clear that, had they been more articulate about the nature of Socialism, they might have expressed sympathy for the idea of workers' control. Such sympathy is often implied in their works.

In his writings on the alienation of labour, Marx asserts that the subordination of the worker to the absolute power of the capitalist is a crucial element in the estrangement of the worker from his work. Alienation for the worker, says Marx, consists in 'the fact that it is not his own work but work for someone else, that in work he does not belong to himself but to another person'.[6] At work, according to

Marx, man is 'under the domination, compulsion and yoke of another man'. Although it is never expressed in so many words, Marx clearly implies that the obvious remedy for alienation stemming from this condition is democratic self-government of the workers in the factory.

Besides his discussion of alienation we might mention Marx's particular abhorrence of the necessary split in capitalist society between mental and manual labour. In predicting the eventual abolition of the division of labour, Marx foresaw the elimination of the exclusive separation of labour into its manual and mental spheres. Clearly, this vision entails some conception of the administration and control of the factories by the men who labour in them.

From Engels we get snatches of sentiment for workers' control. In his introduction to Marx's *Civil War in France*, he takes especial note of the decree of the communards for the utilisation of the factories which the manufacturers had closed down. According to Engels the decree envisaged 'the operation of these factories by the workers formerly employed in them'. This, says Engels, was 'by far the most important decree of the Commune' and if the communards had been able to carry it out 'must necessarily have led in the end to Communism. . . .'[7]

In 1874 Engels published a short essay entitled 'On Authority'.[8] In this essay Engels argued: *1*, that an industrial system imposes a definite need for authority within the factory, that the need for authority is inherent in the factory system and is not peculiar to one or another type of social organisation; *2*, though authority is absolutely essential in the factory even under Socialism, one must not overlook the possibility and the desirability of having that authority democratically constituted.

The following passage, wherein Engels discusses the hypothetical operation of a cotton-spinning mill under Socialism, illustrates the two points mentioned above. All the workers in the mill, Engels argues,

> are obliged to begin and finish their work at the hours fixed by the authority of the steam, which cares nothing for individual autonomy. The workers must, therefore, come to an understanding on the hours of work; and these hours, once they are fixed, must be observed by all, without any exception. Thereafter particular questions arise in each room and at every moment concerning the mode of production, distribution of materials, etc., which must be settled at once on pain of seeing all production immediately stopped; whether they are settled by decision of a delegate placed at the head of each branch of labour *or, if possible, by a majority vote*, the will of the single individual will always

have to subordinate itself, which means that questions are settled in an authoritarian way.[9]

In his preface to this essay, Lewis Feuer claims that Engels here 'gave expression . . . to an authoritarian principle latent in his and Marx's philosophy'. This is incorrect. Feuer sees only Engels' first point (the need for industrial authority) while overlooking the second (the democratic source of that authority under Socialism). If Engels seemed to give priority to the former, it was undoubtedly because he wrote this essay expressly as an answer to the anarchists' views on the dispensability of all authority. Actually, when Engels argues that it is impossible to have industrial organisation without authority, he is being no more nor less authoritarian than contemporary industrial sociologists who make the identical argument. This is certainly true, to take only one classic example, of Chester Barnard's acclaimed *Functions of the Executive*. And in an essay which has been praised by those who see authoritarian tendencies everywhere in Marx and Engels, Hannah Arendt wrote: '. . . it is quite doubtful whether the political principle of equality and self-rule can be applied to the economic sphere of life as well. It may be that the ancient political theory, which held that economics, since it was bound up with the necessities of life, needed the rule of masters to function well, was not so wrong after all.'[10]

Returning to the original issue, we see that there were allusions in Marx and Engels to some kind of economic democracy. But at best these were indirect and oblique, and for the Yugoslavs to speak continually about the 'Marxist theory' of workers' management is gross exaggeration, whatever other functions it may serve.

As with Marx and Engels, so too with Lenin. The Bolsheviks did advocate a kind of 'workers' control' between March and November 1917, but it was of a very special form. First of all, the purpose of this workers' control was to keep a check or a watch on the capitalists who had not yet been expropriated. Secondly, workers' control was a phenomenon of transition and coincided with the phase of 'dual power' in the state. Thirdly, it was to cease when the proletariat had been victorious in establishing their dictatorship. Trotsky well describes this early Bolshevik conception of the nature of workers' control. In such a system

> control* is in the hands of the workers. This means that ownership and the right of disposition remain in capitalist hands . . . workers' control

---

* Control in this sense means essentially a *check*; it does not mean 'to have direction over'. I am indebted to Hal Draper for clarifying this special use of the word here.

thus means a kind of *economic dual power* in the factory, bank, business enterprise, etc. . . . . What state régime corresponds to workers' control of production? It is obvious that the state would not as yet be in the hands of the proletariat. If such were the case, we would not have workers' control of production but rather control of production by the workers' state as preparation for a régime of statified production.[11]

Though identical in name, this kind of 'workers' control' is a different species from that considered here.

As for Lenin himself, the Yugoslavs are hard pressed to quote him on workers' control.[12] As Deutscher and others have pointed out, Lenin's position was ambiguous and he stood between two extremes when it came to the question of workers' control and the autonomy of the trade unions from the state.[13] He stood between Trotsky, on the one hand, who was opposed to genuine workers' control and independent trade unionism, and, on the other hand, the so-called Workers' Opposition whose ideas smacked of Syndicalism. But to the latter's ideas on the organisation of the economy Lenin was particularly opposed.

True, Lenin's party programme of 1919 stated in its famous point five that

. . . the trade unions . . . ought to concentrate in their hands all the administration of the entire national economy. . . . The participation of the trade unions in economic management . . . constitutes also the chief means of the struggle against the bureaucratisation of the economic apparatus. . . .[14]

So inconsistent is this passage with known Bolshevik doctrine that Deutscher argues that it was probably a 'Syndicalist slip' made by the Bolsheviks out of gratitude to the unions for their impressive performance in the civil war. Needless to say, this part of the party programme was never put into practice. The following year one-man management was proclaimed (and that one man was appointed by the state). And in 1922, the party congress finally and irrevocably removed trade unions from participation in the management of the economy.[15]

As we have seen, it is not to Lenin, nor to Marx or Engels that the Yugoslavs have turned in the reconstruction of their society. It is really to the kinds of ideas advanced by the English Guild Socialists and to a lesser extent the French Syndicalists that the Yugoslavs are most indebted for their innovations in workers' management.

Although the Guild Socialist movement is dead, and has long been so, the ideas behind it, in the now-dusty volumes of G. D. H. Cole, S. G. Hobson and others, written a half-century ago, still have extraordinary relevance to discussions of some of the central social issues of our day, such as work alienation, political and social pluralism, and the meaning of democracy.[16] In spite of this relevance and the light which Guild Socialism could still shed on these problems if the literature were examined anew, the movement is all but forgotten, and Cole, the brilliant thereotician and leading intellectual of that movement, is remembered far more today as the renowned historian of the labour, co-operative and Socialist movements. As one writer has said:

> Most prominent British Socialists, speaking about Cole after his death and appraising his work, talked about his historical writing, his internationalism, his gentle character, his erudition; none talked of his desire to see workers' control of industry introduced as an essential ingredient of Socialism. This, however, was his greatest contribution to Socialist thought.[17]

But although this has been forgotten and Guild Socialism has become extinct from the British political scene, another species has arisen elsewhere, in Yugoslavia, which in many important respects resembles its predecessor, from which it has inherited features both general and particular, but which refuses to acknowledge its ancestry. But it is an ancestry which should be traced and acknowledged.

Even a cursory comparison of the Guild Socialist literature and the ideology—if not the precise practice—of Yugoslav Communism, reveals a number of general similarities. These are:

1. A thoroughgoing democratic society consists of more than formally free political institutions which constitute just the mere beginnings of democracy and which, under capitalism, are of little value and meaning due to such things as economic inequality and the political power of wealth, the inadequacy of political representation alone to represent the manifold interests of citizens, the infrequency of elections, and the inaccessibility and remoteness of representatives and representative bodies.

2. State control of the means of production endangers political democracy and obstructs economic democracy. The evils of bureaucracy under state control are substituted for the evils of private ownership.[18] State control of the means of production does not essentially change the status or the attitudes of the worker *vis-à-vis* his work.

3. Though the workers should manage the means of production, they must do so in the name of, and as the agents for, the community, where true ownership resides.

4. Although the workers in each industry must have primary responsibility for industrial management, the community must have some *check* on the organs of workers' management, in order to guarantee that the general interest is secured. Pure Syndicalism is inadequate because producers are in no way accountable to the community.[19]

5. The Socialist ideal must not be the super-centralism of the collectivists nor the pure localism of the Syndicalists. Instead, the Socialist ideal must be *decentralist*.[20]

6. The plurality of man's associations necessitates democracy at all levels of social organisation as well as in the economy. These organisations, institutions, and associations ought to be independent, free of central state control, autonomous and self-governing. Society must be permeated by a network of self-governing associations. Furthermore, the multiplicity of man's interests calls for *functional* as well as territorial representation in government.[21]

7. The ideal unit of Socialist society is the commune—a geopolitical unit of essentially self-governing cells.[22]

Workers' Management and Political Democracy

A constantly recurring question in this chapter will be : to what extent is Yugoslav workers' management genuine, or, in broader terms, is industrial democracy compatible with a one-party dictatorship? It is tempting to dismiss Yugoslav workers' management by recourse to a simple slogan such as: 'There can be no democracy in an enterprise when there is no democracy in the state.'[23] And although it has the ring of an elementary truism, it is probably sociologically invalid. It is theoretically possible for an otherwise autocratic régime to accord democracy to its citizens in meaningful areas of life in which the exercise of this democracy does not threaten the political survival of the régime. There are a myriad of social and economic organisations which can be organised democratically even in a society in which the fundamental economic and political institutions cannot be called into question. In point of fact, it is in some ways positively functional for a régime to encourage this kind of democracy, for in so doing it introduces a measure of flexibility into an otherwise rigid society, it provides opportunities for the safe channelling of discontent, and gives vent to impulses for free expression. It should not be regarded as a foregone conclusion, therefore, that because Yugoslavia does not have free political institutions, as we envisage them, that no other institutions in that society can possibly be organised in a democratic manner.[24]

The report of the International Labour Office on workers' management in Yugoslavia is, by far, the most thorough, conscientious, and meticulously researched account of that experiment available in English.[25] In its detailed examination of the literature, supplemented by its field research in numerous Yugoslav enterprises (of its own choosing), the report surpasses anything else we have to date, both in the scope of its coverage and its precise attention to detail. A close and careful study of this objective account leads even a sceptical reader to the tentative conclusion that: *1*, workers' management is genuine in the sense of being a fairly autonomous institution and not a front for complete party control; *2*, that the power of workers' management is great and has been growing since its inception in 1950 in such crucial areas as the recruitment and dismissal of the plant's labour force, including the director, the regulation of remuneration, and the distribution of profits; *3*, that workers' management is a workable system of industrial organisation and a valid and viable alternative both to Western capitalism and 'classical' Soviet central planning.

But we shall return to the original issue posed here after a survey of the system's formal structure.

The Structure of Workers' Management

The Yugoslav system of workers' management represents the highest expression of the Titoist ideology. More than any other institution, it symbolises the avowed intention of the Yugoslav Communists to disperse the power of the centralised state, and to create in its place a society of loosely connected, self-governing organisations. Although this system of workers' management is the major element in this shift to decentralism, it has been accompanied by comparable forms of decentralist 'self-government' in universities, hospitals, schools, scientific institutions, libraries, social insurance bodies, apartment houses, and the like. To democratise *society* (in contrast to the state) is the declared aim of the Yugoslav Communists.

The Yugoslavs are not modest in their claims for workers' management. At one and the same time it represents the triumph of Socialist democracy, the achievement of a new humanism, the victory over bureaucracy and its accompanying deformations, the realisation of the decentralist ideal, the abolition of the alienation of labour and the successful fusion of mental and manual work. Basic to the workers' management system is a particular conception of Socialist property. The Yugoslav Communists make a crucial distinction between 'state ownership' and 'social ownership' of the means of production. With both forms, private property does not exist and has been formally 'nationalised'. The essential difference between the two forms rests with the locus of control. State ownership of the means of production signifies that nationalised property is controlled and operated by a centralised state bureaucracy. The workers have no share in the management of the economy and, for this reason, their status remains essentially unchanged from that under capitalism. The workers have merely exchanged one set of masters for another: bureaucrats have replaced capitalists. In addition, state ownership lays a society open to all the dangers to the development of Socialism that were discussed in the previous chapter.

The Yugoslav Communists claim, therefore, that state ownership is actually the 'lowest form of Socialist ownership'. Social ownership, on the other hand, is a higher form and differs from state ownership in one important respect: property is not administered and controlled by a group of self-selected, privileged bureaucrats, but by the workers themselves within the framework of a system of economic self-government.

This principle of social ownership is set forth clearly in the first article of the 'Basic Law Concerning the Management of State Economic Enterprises and Higher Economic Associations by the Workers' Collectives'.

> Factories, mines, transport, commercial, agricultural, forestry, communal and other state economic enterprises, as the common property of the whole Nation, are in the name of the social community, administered by their working staffs. . . .[26]

The Basic Law was enacted in 1950, just two years after Yugoslavia was expelled from the Cominform, and it was to have far-reaching effects upon the structure of the Yugoslav economy and eventually on the whole of Yugoslav society. In its fifty articles it specifies the exact form and framework through which workers' management was to operate. Though it has been revised and liberalised, it still stands as the fundamental document in Yugoslav workers' management.

The law provides for at least two bodies of workers' management in each enterprise: the workers' council and the management board.

The Workers' Council. As stipulated by law, workers' councils are composed of between fifteen and 120 members, depending upon the size of the enterprise in which they exist. Though there are councils in the country at both ends of this continuum, the average number of members is between twenty and twenty-two. This average has remained quite constant since the inception of workers' management.[27] In enterprises employing from seven to twenty-nine workers, the entire collective* comprises the workers' council. In enterprises of thirty or more workers, the council is elected from members of the collective. The Basic Law provided that elections to the workers' council were to take place yearly, but as time passed there arose much feeling that the term of office for the councils should be extended to two years, in order not to impair their efficiency of operation. In April 1964, the Federal Assembly fixed the term of office of council members at two years, with one-half replaced each year.[28] In line with the recent Yugoslav penchant for rotation and replacement, no council member may serve two consecutive terms.

In smaller enterprises, workers are elected at large to the council; more sizeable enterprises, however, are divided into numerous electoral units and workers are elected from these units in proportion to the numerical strength of each. Regardless of the size of the enterprise, elections are run according to universal suffrage, secret ballot, and direct election. An electoral commission supervises and conducts the election by approving the list of candidates, making arrangements for the voting, and announcing and certifying the election results. Originally the electoral commission was appointed by the trade union branch, but since 1952 the outgoing workers' council has been responsible for selecting the five member commission which may consist of any members of the collective except the chairman of the outgoing workers' councils, members of the management board, or any of the candidates.

The exact nominating procedure was not made perfectly clear in the 1950 law but, in general, it originally worked as follows. Either the trade union branch or a body of workers comprising 10 per cent of the work force could put forward a list of candidates. More than one list was permitted but 'as a rule' it was expected that there would be 'a single candidates list for the whole enterprise', as one expert on the law

---

* The collective includes, roughly, all the regular employees.

interpreted it. If there were one list and if there were more candidates than positions to fill, then those candidates with the highest number of votes were elected. According to the 1950 law, if there were two or more lists, a worker could not divide his vote between the two (or more) lists; he had to vote *by list*. Then, those candidates were elected 'who obtained the greatest number of votes on the list . . . for which the majority of the workers and employees voted. . . .'[29] In 1953, the election procedure was liberalised to allow voting by candidate rather than by list; a worker could now divide his votes between lists, if there were more than one, and those candidates with the greatest number of votes were elected regardless of list.[30] Each voter generally has as many votes as there are seats to fill on the council.

In elections to workers' councils, how often has there been more than one list of candidates? Computations from available data on the 1950s suggest that multiple lists occurred in no more than 15 per cent of the elections.[31] This does not mean, however, that workers have no choice and are confronted with a single list of candidates with exactly as many names as there are seats to be filled. One careful estimate suggests that on the average the number of candidates exceeds the number of seats to be filled by between 20 to 50 per cent.[32] Certainly some seats are contested in most undertakings and the workers have an element of choice. The ILO reports that

> . . . the lists submitted to the voters generally include a larger number of names than there are seats to be filled. This was so in all the undertakings visited by the Office commission [about twenty], and the practice was apparently based on a rule which, though unwritten, was nevertheless considered as binding in the undertakings visited.[33]

There is additional evidence that the elections to the councils are legitimate contests rather than merely rubber stamps. The ILO visited a number of firms whose elections' statistics they examined, and they discovered that there were often very large differences between the number of votes received by the various candidates, sometimes amounting to a ratio as high as three to one, indicating that workers saw clear-cut choices among the candidates.

> In certain cases, for instance, the trend of voting seemed to have gone against the supervisory staff, whereas elsewhere the foreman had a clear lead. In one case not a single woman on the list was elected. In another, the candidate who headed the list and was chairman of the outgoing workers' council barely obtained enough votes for re-election.[34]

However, another factor of importance to consider in the electoral process is the role of the trade unions. Traditionally, electoral lists of the plant trade union branch have been decisive in the elections to the workers' councils. For example, in the 1950s, the trade unions customarily sponsored 95 per cent of all candidate lists for elections to the councils, with the result that about 97 per cent of all members elected were chosen from these lists.[35]

In the early 1960s the trade unions were deprived of their power to select candidates, but for the earlier period, most Western observers constructed the obvious syllogism: the party dominated the unions; the unions controlled the elections to the workers' councils; therefore, the party ruled the councils. Naturally, the Yugoslavs denied this.[36] The basic error, they claimed, was a misunderstanding of the meaning of the 'trade union list' which did not comprise the exclusive preferences of the union leadership. Actually, some time before the election, groups of workers put forth their candidates to the workers' council. After all the nominations had been made, the union combined them all into one list, thereafter known as the 'trade union list'.

The ILO noted a fairly similar nomination procedure in which the unions had considerable but not total power.[37] The trade union branch drew up its list of suitable candidates for election to the council which it then submitted to a meeting of the collective. The workers discussed the candidates and proposed additional names for the list and deletions from it. According to the ILO, such meetings apparently led to considerable changes in the original trade union list and thus reflected the choices of both the union and the workers.

At any rate, according to the provisions of a law adopted in 1964, the trade union branch is by-passed altogether in the nominating procedure and its former power is now vested in the collective.[38] The law provides that at meetings of the entire work force (or in department meetings in larger enterprises), anyone is allowed to nominate a candidate provided three other workers second the nomination. The workers attending the meeting then vote on whether the prospective candidate shall receive a nomination. Upon completing the list of nominees, the workers take a final vote by secret ballot.[39]

Even if these regulations are respected by the trade union branch however, it does not signify that the unions are impotent where workers' management is concerned. They do have great power. They may propose the recall of members of workers' management bodies, they are empowered to propose the recall of the firm's director, they often initiate proposals which are then submitted to the workers' council for consideration, they are one of the bodies which must approve the wage distribution and the rules on labour relations which workers' management organs have determined, etc.

Nevertheless, even though the trade union branch might still select all or most of the candidates for election to the workers' councils—by overt or covert means—their power is limited by the fact of rapid turnover on the councils. Within a few years—if not already—a majority of all the regular employees within a firm will have been members of the workers' council or management board because of the rules on turnover and replacement. Trade union power to control the personnel on workers' management is thus, in the long run, rather small.

Jiri Kolaja's research, conducted in two Yugoslav factories, suggests that the trade union is, actually, rather dependent upon the workers' councils, due, in part, to the fact that the councils have power to increase or decrease the amount of money which the trade union receives for its activities[40] This tends to make the union subservient to the councils.

Moreover, less than two per cent of workers questioned in one of the factories believed the union was the most influential force in the enterprise. Reflecting this, few workers took their grievances to the union, but went directly to the management board or to the director. This generally confirms the findings of the ILO which will be discussed subsequently. Kolaja believes that the major function of the union in both factories he studied was to assist individuals with minor personal economic problems. The ambiguous position of the unions undoubtedly stems from the fact that their functions have been appropriated by other bodies within the enterprise.

Once elected to a workers' council, the member does not become part of any new class. True, he cannot be fired or transferred during his term of office—this superseniority assures his independence and protects him from threats. Nevertheless, the council member is subject to recall at any time, for any number of offences, on the initiation of any number of sources. In 1956, for example, about one thousand members of workers' councils (or 0·8 per cent of the total) were recalled at the instance of the collective, the unions, workers' managements bodies, the director, and the party, for reasons of laxity, economic crimes and the like. Furthermore, recall of a council member is usually accompanied by considerable publicity. The Yugoslav press is fond of publicising cases in which an indignant body of workers recalls its representatives from the council, the board, or even the director himself.

This general lack of privilege of a council member is supplemented by the fact that he is not paid for his services. Moreover, meetings are most often held after working hours so that the member does not get much opportunity to miss work. If he is off the job, however, while pursuing his duties on the workers' council, he is indemnified for his loss.

Soon after the election, the new workers' council meets and chooses its chairman. To hold his power down, the law provides that the chairman may not concurrently be a member of the management board. The chairman is responsible for calling meetings which in no case can be held less frequently than once every six weeks. These meetings are attended by members of the management board and the director, and may be attended by any interested workers in the enterprise, plus representatives of the party or the union.

Besides enjoying the right to elect and recall members of the management board, the workers' council has wide-ranging power with respect to the operation of the enterprise which are almost too numerous to mention, but which include the following major responsibilities.

1. The council adopts the basic bylaws of the enterprise which include: the name of the undertaking, the location of its head office, and its activities; the 'composition, powers, and operation of its workers' management bodies'; the rights and duties of the director; the internal organisation of the enterprises; financial management and utilisation of assets; labour relations (see below); 'procedure for the adoption of the annual plan of the undertaking, its rules of remuneration and its final accounts for the financial year'.[41] The bylaws are usually drawn up by the management board or a commmittee of the workers' council, adopted by the council and approved by a local government body which scrutinises it only for its legality, not its desirability.

2. The workers' council is empowered to adopt the annual economic plan of the enterprise which includes both material pertaining to the physical volume of production and sales for the coming year as well as financial estimates and cost calculations. The council also is empowered to scrutinise and approve the periodic reports of the management board and the director.

3. The council must also adopt rules pertaining to labour relations which include

> *a*, the method of recruiting workers; *b*, the allocation of workers to particular jobs; *c*, annual and special holidays; *d*, the workers' liability; *e*, labour discipline. . . . *f*, occupational safety and health; *g*, special protection for women and young or disabled workers; *h*, the termination of labour relations; *i*, the right of appeal and grievance procedure; and *j*, the competence of the various organs of the undertaking that are empowered to take decisions on labour relations.⁴²

The rules regulating labour relations which the workers' councils were empowered to adopt by liberalising legislation of 1957, must be submitted to a committee of the local government and the trade union branch for approval.

Under the 1957 Law on Labour Relations, the council, or its designated committee, is in charge of hiring and dismissal. The director usually specifies to the council how many men he needs and with what qualifications and the council or its committee does the hiring. With regard to dismissal, the director may propose to fire a worker, but it is not effective unless the council concurs. Redundancy dismissals, though rare, are also handled by the workers' council.

A committee of the workers' council is in charge of all cases of serious discipline. The director is permitted to issue a warning or a reprimand and may also impose a fine on a worker of up to five per cent of his monthly income. But with respect to offences which might warrant further discipline, a committee of the workers' council, composed of two members of the council and one member of the trade union branch, bears responsibility. This same committee can hear and decide appeals by workers against disciplinary action which has been taken by the director.

4. The council is also in charge of adopting the basic remuneration schedules of the enterprise, a complex affair, which is directed by the government only in the sense that certain guidelines are set up which include: *1*, minimum wages; *2*, maximum ratios between the highest paid and lowest paid workers in the enterprise; *3*, suggested ratios of remuneration for workers at the four skill levels: unskilled, semi-skilled, skilled, and highly skilled; *4*, compulsory consideration by the council of how the proposed wage scales will affect prices, productivity, the financial status of the firm, etc.; *5*, mandatory approval of the scales by the trade union branch and a representative of the commune in which the enterprise is located.⁴³

5. The council is also empowered to approve the final balance sheet and distribute the net income of the enterprise into various channels: supplemental wages and salaries; a 'joint consumption' fund in which money is allocated for such purposes as housing construction, children's institutions, household services, scholarships for training workers, etc.; the investment fund; the reserve fund (used to meet future business losses and to cover wages).[44]

6. The workers' council also participates in the selection of the director. Since 1950, the unmistakable trend in workers' management legislation has been in the direction of according greater power and responsibility to the elected workers' representatives. One sign and symbol of this is the changes that has come about in the procedure for the selection of the director of an undertaking. Before 1950, of course, during the period of administrative management and preceding the development of workers' councils, the director was a state official who was appointed by those in the economic hierarchy above him; he was in no sense responsible or answerable to the workers in the enterprise which he headed.

The 1950 legislation introducing workers' management did not give the workers in an enterprise any greater control over the selection of their director than they had previously. Directors were now selected by the management board of a so-called industrial group to which an enterprise belonged. In 1952, the power to select enterprise directors passed to the local government (district and commune people's committees) in a general move to decentralise decision-making. In 1953, an act established the principle that directors were to be chosen according to a system of open competition, on the basis of education, experience and competence, with the selection committee composed one-third of representatives of the enterprise workers' council, and two-thirds of representatives of public authorities, trade unions, economic chambers, etc. In 1957, the workers' councils were given additional power on the selection committee, entitled to one-half the membership, with the other half appointed by the local people's committee. Under this arrangement, the selection committee made its choice known to the municipal people's committee which made the final decision. As of 1964, however, the selection committee, composed as before, notifies the *workers' council* which makes the actual decision. In addition, the 1964 Act sets the director's tenure, previously unlimited, at four years. The council may reappoint the director for an additional term if it desires.

The workers' council has the right to propose the removal of a director. The legal grounds for so doing are cases where: *1*, the director has clearly violated the law; *2*, the enterprise cannot meet its financial obligations to the community (taxes); *3*, there is inefficiency of the enterprise due to the director's incompetence.

Previously, if a worker's council wanted to dismiss the firm's director, its recommendation had to be reviewed by the local people's committee. That body could refuse to accept the council's decision and, in the event of a real conflict between director and council, the people's committee was empowered to dissolve the workers' council and order new elections. If the newly-elected workers' council also demanded the dismissal of the director, then the people's committee had to accede. Now, according to one report, the final decision on the recall of the director lies with the workers' council, not the representatives of municipal government, and a director may be dismissed by the workers' council on the recommendation of one-third of the collective, the workers' council itself, the commune assembly or its committee.[45] According to another report, however, a director's dismissal is now in the hands of a commission with a representation similar to the original selection commission (one-half of whose members are chosen by the workers' council).[46] If this commission recommends dismissal, the workers' council may then approve this decision, but it may also decide to retain the director after all. If, however, the commission votes to keep the director, the workers' council cannot override this decision.

If a director feels he has been dismissed illegally, he may sue in court for damages, but not for re-instatement to the firm. A director will sometimes do this in order to clear his name, with a view to a subsequent application for a directorship of another enterprise.

To illustrate the diversity of topics which workers' councils discuss, we have listed below the agendas for some 6,000 workers' council meetings during the year 1956.[47]

Plans of the undertaking and final accounts for the financial year	16,807
Rules concerning remuneration scales	15,470
Reports of the board of management	20,134
Investment and reconstruction plans	15,212
Utilisation of the funds of the enterprise	12,404
Production costs, quality and marketing	20,286
Output norms, productivity and improvement of working methods	12,341

Labour relations	20,285
Occupational health and safety	10,953
Labour discipline	16,119
Social insurance	7,185
Vocational training	8,679
Distribution of income	9,002
Economic offences	4,941
Communal affairs	2,352
Other questions	21,887

Certain topics are likely to generate intense interest among the council members and workers who may turn out in great numbers for the meetings.

> In one undertaking visited by the [International Labour] Office mission it was reported that the session of the council at which the final accounts for the financial year (including the use to which the net income was to be put) were approved normally lasted three days. In another undertaking a four-day session was necessary to reach a decision on the dismissal of an unpopular chief of personnel. In yet another undertaking a resolution that the director be removed from his post was passed after a long discussion by a majority of only one vote.[48]

We have alluded to the role of the trade union previously. One of its functions is to restrain the workers' natural inclination to distribute the income of the enterprises in the form of wages and salaries and instead to attempt to divert these funds toward re-investment in the enterprise. This has led to a unique situation in Yugoslavia which deserves further study: 'management' (i.e. workers' management) often strives for higher wages and better conditions while the unions often press for lower wages, longer hours, shorter work-breaks, and less liberal working conditions. The roles of union and management in Yugoslavia have become somewhat topsy turvy, leading to some bizarre consequences.[49] This reversal of function, with the trade union taking a managerial role and the workers' management bodies behaving like trade unions, is due to the fact that the trade unions, under strict party control, never offered an effective outlet for the expression of trade union issues, i.e. they did not truly represent the trade union interests of the workers. The workers' management bodies (councils and boards), on the other hand, which are more democratically constituted than the unions, became a channel for the expression of trade union demands. As Adolph Sturmthal has written:

... in Yugoslavia where the councils were created by the régime and intended to be merely managerial devices, many employees endeavoured to use them essentially for union functions.[50]

In a survey of workers in a number of enterprises in Croatia in 1958, it was discovered that over half the workers questioned (57 per cent) said they generally approach a workers' management body when they feel they have a grievance, while only 21 per cent said that they appealed to their trade unions.[51]

There is no question but that workers' councils have increased the scope of their activities and acquired greater power over the years. The ILO reports, for example, that meetings of the councils have become more frequent in recent years, that the minutes of their meetings, some of which the ILO mission examined, have become increasingly complex and voluminous, and that, because of legislation passed since 1950, the councils are dealing with a growing number of issues. Much legislation actually forces the councils into action by rendering decisions of the enterprise invalid which have not been formally approved by the council.[52] And Sturmthal reports on an interesting 'maturation' of the councils in the last decade and a half. When the councils were first formed, in the early 1950s, the meetings

were taken up overwhelmingly by personal issues, many of them the grievances of one or two individuals. During the next stage, the discussions focused primarily upon methods by which the short-run incomes of the workers in the enterprise ... could be increased. Only gradually did interest shift to long-term consideration of the economic, financial, or technical problems, which are the real assignments of the councils.[53]

The Management Board. Each year, the workers' council chooses its executive organ, the management board of the enterprise. The board is smaller in number than the workers' council, ranging from five to eleven members, plus the director who is an *ex officio* member. The members of the management board need not be chosen from the ranks of the workers' council but in practice they usually are. The election procedure is usually as follows. A member of the council may nominate, orally or in writing, as many persons as there are seats on the board. The names of all the nominees are placed on a list, and the candidates receiving the greatest number of votes are elected. The ILO mission observed that in most cases the number of candidates for the management board exceeds the number of available seats. As with the workers' council, the voters have marked preferences for certain candidates. In no case did the ILO mission observe a situation where a candidate or a group of candidates was elected by acclamation.[54]

To prevent the formation and crystallisation of a bureaucratic élite within the enterprise, the law provides that: *1*, only one-third of the members of the management board may be re-elected; *2*, those who are re-elected may serve for no more than three consecutive terms; *3*, finally, in order to keep workers' management in the hands of workers and out of the hands of white collar experts and technicians, at least three quarters of the members of the management board must be 'workers directly engaged in production'. All indications are that these provisions are upheld in practice.[55]

Some regulations pertaining to workers' councils also apply to the management boards: meetings regularly take place after working hours; members are not paid for their work; members may not be fired or transferred during their term of office.

The management board elects its chairman who cannot be the director of the enterprise. The chairman calls meetings at regular intervals but in no case less than once a month. In recent years, the management boards have been meeting more frequently. In larger enterprises weekly meetings are common and in some enterprises daily meetings are typical.

The management board generally sees to the proper operation of the enterprise and has these special functions which are sketched very generally here.

a, the board presents reports to the workers' council on the management of the undertaking and prepares proposals on matters that lie within the competence of the council (for example, draft annual plan of the undertaking, draft rules of the undertaking, proposals concerning the purchase or sale of capital goods, the investment plan, etc.);

b, in execution of the general policy laid down by the workers' council, the board has duties specified in the legislation and in the bylaws of the undertaking (fixing of production targets under the plan; appointments to managerial posts within the undertaking; use of certain of the undertaking's funds; decision in the first instance on appeals by workers of the undertaking, etc.); it takes the necessary measures to put the decisions of the workers' council into effect and may in general consider any questions concerning the day-to-day management of the undertaking;

c, the board supervises the work of the director of the undertaking and his subordinates, and, whenever the post is vacant, directs the undertaking until it hands it over to his successor.[56]

In 1954 management boards gained important powers at the expense of enterprise directors. In that year the boards were empowered to appoint all the executives of the enterprise, a privilege once enjoyed by the director, either by means of an open competition of candidates applying from outside the enterprise, or by selecting personnel from among the staff of the enterprise.

The Director. We mentioned the selection and removal procedure of the director earlier. The director is the chief executive of the firm and is responsible for organising production and carrying out the plan approved by the workers' management bodies. He represents the enterprise in dealings with the state and other parties and has jurisdiction over the finances of the firm. However, his powers are strictly limited by the organs of workers' management. With respect to his right to represent the enterprise before third parties and to sign contracts for the firm or to sue in the name of the firm, he must share his authority with the management boards and the workers' councils. For the most important of these matters,

> he must obtain the prior consent of the board of management or workers' council, and in some instances must also produce an extract from the minutes of their meetings as evidence of their approval. In some cases, for instance when proceedings are instituted against an undertaking, the board of management is the only representative recognised by the courts.[57]

If the director feels that any decisions taken by the management board or the workers' council are contrary to law, he is empowered to postpone execution of the decision until the 'competent state organs', which he must inform, have rendered a verdict. This provision should not be regarded as 'the key' to the director's total control over the organs of workers' management. Various surveys have indicated that this power is used very sparingly, indeed, by the director who usually does not want permanently strained relations between himself and the council or board. One survey of enterprises in Belgrade uncovered only one case in which the director had suspended a decision of workers' management. And the ILO mission also discovered one instance in which a director interpreted the provision as giving him unlimited veto power. The director was eventually replaced.[58]

Brief mention should be made of efforts to carry decentralisation and workers' management beyond the level of workers' councils and management boards at the enterprise level. Attempting to involve workers themselves directly in management without intermediaries of elected representatives, the régime has established within enterprises the so-called economic units, usually comprising between twenty and one hundred workers. Where possible, all workers in each unit constitute that unit's workers' councils; in larger units a workers' council and other unit leaders are elected.

The economic units are intended to bring participation down to the most direct and intimate job level. They generally take responsibility for reducing costs, raising production, and introducing new methods and techniques. They negotiate with other economic units on matters related to production and the co-ordination of activities. In certain cases they have jurisdiction over the use of investment funds and decide what new machinery should be purchased for their use. They are often responsible for the hiring and dismissal of workers. Annual income is distributed to those economic units involved directly in production on the basis of their calculated contribution to enterprise production as a whole. And within the units income is distributed to individuals according to formulae established by the workers themselves.

The Unintended Consequences of Workers' Management

To return to the basic question asked by Western observers: is Yugoslav 'workers' management' really workers' management? Those who say 'no' have argued that two conditions must be met for genuine workers' management to operate: *1*, those who are elected to workers' councils must actually represent the wishes of those who have elected them; *2*, those who are elected must be able to exercise their legal rights when in office. On both these counts, it has traditionally been argued, workers' management in Yugoslavia fails. First, elections are undemocratic: there is usually one list of candidates and that is supplied, one way or another, by the trade union. Thus, those who are elected do not truly represent the wishes of the electorate. We discussed and qualified this argument earlier.

Even if elected fairly, the argument continues, the members of the councils and boards are not free to exercise their legal rights. They are blocked by the trade union branch and especially by the party. Regarding the latter, one critic writes:

> Factory management through works' assemblies and committees . . .
> means in reality that the Party cells take over the individual factories. . . .
> The factory cells—an organised minority of Communists—dominate
> workers' assembly, works' councils and managing committees, because
> no worker who does not belong to the Party would dare oppose it
> consistently on an important question.[59]

If the party somehow fails, the director is sure to prevail over the council and board as a result of his superior training, education and technical skill, his control over finance and his collusion with the technical staff.

It is doubtful whether this extreme position can be defended. This is not to say that workers' management is as free and independent as the Yugoslavs claim it is; this is certainly not true. Nevertheless, we must recognise that workers' management has led to important developments within the Yugoslav economy which were both *unforeseen* and *unwanted* by the government and party. These developments simply cannot be explained if one assumes that workers' management is merely a façade behind which lies the power of the party, the union, or the director. These things could only have occurred if workers' management did have some genuine autonomy. Let us trace some of these unintended developments through the entire period of workers' management in Yugoslavia.[60]

1. During the 1950s, wages increased at a very rapid rate, exceeding the rise in productivity. Clearly such things could not have happened had workers' management been under the thumb of the party. In addition to these wage increases, workers' councils have voted their workers large bonuses from the surplus profits of the enterprises. In 1953, for example, in the Belgrade area, extra wage payments varied from one to four month's salary. McVicker claims that '*the régime had never intended*' bonuses to go so high, for it 'rightly feared inflation, and preferred to see most extra profits used for planned industrial improvement. . . . Therefore, in 1954, the major responsibility for disposal of surplus profits . . . was shifted from the workers' councils to the local political-administrative authorities, the people's committees.'[61] Nevertheless, in 1957, it was officially reported that 'industrial undertakings distributed to their workers, on an average, $2\frac{1}{2}$ month's remuneration in addition to the regular twelve month payments. . . .'[62]

2. In spite of the efforts of the régime, inflation hit hard during the mid-1950s. In 1954 wholesale and retail prices rose on the average of one per cent a month; and in the first six months of that year alone, prices were up 8–9 per cent. These increases were not at all foreseen by the Federal Plan of 1953 and 1954. Workers' management was, of course, primarily responsible for the price boosts. In the mid-1960s, Yugoslavia suffered an even greater round of inflation, with official figures indicating rather alarming annual increases in the cost of living of over 22 per cent between 1964 and 1966.[63]

3. Monopolistic practices in the best tradition of Western capitalism

have blossomed under workers' management. *Borba*, the Belgrade
party newspaper, accused firms which were the exclusive producer of
some goods of using their economic power irresponsibly. These firms
often 'blackmailed' their customers into paying high prices and
accepting inferior quality goods and/or more goods than they actually
needed. As a result of monopolistic pricing, price collusion and other
devices to create favourable market conditions, the government resorted
to 'anti-trust' legislation which prevented the formation of cartels and
established maximum prices on a great number of items. Some ingenious firms responded to these decrees by switching production
away from price-fixed goods. Neal cites the case of one leather products
firm in Slovenia which turned the bulk of its manufacturing from
shoes (which were price-fixed) to luggage and briefcases. Apparently
these practices were widespread enough to call forth regulations from
the government permitting the dissolution of workers' management
bodies found to be engaging in them. Reporting on the conditions
under which workers' management organs may be dissolved, the ILO
includes those which result from 'unlawful conspiracy relating to
prices or the sharing of markets, as well as for other similar practices
intended to create a market monopoly or to obtain benefit from such a
situation. . . .'[64] The following case illustrates the use of the market
power of a large edible oils' producer to capture a large share of the
market by reducing prices 'artificially' to drive out competition. A representative of a small edible oils' factory presented his case as follows.

> The big producers are competing with us unfairly. No matter which
> customer we contacted [offering their product at the price set by big
> producers] the answer was that others were selling more cheaply. Our
> collective accordingly decided that we should sell at any price provided
> it would cover our costs.
> The representatives of the big oil factories then threatened to sell
> their products at a discount in the areas supplied by the small factory
> and were told that the small factory would not accept an ultimatum and
> if necessary would cut its own price still further.[65]

The second case illustrates both the operation of a boycott, in which a
firm refused to sell to its customers at current prices, and the role of a
representative of workers' management in settling the issue. In this
instance

> . . . an undertaking which was largely dependent on regular supplies
> of small quantities of a special alloy was notified by its supplier (which
> also happened to be the only producer in the country) that all deliveries
> would be suspended because its own production was barely adequate

for its new development programme. The director's protests had no effect and the chairman of the workers' council had to pay two visits to the supplier to plead his case with the latter's director and workers' council. He finally won them over, but only after bringing the case out into the open in one of the daily newspapers.[66]

In any case, monopolistic abuses were prevalent enough to call forth a provision in the new constitution itself which prohibited '. . . the association or merging of working organisations . . . which is directed towards preventing or restricting a free exchange of goods and services in order to attain material or other advantages . . . or which create other unfair business relations. . . .'

4. Investment has not always taken the form most desired by the party. In response to popular pressure, new investment has often been channelled toward the production of consumers' goods, and established factories often turn to the production of popular items. Neal cites the case of two canning factories in Croatia suddenly adding equipment to produce the popular sweet, 'Turkish Delight'. And, indeed, on a national scale, the overinvestment crisis of the Yugoslav economy in the 1960s, which so disturbed party and government leaders and was so contrary to their intentions, was an apt testimony to the autonomy of workers' management.

5. Other miscellaneous deeds of workers' management which run counter to the wishes of the party are reported in the literature. For example, some firms have artificially reduced the size of their work force to increase profit shares for the remaining workers. This helped to lead to a fairly serious unemployment situation during the early 1950s. Ward reports on the persecution of directors by bodies of workers' management. Apparently job satisfaction among some members of the new class is rather low: in 1956 10 per cent of all the directors who had been removed had removed themselves, i.e. had quit. Many preferred technical jobs at lower levels in the firm; others sought employment in the state administration. Workers' management bodies will use their control over the hiring and firing of the director's staff—a power they acquired in 1954—as a weapon over his head. The size of his salary is used in the same way. Ward and the ILO report the atypical but significant case of one director of a coal mine whose salary was 20 per cent below that of 'his' miners. The ILO observed that

. . . there can be little doubt that workers' management in practice has led to a strong egalitarian attitude towards the remuneration of directors, and of executives in general. The same appears to be true of

the other perquisites and emoluments such as *per diem* allowances, fares
while travelling on business, entertainment, etc., which are regulated
with growing strictness and often require the approval (sometimes
beforehand) of the workers' management bodies.[67]

Now that the directors' salaries are regulated by the workers' management organs—and thus receive substantial publicity among the rank
and file workers—extreme inequalities in the distribution of personal
income in undertakings has been largely reduced, and various bonus
schemes for executives, once common, have been eliminated. The ILO
concludes that the inroads of workers' management power have meant
that the position of director 'has lost some of the material and political
attractions and prestige it once had'.[68]

6. As stated earlier, the law prohibits any compensation being paid
to members of workers' councils or boards of management, apart from
reimbursement for travelling expenses and compensation for loss of
wages resulting from attendance at meetings during the working day.
Nevertheless, in spite of the law, workers' management organs in
some undertakings have occasionally decided, more or less secretly, to
vote themselves so-called 'attendance allowances'. And it is estimated
that approximately seven million dinars were spent in 1956 for this
illegal compensation, the bulk of it among firms in the industrialised
Republic of Slovenia.[69]

7. Final proof of the autonomy of workers' management are the
critical remarks made in the Yugoslav press concerning the abuses
which have been mentioned here. Generalised criticisms of workers'
management which have appeared in the Yugoslav press fall into
categories such as: *a*, 'primitivism', which denotes an excessive reaction
by workers' management against the technical or administrative staff,
accompanied by attempts to reduce their numbers or their activities to
a point which endangers the efficient operation of the enterprise; *b*,
'bureaucratisation' of workers' management organs, involving the
appropriation of various material or non-material privileges for those
elected to management; *c*, 'particularism', whereby the workers'
management bodies pursue the interests of their enterprise exclusively
and to a degree which interferes with or injures the public interest.
Such behaviour is considered a reversion to a petty bourgeois or a
producers' co-operative mentality wherein the employees believe the
company should be run for their benefit and profit alone.[70]

It may be argued that all of these abuses merely demonstrate the
autonomy of the *firm* but not necessarily the autonomy of workers'

management within the firm. Reasoning along these lines, analogies may be drawn between the Yugoslav and the Soviet firm, and the argument made that abuses of the Yugoslav firm no more prove the existence of an independent workers' management than do the often flagrant abuses of the Soviet firm.

The abuses of Yugoslav enterprises, however, are basically different from those typical of Soviet enterprises. The latter are often measures designed to circumvent the assigned plan or to make its fulfilment easier and are schemes which are in the direct interest of those held responsible for carrying out the plan, viz. the director and his immediate staff. Yugoslav firms, on the other hand, have no centrally assigned production targets, either to meet or to evade; and the abuses of these enterprises almost always take the form of actions which benefit the workers (or their representatives) directly, and are almost invariably, from their very nature, the concoction of the workers' management representatives. These abuses, therefore, do point to the autonomy of workers' management.

Again, the purpose of citing these developments has not been to suggest that workers' management is destroying the Yugoslav economy and is totally at odds with the wishes of the party. Obviously this is not true. These negative developments give a one-sided picture of the operation of workers' management, and yet they illustrate that workers' management does not act merely as a willing tool in the hands of the party. It must be granted some measure of real independence. Furthermore, looked at from the point of view of the survival interests of the régime, it would be folly for it to create a structure which is in its design a model of democracy and mass participation, only to subvert its principles and render the entire structure fraudulent for the entire working class to see. The mass unrest and discontent which such a situation would generate would be difficult to exaggerate.

The Composition of Workers' Management

Magnitude. Between 1950 and the early 1960s over a million Yugoslav workers served in workers' management, participating either on workers' councils or the higher management boards. In addition, thousands more have served on the standing commissions of workers' councils and other *ad hoc* bodies of workers' management. These million comprise somewhere between one-third and one-half of all workers in the Socialist sector of the Yugoslav economy.[71]

Party Membership and Workers' Management. The party's chief publication, *Komunist,* announced in 1959 its strength within workers' management. On the workers' councils in 1958, there were some 60,000 party members, comprising about 27 per cent of the total council membership, while on the management boards the party had about 25,500 members, constituting 37 per cent of total board membership.[72] Thus, party members constitute a minority on the workers' management bodies, although they are significantly overrepresented in relation to their proportions in the work force. Of course, there is a great deal of variation from factory to factory. The Zagreb Institute of Social Management, in a survey of eighteen factories in that city, found that party membership on the workers' councils ranged from a low of 8 per cent to a high of 65 per cent.[73]

Over time the proportion of party members on workers' management has probably fallen, on the average, because of the rapid turnover and the inclusion of a great part of the work force on the management bodies. For example, Neal claims that in 1954 party and union officials reported to him that in the major cities probably 'between 60 and 70 per cent' of the members of workers' councils were party members.[74] Ward reports official data from Croatia, also for 1954, which show that about 35 per cent of the members of the workers' councils in this Republic were party members.[75] This is a much lower figure than Neal's but is still higher than national figures for 1959, five years later.

Of course, party domination does not depend upon holding the majority of seats; the question of representation is interesting and important, but it is not crucial. The Yugoslav League of Communists does not need majorities in order to rule. In the trade unions in the mid-1950s for example, only 300,000 out of the 1·7 million union members belonged to the party—a small minority.[76] But there is no doubt where the power lies.

The case of workers' management is more complicated. Party members in the factories these days are often subject to two sets of contradictory expectations. On the one hand, they are expected to do everything they can to encourage interest and participation in workers' management.* But they are also instructed to see to it that workers' management makes the 'correct' decisions. Also, party members are no

---

* For example, in redundancy cases, the Party has seen to it in many factories that one minor criterion used to determine whether a worker will be retained or dismissed is the extent to which he has been active in workers' management.

longer supposed to dictate, dominate or coerce, but to convince and educate by power of example, etc. But what happens when workers do become interested, do begin to participate, but do not make the 'right' choices? Party members are then faced with a dilemma, the resolution of which depends upon the particular conditions in each enterprise. The party may decide that proper decisions take priority over genuine participation and may thus manipulate or even coerce. On the other hand, they may opt for the other set of priorities, the stimulation of interest and participation, and may, consequently, merely exhort or even allow the exercise of autonomy.

Workers in Workers' Management. By law, 75 per cent of the members of the management boards are required to be 'workers directly engaged in production'. This requirement has been fulfilled in practice. In fact, the workers' councils show the same domination by 'workers at the bench', even though this is not required by law.[77]

In their study of the American trade union locals, Sayles and Strauss observed that highly skilled and well paid workers predominate in union office. Local presidents, chairmen of grievance committees, shop stewards, and other officials very often derive from the 'aristocracy' of the work force.[78] This is generally attributable to a mixture of status considerations and competence for the job.

In Yugoslavia the same pattern exists with regard to the composition of the organs of workers' management. There, too, the highly skilled and skilled workers predominate; semi-skilled and unskilled workers are few in proportion to their numbers in the work force (see Table 1). Although the highly skilled and skilled workers constituted less than half of the Yugoslav labour force in 1960, they comprised nearly three-quarters of the members of the workers' councils and 80 per cent of the members of the management boards. At the same time, while semi-skilled and unskilled workers made up about half the labour force, they comprised only about one-quarter of the members of the workers' councils and one-fifth the members of the management boards.

The trends are exaggerated with respect to presidents of the workers' councils and management boards, of whom about one-third are highly skilled workers and an additional 50 per cent are classified as skilled.

Again, as in America, status considerations and competence are certain to be the most important factors. Status ambiguities are disconcerting; it is awkward to look down on someone at his job and up to

TABLE I: PARTICIPATION OF WORKERS IN WORKERS' MANAGEMENT, BY LEVEL
OF SKILL, 1960[79]

Level of skill	Per cent in labour force	Per cent on workers' councils	Per cent on management boards
Highly skilled	10·1%	19·6%	28·6%
Skilled	38·3	53·3	51·8
Semi-skilled	25·0	17·6	13·3
Unskilled	26·6	9·5	6·3
Total	100·0%	100·0%	100·0%
SUMMARY DATA:			
Highly skilled and skilled	48·4%	72·9%	80·4%
Semi-skilled and unskilled	51·6	27·1	19·6
Total	100·0%	100·0%	100·0%

him on a workers' council. It also undermines the legitimacy of an institution to have it represented by individuals of low status.

Also, it must be remembered that Yugoslavia was left with a heritage of a backward labour force. Only thirty years ago 75 per cent of the economically active population were peasants; in 1955 about 25 per cent of the industrial labour force were part-time peasants.[80] And as recently as 1953, approximately one quarter of the population over ten was illiterate. In spite of the efforts of the régime to provide basic education for the workers with regard to the administration of the economy—in the form of workers' universities, seminars in the plant, etc.—it is obvious that a large proportion of workers are incapable of understanding—much less supervising—the operation of an enterprise.

White Collar Workers Serving in Workers' Management. White collar workers—'employees'—play a relatively minor role in workers' management. Not only are 75 per cent of the members of workers' management usually manual workers, but between 70–80 per cent of the chairmen of workers' councils and management boards are also workers.[81]

Though the representation of white collar workers is relatively minor, the *pattern* of their participation follows generally that of worker participation. That is, in both groups, those with higher levels of skill and training are more likely to serve on councils and boards than those with less skill and training. The pattern for white collar workers, however, is less pronounced than that for manual workers, and there are even occasional reversals.

TABLE 2: PARTICIPATION OF EMPLOYEES IN WORKERS' MANAGEMENT, BY LEVEL OF TRAINING, 1960[82]

Level of training	Per cent in labour force	Per cent on workers' councils	Per cent on management boards
University or advanced	20·5%	17·7%	34·2%
Secondary School	39·6	50·7	45·6
Lower training	27·4	29·0	19·1
Auxiliary clerks	12·5	2·6	1·1
Total	100·0%	100·0%	100·0%

Women in Workers' Management. In their research on the local union, Sayles and Strauss report that women are elected to union office very rarely and then only when the rank and file are overwhelmingly female.[83] Important factors which account for this are: *1*, status considerations. Theodore Caplow rightly observed that men abhor having women in positions of authority over them. This often merges into simple discrimination rationalised by the attitude that women belong in the home. *2*. There is also the important factor of traditional female apathy toward union affairs. *3*. One cannot neglect the nature of union meetings, and the times and places they are held. Meetings take place at night, often in dirty, dingy halls, at which the 'stag' element prevails. Many women are probably fearful of going home late at night, after the adjournment of a long union meeting. They are probably equally reluctant to spend their time in the kinds of places in which meetings are held, and they are also somewhat repelled by the excessive masculinity of the meetings.

How many of these factors also characterise the Yugoslav scene is difficult to judge.* There are probably status considerations, elements of male chauvinism which are a heritage from the severely patriarchal mores and legal code of pre-Communist Yugoslavia, perhaps reinforced by female apathy. But whether the causes are the same or not, the effects are similar to the American trade union local. Women do

---

* I cannot comment on the nature of the meetings. As to place, they are held in the factory itself which would probably not discourage female participation. As to the time, they are usually held after working hours, and as the work day generally runs from 6.00 a.m. to 2.00 p.m., most meetings probably fall during the middle of the afternoon rather than at night. However, domestic responsibilities, rather than the lateness of the meetings, may keep some women from accepting nominations.

not serve on workers' management in the same proportions as they participate in the labour force. Although women comprised more than a quarter of the labour force in 1958 they had only 16 per cent of the seats on the councils and 10 per cent on the boards. Furthermore, only 5 per cent of the presidents of the councils and the boards were women: less than 1 per cent of all enterprise directors were women.[84]

The differences between male and female representation may be due to other factors as well. Women workers, for example, are on the average less skilled than men. Thus, only 1·5 per cent of the women in the labour force are classified as highly skilled as compared to 10 per cent of the entire labour force.[85] As highly skilled workers are more likely to participate in workers' management, part of the female under-representation may be accounted for in terms of differences of skill and not of sex.

The proportion of women in workers' management increased slightly in the first decade of the system's operation. In 1952, 13 per cent of the members of workers' councils were women. This fell briefly in 1954 to 10 per cent but increased consistently thereafter and by 1960, about 18 per cent of the total elected membership was female. While women seem to be making moderate gains in representation, it should also be remembered that female participation in the labour force is also increasing and so slightly greater proportions on the councils are to be expected.

In summary, the following groups are represented disproportionately in workers' management: party members; highly skilled and skilled workers; white collar workers with university, advanced or secondary school training; and males. The data also indicate that the age group from the mid-20s to the mid-40s seems to dominate the councils and the boards—i.e. workers in the prime of their working lives, with workers both older and younger less well represented.

Among its other functions, workers' management in Yugoslavia is unquestionably a unique vehicle of upward social mobility, for talented workers are able to develop and demonstrate their managerial competence by serving on workers' councils, management boards, or miscellaneous workers' committees. Western sociologists have often observed that there are two discrete promotional ladders in modern business enterprise, the factory hierarchy and the office hierarchy, and that while there may be upward mobility within each one alone, there is almost none between factory and office. That is, the office ladder and the factory ladder are separate and distinct today and it is almost impossible for the worker on the factory floor to ascend, by means of hard work, diligence, ingenuity or any of the other traditional virtues, to the office.[86] There is, in that special sense, a caste system in industry. What is unusual about workers' management in Yugoslavia is that it tends to connect the severed link between office and factory and allow exceptionally able workers to move up into the office, into the managerial staff, occasionally even as director. Although I have seen no data on the frequency of this movement, individual cases are very often cited in the literature. Some observers have even claimed, remiscent of Young's *Rise of the Meritocracy*, that the very success of workers' management may lead to its own defeat, as talented workers are drawn from workers' councils and boards into management, thus depleting the pool of qualified workers' representatives. Though undoubtedly exaggerated, this argument does call attention to workers' management as a new instrument for occupational mobility, unavailable to workers elsewhere.

Productivity

Western students of the Yugoslav economy during the 1950s were generally sceptical of the power of workers' management to increase labour productivity. And true enough, the record of the Yugoslav economy during much of this period was poor. Overall labour productivity in 1951 was lower than in 1950, and, taking the year 1952 as equal to 100, productivity in 1953 fell to 97 and in 1954 declined further to 95.[87] On the basis of these figures, Ward claimed that there was 'no evidence that creation of workers' councils changed the attitudes of the workers toward the factories in a way which stimulated their productivity'.[88]

But was this hasty judgment warranted? The system of workers' management, although formally introduced in 1950, did not really take hold until 1952 when detailed administrative planning was abandoned. And certainly, during the early 'fifties, the Yugoslav economy was under extraordinary strains and pressures. Ward himself grants that 'Yugoslavia was still in considerable difficulties as a result of droughts [1947, 1950, 1952] and the Cominform blockade . . . and the uncertainties attendant upon these problems may have made any organisational system perform poorly in terms of productivity.'[89]

But his willingness to make allowances for the extraordinary situation in which Yugoslavia found herself is limited; even 'when all this is said, the performance over the period 1950–1954 is nonetheless disappointing'.[90]

However, the performance of the Yugoslav economy since Ward wrote calls his conclusions into serious question and now makes his judgments on the efficacy of workers' management seem premature and inaccurate. By the mid-1950s, when Yugoslavia had recovered from the shock of being severed from the Soviet camp and had established trade relations with the West, the economy completely reversed its previous trends and began to perform at extremely high levels. For example, the gross national product, which grew at an annual rate of only 2·4 per cent between 1948 and 1952, reached an average annual rate of growth of 10·4 per cent in the years between 1953 and 1959.[91] United Nations data indicate that the Yugoslav economy during the late 1950s captured the world's record for the greatest increase in *per capita* gross national product. According to the United Nations *Economic Survey of Europe* (1959) and their *Economic Bulletin for Europe* (November 1960), the Yugoslav *per capita* increase in gross national product from the period 1951 to 1959 (part of which time the economy was performing poorly) was three to four times more rapid than that of the countries of Western Europe and considerably more rapid than that of the Eastern European Communist countries. Industrial production, which remained in the doldrums from 1949 to 1953, tripled from 1952 to 1961.[92] And labour productivity, which Ward had pointed to significantly as having fallen from an index of 100 in 1952 to 95 in 1954, had by 1957 reached 123 and by 1961 passed 143.[93] More recently, between 1964 and 1966, labour productivity increased at the very rapid annual rate of 7·2 per cent.[94]

Behind all these abstract numbers lie unmistakable improvements in the level of living of the average Yugoslav citizen. Referring to the late 1950s, Hoffman and Neal remark that: 'One of the most dramatic aspects of the new Yugoslavia is the advance in the standard of living of most people as compared with the early post-war years'.[95] The production and importation of consumers' goods have risen very sharply over the years, and increased purchasing power has made these goods more accessible than ever before. While the Yugoslav standard of living naturally lags behind that in Western Europe, it is the envy of many visitors from Soviet bloc countries.

There is, of course, no gainsaying that the Yugoslav economy has its afflictions.[96] There is, first, the serious overinvestment problem which helped to stimulate the economic reform of 1965. Second, the economy has recently been plagued with inflationary problems, as mentioned earlier. Third, there is unemployment on a fairly large scale which has been partly responsible for the scattering of several hundred thousand workers—mainly unskilled and semi-skilled—abroad in search of work. And there is, finally, the continuing balance of trade problem.

Nevertheless, the economy continues to grow. Using the GNP in 1960 as an index of 100, the figure for 1954—the last year Ward examined—was only 52 but had increased to 149 by 1964.[97] And real personal income rose by 10 per cent annually between 1964 and 1966.[98]

Naturally, it would be going beyond the data to assert that the remarkable improvement in the performance of the Yugoslav economy has been due to the system of workers' management; the connection between them is too indirect. Yet one can cautiously argue that extremely large increases in labour productivity in recent years have taken place alongside the development of a system of workers' management, that the two have not been incompatible, but coincident.

Actually, of course, a causal connection is not unlikely; due to the structure of workers' management, one would expect it to have a favourable influence upon labour productivity. The ILO mission noted in this regard that schemes of modernisation and mechanisation

> do not appear to have come up against any resistance from the collectives or [workers'] management bodies. In fact, they seem to set their hearts on it as soon as enough money is available. This attitude seems mainly due to the fact that they [the workers] themselves control the volume of unemployment in their undertaking and that any initiative they display has an effect on their earnings [through 'profit'-sharing].[99]

It is interesting in this context that labour productivity and economic performance are actually being *de*-emphasised by many Yugoslav writers today. Workers' management is lauded as much for its 'humanistic' features as for its alleged efficiency.[100] This evolution away from a total concern with performance is unusual in the Communist world.

Survey Research

Sociologist Jiri Kolaja, who studied a Polish textile factory and its workers' council in 1957, also carried out similar research in Yugoslavia, to which we have alluded earlier. The factory in which Kolaja conducted and reported his first interviews is a major producer of dyes and polish and employs over five hundred men and women.[101] Kolaja asked a sample of seventy-eight workers and employees the following question: 'Who has the greatest influence in the management of the enterprise?' Western readers might predict that the director, the party, or the union would be named most often. Accordingly, it is significant that the majority of the respondents (57 per cent) stated that the workers' council was most influential in the management of the factory.* Thirty-four per cent named the director, only five per cent named the party, and, as mentioned earlier, less than two per cent named the union as having the greatest influence. One could claim that fear of invoking the party or the union as *de facto* ruler in the enterprise biased the responses, but in contemporary Yugoslavia one has pretty much to discount this possibility.

Kolaja also asked a series of projective questions designed to elicit the opinions of the respondent himself. For example he asked his sample of workers, 'how many persons [in the factory] think that the profit should rather be distributed [to the workers] than invested [in the factory]?' The results seem to be consistent with the findings of Western sociologists with respect to the deferred gratification pattern and its relation to social position. The lowest occupational groups (unskilled and semi-skilled) were least likely to want to postpone gratification (by reinvesting factory profits) and most likely to want immediate distribution of the profits to the workers. Of course, this may very well reflect economic need as well as the psychology of immediate gratification. In general, Kolaja's finding here is consistent with stories in the Yugoslav press regarding the difficulty of convincing the unskilled, often illiterate and recently urbanised peasant that much of his factory's profits should be ploughed back into the firm rather than distributed immediately to the workers.

In another question Kolaja tried to measure the extent to which the workers and employees identified with the factory and had a feeling of ownership toward it (see Table 3). Again there are differences according to level of skill, but at all levels identification seems to be high.

It is interesting to compare these responses to those Kolaja received from Polish workers on a similar question. In the Polish textile factory, when asked if they felt the factory belonged to them, the workers reacted with surprise, bewilderment and humour. A typical response was: ' "This factory mine? What a queer idea."[103] Another, equally

* Kolaja does not report whether he supplied the alternatives or left them open-ended.

TABLE 3: HOW MANY EMPLOYEES FEEL THAT THE FACTORY IS THEIR PROPERTY?[102]

Estimate	Unskilled and semi-skilled	Skilled and white collar	Executives
All or many	50% (12)	72% (31)	82% (9)
One half or few	50% (12)	28% (12)	18% (2)
Total	100% (24)	100% (43)	100% (11)

representative, was: "What an idea! Only the plant director can have a feeling of ownership. This is his factory." '[104]

The greater identification of Yugoslav workers with their factory undoubtedly stems from the system of workers' management in that country. In Poland, the workers' councils were a fleeting and transitional phenomenon. Created as a result of the demands of Polish workers in 1956, the government never really accepted them and almost immediately began chipping away at their power. They were not buttressed by any officially accepted ideology as in Yugoslavia; the councils were, on the contrary, in the nature of concessions and tactical expediencies of the régime. Thus, they never took root firmly in Polish soil. Moreover, their powers were sharply limited from the beginning; in contrast to the Yugoslav situation, the Polish councils had to work within the framework of the national economic plan, which really left them very little to do.

Though Kolaja believes that Yugoslav workers had a more highly developed sense of identification with their factory than did Polish workers, he feels that the identification is nevertheless quite low. In informal conversations with workers, he asked whether they thought most workers would quit and take a job in another factory if they were offered more pay. The most common attitude Kolaja found is conveyed by one respondent's reply: ' "Of course they would leave, if they can get more money elsewhere. What difference does it make? All these factories are our property. *In another factory you will also find a workers' council.*" '[105]

Kolaja states that this attitude shows diffuse feelings of ownership and weak identification with their particular factory. Perhaps it does. But equally important—and this is the point Kolaja overlooks—this statement shows very strong identification with the workers' council system *as such* and with the idea of 'social ownership'. Indeed, according to Yugoslav law and the prevailing ideology, the workers *do not* 'own' the factories and thus *should not* feel that the factories in which they work are 'theirs'. The Yugoslavs are very explicit on this point. The means of production are not to be regarded, in any sense, as the personal property of the work force. In law as well as in practice the workers possess merely the right to use and manage the enterprise as agents for the entire community. Thus, Kolaja's entire orientation here with respect to ascertaining feelings of ownership seems misconceived.

In a later work,[106] Kolaja describes in greater detail his study of the dye and polish factory discussed above, and also reports his research in another enterprise in the Belgrade area, this one manufacturing inexpensive cotton material and employing some 1,600 workers. In both factories he attended meetings of the workers' management bodies, examined the minutes of previous meetings, interviewed workers or administered questionnaires to them, and so on.

Kolaja concludes from his study of these two factories that workers' management does not function in the manner in which the formal structure suggests. His general conclusions are as follows. *1*. The director of the enterprise and his staff were the most active participants in the meetings of the workers' management bodies and almost always had their suggestions approved by these bodies; nevertheless, workers were free to express their views when they so desired. *2*. There seemed to be a substantial amount of *apathy* among members of the workers' management bodies toward the administrative and managerial problems of the enterprise, while interest and enthusiasm were shown primarily with regard to problems directly concerned with the workers' welfare, e.g. wage norms, premium payments, apartment house allocations, and the like. *3*. There seemed also to be a considerable amount of *apathy* and *ignorance* among the rank and file workers regarding most of the activities of the workers' management organs. *4*. Kolaja concluded that the chief function of workers' management was that it *facilitated communication* between management and the work force, and he judged that more information about the management and operation of the plant is accessible to the average Yugoslav worker—if he cares to avail himself of it—than is available to his counterpart in Britain, the United States, or the Soviet Union.

It would be erroneous to infer from this study that Yugoslav workers, after all, even when given the opportunity, are not interested in workers' management. First, Kolaja's sample is quite small, consisting of merely two factories. Second, it is doubtful whether the work force in these two factories is representative of others. Both plants which Kolaja investigated were overrepresented by female workers, who would be expected to be more apathetic with respect to workers' management, given the traditional subordinate role of women in pre-revolutionary Yugoslavia. As one woman said to Kolaja rather apologetically when he asked her about some aspect of workers' management in her plant: 'We have children; this is of no interest to us'. This pattern of female apathy toward trade union and factory matters is also typical of the American scene, as is well known.

In 1958, women comprised about 27 per cent of the Yugoslav labour force, but in the textile factory Kolaja studied in the same year, some 80 per cent of the work force was female. In the other factory, the proportion of women was lower, but nevertheless somewhat higher than in the labour force as a whole. This fact cannot be disregarded when assessing the apathy and ignorance of workers whom Kolaja observed.

Third, it is difficult to reconcile Kolaja's overall conclusions regarding the importance of workers' management with his finding, stated earlier, that over half the workers questioned in one factory believed the workers' council to be the single most influential force within the enterprise.

Nevertheless, in spite of these qualifications, it is undoubtedly true that many workers in Yugoslavia are apathetic regarding the system of workers' management and are interested only or primarily in economic issues closest to their own lives. This, certainly, is at least partly a consequence of the poverty, backwardness and ignorance of the population.

As we observed earlier, until the war some 75 per cent of the labour force consisted of semi-literate peasants, and much of the industrial labour force today is made up of a recently urbanised peasantry. As late as 1958, 80 per cent of the population did not have as much as an elementary school education (8 years), and only $2\frac{1}{2}$ per cent had completed college.[107] Given this cultural level, one need not be surprised that a considerable amount of apathy and ignorance exist with respect to the operation of workers' management. It is entirely likely that greater interest and involvement in the system will develop with increasing material prosperity and the gradual development of a more highly skilled and educated population. The data presented in this chapter indicate that workers with more skill and education are more likely to participate in workers' management than less skilled or educated workers, and are less likely to define it primarily as an instrument to enhance their own private economic well-being.

In the early 1960s, sociologists from the Institute of Social Science in Belgrade conducted a survey of more than 5,000 workers selected from 255 enterprises in Yugoslavia on the subject of workers' management.[108] Although it smacks somewhat of an 'official survey', with attractive answers for the workers to gravitate towards and conclusions nicely harmonising with the régime's official ideology, the results are nonetheless interesting and do contain some views—albeit a minority—which do not support the prevailing orthodoxy. As perhaps might be expected, the findings suggest greater interest and involvement in workers' management than Kolaja found in his research.

Of the 5,000 workers questioned, about 1,100 or 22 per cent were or had been members of workers' councils, while the remainder had not yet been. To the question of whether they would be willing to stand for election for the councils, a majority (54 per cent) replied in the affirmative while a little more than a third (36 per cent) said they were unwilling. Those who were interested in becoming council members were asked to give their reasons, and these are listed in Table 4. Workers seem to be interested in serving on workers' management either in order to seek their own personal advancement (about 20 per cent of the cases) or for more 'social-altruistic' reasons (the bulk of the cases).

Those who stated that they did not want to run for a seat on their workers' council were asked to explain. Most reasons related to per-

TABLE 4: WHY WOULD YOU LIKE TO BECOME A MEMBER OF YOUR WORKERS' COUNCIL?[109]

Social-altruistic reasons		
Interested in the work and problems of the council	25%	(564)
To acquire a better understanding of the problems, tasks and workers of the enterprise	22%	(492)
To be in a better position to criticise injustices and remove them	21%	(464)
To protect the interests of the workers in the enterprise	10%	(227)
Reasons of personal advancement		
To improve themselves by serving on the council	9%	(197)
For personal prestige	7%	(162)
To get on at work, get a better post or an easier job	5%	(121)
Total	100%	(2,227)

sonal inadequacies of one kind or another. Twenty-four per cent of those who did not want to serve felt they were too old, 3 per cent considered themselves too young, 36 per cent said they had insufficient experience, knowledge, or ability to carry out the tasks. A sizeable proportion (21 per cent) felt they were too busy to take on the responsibility due to other activities such as school, other jobs, etc. Finally, 17 per cent said that they had no desire to 'worry about other people's problems' or considered council work a waste of time.

The majority of the workers, 74 per cent, believed that workers' management had improved the workers' position in the enterprise, while 5 per cent thought it had not, and 21 per cent, a rather large figure, did not give a definite answer. Those who believed that workers' management had led to favourable changes were asked to mention the major improvement which it had brought about. A number of items were mentioned: a more equitable distribution of income (24 per cent); greater care of the worker, his conditions of work, etc. (18 per cent); greater freedom of the worker as a producer (11 per cent); raising the workers' level of education and awareness (4 per cent); better organisation of work and improvements in the business aspects of the enterprise (16 per cent); general improvements of living standards and conditions (8 per cent); greater opportunity for correcting abuses and injustices (1 per cent); miscellaneous improvements (18 per cent).

A large majority of the workers, 76 per cent, believed that their workers' councils had sufficient power 'to maintain complete control of the management of the enterprise'. And 82 per cent agreed with the statement that there were no serious obstacles preventing workers' representatives from playing a more active role on the workers' councils and management boards.

The sociologists sought to discover whether membership on the workers' councils brought with it privilege-seeking or assertions of superior status. According to the survey, it did not in the majority of cases. Ninety-one per cent of the workers reported that the behaviour of their colleagues had not changed since they were elected to the councils, and some workers (3 per cent) reported that their councillors were now more willing to offer explanations and to help out generally, were more thoughtful and had become better workers. A minority of workers, however, had complaints about the behaviour of their colleagues on the workers' councils. Four per cent of the workers said that some council members had 'become high-and-mighty, conceited and uncomradely in their behaviour'; an additional one per cent claimed that some of their fellow workers on the council now pursued their own interests often at the expense of the other workers, and another 2 per cent claimed that their fellow workers on the council 'had become officious, neglected their former friends and kept company only with officials and executives'.

Conclusions

David Tornquist, an American writer who recently lived in Yugoslavia for two years more or less as an ordinary citizen working for a Belgrade publishing house, has given us a perceptive report on the tone and feel of Yugoslav society today.[110] Exploring numerous aspects of social life there, he visited several enterprises in the Belgrade area—a machine tool factory, a children's hospital, and a pharmaceutical company—in order to assess the operation of workers' management. He writes also of his own experiences with workers' management as it operated in the publishing firm for which he worked. Although he is sociologically less sytematic than Kolaja, his observations, examples and anecdotes show political sophistication and sociological insight and thus give us far more of the sense of the system in actual operation than does Kolaja's study.

For the last time now we will ask: Is workers' management in Yugoslavia genuine? In some firms—Tornquist's own publishinghouse included—workers' management worked poorly or not at all: the director, the party, the union—or some combination of these—clearly ran the show. In others, however, workers' management actually began to approach the model set down for it by the formal system. And throughout, one must not dismiss the formal system as meaningless and irrelevant. There is no question but that the legal and moral framework for workers' participation is firmly implanted in Yugoslav society: it is enshrined as perhaps the crowning principle of the 1963 constitution; it is a cornerstone of the party programme; it is incorporated in the laws of the land; and the party and government, in all their manifestations, constantly push the ideas of participation before the people and exhort them to take ever greater initiative. Uninterested, apathetic workers are condemned and called 'little citizens' and the working class hero today is one who actively participates in workers' management.

We have argued earlier that one should not overlook the importance of ideology and form, regardless of how 'insincerely' the ideology and the forms were originally meant to be, for these things begin to take on a social reality beyond what was initially intended. What seems to matter in contemporary Yugoslavia is that the legal and the moral framework for workers' management now exists, and it is this framework which provides the stage, the setting and the context in which the struggle for control of the factories is carried out. Because the formal structure and the ideology permit and even encourage a high degree of participation, all that is required for genuine workers' management in a factory is the sheer *determination* of the workers themselves. If they are bold enough, interested enough, self-confident enough, and aggressive enough, they can take power through the machinery of workers' councils, management boards, and economic units, and they can hold power and wield it.

One can plainly see that workers' management in Yugoslavia has neither been a clear-cut failure nor a clear-cut success. There is undoubtedly tremendous variation from one enterprise to another, depending upon the constellation of forces in the factory. In many cases—perhaps the majority—workers' management has little power and remains a mere form; but in some it has actually begun to operate in line with law and ideology.

As we said, the framework for workers' management is there, but all the framework can do is to set the stage for the battle. What determines the outcome of the struggle for control in the factory? Unfortunately, we do not have the data which would tell us in what kinds of situations the workers are more likely to win out and in what situations the director and his staff are likely to prevail. We do not know the importance of such obviously crucial variables as: size of the enterprise, nature of the product, region of the country, social composition of the work force, economic position of the firm, etc. Apparently, however, a great deal depends on the personalities and attitudes of the director and his staff and the 'level of consciousness' of the workers themselves. In many cases, the workers are apathetic, lead privatised lives (as in the West), are ignorant, uninformed, basically uninterested, easily intimidated by the authority and traditional prerogatives of the director. They may be too fearful and timid to assert their legal rights within the factory, and so may capitulate to stronger forces.

At the same time, just as the workers may be weak, their director may be strong, arrogant, or domineering. He may use the union and the party to dominate workers' management. He may go his own way, withhold vital information from the workers' council or the management board, or overwhelm the workers with an avalanche of unexplained, purposely abstruse, and tediously presented facts and figures. He may be autocratic at meetings and openly violate the legal provisions of workers' management, but go unchallenged by a docile work force.

In those factories where the system is working well, however, workers' representatives can apparently understand the operation of the enterprise and make sensible, responsible and restrained business decisions, thus offering some refutation to the generally accepted notion that workers are simply incapable of running a factory intelligently. Tornquist provides a vivid account of lively, intelligent and productive meetings of the management board in a children's hospital, and, in a pharmaceutical company, describes in rich detail the eminently fair, concerned and responsible manner in which workers and their representatives went about the unpleasant and painful task of making redundancy dismissals. Naturally, there are abuses, and the régime itself is the first to admit it. But what is surprising is not the abuses but that the system works as well as it does, given the low level of education, the poverty, the backward peasant origins, and the lack of democratic tradition of the Yugoslav working class. If workers' management is genuine only in a small minority of factories in Yugoslavia today, we may tentatively expect their numbers to increase in the future due to inevitable changes in the social composition of the working class, mentioned earlier, which are usually associated with higher rates of social participation: increased literacy and education, higher levels of skill, and growing prosperity. And we should not forget the cumulative impact on the working class of the relentless political saturation of this workers' management ideology.

What are the immediate prospects for workers' management in Yugoslavia? We argued at the outset that workers' management now seems an inextricable aspect of Yugoslav Socialism, and the most recent events in that country tend to confirm this view and suggest that Yugoslavia is proceeding gradually toward greater decentralisation and grass roots participation in the management of the economy. The celebrated economic reform of 1965, for example, continued the trend of giving more power to individual enterprises—and thus to workers' management—at the expense of the federal government. Of particular relevance to workers' management, the reform ended centrally fixed prices on all but a few commodities, reduced taxes on enterprises and gave them and largely autonomous banks greatly increased power over investment decisions, with a concomitant decline in the investment role of the central government bodies.[111]

Just as significant, Vice President Aleksandar Ranković, for years head of the security police and the man most observers consider the major opponent of economic and political reform, was dismissed from all party and government offices in July 1966, followed by several hundred officials accused of obstructing the economic reform.[112] Finally, Tito himself, long an apparent mediator between liberal and conservative elements within the party had, by the beginning of 1968, clearly begun to swing his influence behind the reformers as he first warned and then had dismissed some four hundred conservative members at middle levels of power, accused of undermining economic liberalisation.[113]

Many of the conservatives are remnants of the partisan generation, still living in the orthodox, Communist past and unable to adjust to the government's gradual liberalisation and decentralisation. They are men who, because of their wartime exploits, were elevated to positions of power and influence after the war, and for whom it has been difficult to move beyond the glory and the heroism of the partisan struggle. Their conception of Communism remains more rigid, authoritarian, and centralist than what is currently evolving in Yugoslavia. These elements are clearly in retreat now, and the liberals undoubtedly represent the dominant force within the party. With the reformers in control, the ninth party congress, scheduled for late 1968, can be expected further to enrich the institutions of workers' management.

Sociologists have written long and often that the industrial revolution, mass production methods, and the ensuing division of labour and subdivision of tasks, have all conspired to atomise and fragment the worker's consciousness so that he is unable to gain a perspective on the entire productive process to which he contributes only an infinitesimal part. His vision is artificially narrowed. Drowned in the mechanical sea about him, the worker loses his sense of integration with his work environment. To the extent that workers' management is successful, it enables—or rather, compels—the worker to see beyond the narrow horizons of his minute task and to take on a greater perspective which encompasses his economic unit, his department, his factory, his industry, and, in fact, the entire economy. For indeed, management of the business enterprise depends for its success on the acquisition and mastery of the larger perspective.

Genuine workers' management, then, tends to be an *integrative force* which, in addition to the benefits discussed in earlier chapters, may for the first time begin to offset the technological splintering and fragmentation which has been imposed upon the factory worker since the beginning of the industrial revolution.

Notes and Sources

Notes to 1 *Introduction: The Relevance and the Future of Workers' Management*

1 G. D. H. Cole, *The Case for Industrial Partnership* (St Martin's Press Inc., N.Y. 1957), p. 19.

2 Statements of disillusionment are common. On England, e.g. see Hugh Clegg, *A New Approach to Industrial Democracy* (Blackwell, London 1960), p. 36; on France, see Adolph Sturmthal, *Workers' Councils* (Harvard Univ. Press, Cambridge, Mass. 1964), ch. 2; on Israel, see Georges Friedmann, *The End of the Jewish People?* (Doubleday & Co. Inc., N.Y. 1967), pp. 102 ff; on India, see K. M. Chanana, 'Worker Participation in Management', *Modern Review*, 118 (July 1965), pp. 41–6, or N. Das, *Experiments in Industrial Democracy* (Asia Publishing House, N.Y. 1964).

3 See, e.g. Walter Preuss, *Co-operation in Israel and the World* (Jerusalem 1960).

4 One of the few good accounts can be found in Ferdynand Zweig, *The Israeli Worker* (Herzl Press, N.Y. 1959), pp. 221–32.

5 For a discussion of recent stirrings in the long-dormant workers' control movement in Great Britain, see Tony Topham, 'The Campaign for Workers' Control in Britain', *International Socialist Journal*, 2 (August 1965), pp. 469–82.

6 I am grateful for this idea to G. D. H. Cole, op. cit., p. 7 and Royden Harrison, 'Retreat from Industrial Democracy', *New Left Review*, 1 (July–August 1960), pp. 32–8.

7 *Strategy for Labor: a Radical Proposal* (The Beacon Press, Boston, Mass. 1967), pp. 12–13.

8 Ibid., p. 30.

9 See Lelio Basso, 'Perspectives of the European Left', *Studies on the Left*, 7 (March–April 1967), pp. 13–45.

10 The best book on the American New Left to date is Jack Newfield, *A Prophetic Minority* (New American Library Inc., N.Y. 1966).

11 Joseph Lelyveld, 'Dadaists in Politics', *New York Times Magazine* (2nd Oct. 1966), pp. 32 ff.

12 See *New Left Review*, No. 43 (May–June 1967), pp. 3–25.

13 Gorz, op. cit., p. 74.

14 *The New York Times*, 10th Feb. 1968, p. 2.

15 Ibid.

16 Neal Ascherson, 'Unmodern Man', *New York Review of Books*, 10 (1st Feb. 1968), p. 10.

17 Newfield, op. cit., pp. 83, 91–2.

18 Quoted in Hal Draper, *The New Student Revolt* (Grove Press Inc., N.Y. 1965), p. 227.

19 For a detailed illustration of this thesis, see my *Workers' Management in Comparative Analysis* (Ph.D. dissertation, Univ. of California, Berkeley, 1966), esp. ch. 10.

20 See e.g. Peter Worsley, *The Third World* (University of Chicago Press, 1964); Paul E. Sigmund, Jr. (ed.), *The Ideologies of Developing Nations* (Frederick A. Praeger, N.Y. 1963).

Notes to 2 *The Forgotten Lessons of the Mayo Experiments: I*

1 For a summary of the barrage of criticism directed against the ideology of the Mayo school, see Henry A. Landsberger, *Hawthorne Revisited* (New York State School of Industrial and Labor Relations, N.Y. 1958), ch. 3. The ideological foundations of this school are found primarily in Elton Mayo, *Human Problems of an Industrial Civilisation* (The Macmillan Co., N.Y. 1933); *Social Problems of an Industrial Civilisation* (Harvard Graduate School of Business Administration, Boston 1946); *Political Problems of an Industrial Civilisation* (Harvard Graduate School of Business Administration, Boston 1947); T. N. Whitehead, *Leadership in a Free Society* (Harvard University Press, Cambridge, Mass 1936); F. J. Roethlisberger, *Management and Morale* (Harvard University Press, Cambridge, Mass. 1941).

2 Mayo, *Human Problems*.

3 F. J. Roethlisberger and William J. Dickson, *Management and the Worker* (John Wiley & Sons, N.Y. 1964 edition).

4 William F. Whyte, *Men at Work* (Dorsey Press, Homewood, Ill. 1961).

5 For a summary of these illumination experiments, see Roethlisberger and Dickson, op. cit., pp. 14 ff.

6 Ibid., p. 21. This selection procedure is, of course, open to question.

7 See ibid., ch. 6.

8 Ibid., p. 77.

9 Argyle claims that in spite of all the evidence to the contrary, there remains a distinct possibility that physical factors did account for some of the changes. See Michael Argyle, 'The Relay Assembly Test Room in Retrospect', *Occupational Psychology*, 27 (1953), pp. 98–103.

10 Mayo, *Human Problems*, pp. 62–3. It should be noted, however, that though daily and weekly output increased, *hourly* output decreased. See

Figure 1. Daily and weekly output were able to rise, in spite of decreased hourly output, because the workers were now working more hours than in previous periods in which they had rest pauses, short days and weeks. There is no doubt that this drop in hourly output was clearly intended and consciously designed by the workers, as they feared—despite reassurances—that if they performed too well during this period none of the privileges of previous periods would be restored. See Roethlisberger and Dickson, p. 72.

11 Mayo, *Human Problems*, p. 64.

12 Roethlisberger and Dickson, op. cit., chs. 5–6. This statement needs some qualification. The researchers attempted to assess the effects of the changes in the piece rate system upon the workers in the Relay Assembly Room by setting up two control groups. Experience with these control groups suggested to the researchers that the change in the piece rate system did have some limited effect upon the productivity of the workers in the Relay Assembly Room. However, the design of these control groups was such as to render this conclusion questionable. See Roethlisberger and Dickson, ch. 6.

13 Ibid., p. 83.

14 Ibid., pp. 83–4.

15 Mayo, *Human Problems*, p. 65.

16 Ibid.

17 Roethlisberger and Dickson, op. cit., p. 67.

18 T. N. Whitehead, *The Industrial Worker* (Harvard University Press, Cambridge, Mass. 1938), vol. 1, p. 102.

19 Ibid., p. 104.

20 Roethlisberger and Dickson, op. cit., p. 181.

21 Ibid., p. 22.

22 Quoted in ibid., p. 32.

23 Mayo, *Human Problems*, p. 58.

24 Ibid., p. 62.

25 Ibid.

26 Ibid., p. 69.

27 See Abraham Shuchman, *Codetermination: Labor's Middle Way in Germany* (Public Affairs Press, Washington 1957) for a continuum of workers' participation which has grown out of the codetermination literature in Germany.

28 Whitehead, op. cit., p. 113.

29 Roethlisberger and Dickson, op. cit., p. 60.

30 Ibid., p. 63.

31 Ibid., p. 51.

32 Ibid., p. 50.

33 Ibid., p. 71.

34 Mayo, *Human Problems*, p. 75.

35 Landsberger, op. cit., makes roughly the same observation. He refers to the 'unsatisfactory treatment of employees' and imagines that most workers regarded the Hawthorne works as a 'semi-sweated beehive', (p. 55). He says also that '. . . . the data presented in *Management and the Worker* . . . are such as to leave the reader with the impression that Western Electric was a thoroughly unpleasant place at which to work during these years and that the authors knew it'. (p. 53).

36 Roethlisberger and Dickson, op. cit., p. 417. See pp. 417 ff. for more comments expressing the undercurrent of fear which seemed widespread among Hawthorne workers. This apprehension mounted after the onset of the depression.

37 See Shuchman, op. cit., ch. 1.

38 Mayo, *Human Problems* p. 163.

39 Roethlisberger and Dickson, op. cit., p. 189.

40 Ibid.

41 Ibid., p. 67.

42 Whitehead, op. cit., p. 104.

43 Quoted in Mayo, *Human Problems*, p. 65.

44 Roethlisberger and Dickson, op. cit., p. 154.

45 Mayo, *Human Problems*, pp. 70–1.

46 Landsberger, op. cit., pp. 15, 49.

47 Quoted in Mayo, *Human Problems*, p. 79.

48 Roethlisberger and Dickson, op. cit., p. 265.

49 Ibid., p. 266.

50 Ibid., pp. 267–8.

51 Ibid., pp. 268–9.

52 Ibid., p. 374.

53 Ibid.

54 Ibid., pp. 561–2.

Notes to 3 *The Forgotten Lessons of the Mayo Experiments: II*

1 Elton Mayo, *The Human Problems of an Industrial Civilisation* (The Macmillan Co., N.Y. 1933).

2 F. J. Roethlisberger and William J. Dickson, *Management and the Worker* (John Wiley & Sons, N.Y. 1964 edition).

3 In a footnote, Roethlisberger and Dickson state that the experiment did continue beyond 1929 although they treat it only up to that point. See p. 29. There are also occasional buried references in Mayo, *Human Problems*.

4 Henry A. Landsberger, *Hawthorne Revisited* (New York State School of Industrial and Labor Relations, N.Y. 1948), p. 9.

5 T. N. Whitehead, *The Industrial Worker* (Harvard University Press, Cambridge, Mass. 1938), vol. 1, pp. 138–85.

6 Ibid., p. 170.

7 Ibid., pp. 170–1.

8 Ibid., p. 153.

9 Ibid., p. 157.

10 Ibid., p. 158.

11 Comment recorded on 29th May 1930. See ibid. p. 150 and also p. 168 for other remarks similar in tone.

12 Ibid., p. 140.

13 Ibid., pp. 142 ff.

14 Ibid., p. 164.

15 Delbert C. Miller and William H. Form, *Industrial Sociology* (Harper & Row, N.Y. 1964), 2nd ed., p. 660.

16 Seba Elbridge *et al.*, *Fundamentals of Sociology* (Thomas Crowell, N.Y. 1950), p. 643.

17 Ely Chinoy, *An Introduction to Sociology* (Random House, N.Y. 1962), p. 94.

18 Adapted partially from Michael Argyle, 'The Relay Assembly Test Room in Retrospect', *Occupational Psychology*, 27 (1953).

19 Earl H. Bell, *Social Foundations of Human Behavior* (Harper & Row, N.Y. 1961), p. 132.

20 Ibid., p. 559.

21 Arnold W. Green, *Sociology* (McGraw-Hill Book Co. Inc., N.Y. 1952), 1st ed., p. 242.

22 Ibid.

23 Elbridge *et al.*, op. cit., p. 690.

24 Joseph Quinn, *Sociology, a Systematic Analysis* (J. P. Lippincott Co., Philadelphia 1963), p. 147.

25 See Charles B. Spaulding, *An Introduction to Industrial Sociology* (Chandler Publishing Co., San Francisco 1961), p. 217.

26 C. Wright Mills, 'The Contributions of Sociology to Studies of Industrial Relations', in *Proceedings of the First Annual Meeting of Industrial Relations Research Association* (1948), pp. 212–3. See also Mills' *The Sociological Imagination* (Oxford University Press, N.Y. 1959), pp. 92–5.

27 Mills, 'The Contributions of Sociology . . .', p. 213.

28 Argyle, op. cit., p. 103. See also Alex Carey, 'The Hawthorne Studies: A Radical Criticism', *American Sociological Review*, 32 (June 1967), pp. 403–16.

29 Landsberger, op. cit., p. 101.

30 Ibid., p. 102.

31 Mills, 'The Contributions of Sociology . . .', p. 218. For other charges of manipulation, see Louis Schneider, 'An Industrial Sociology—For

What Ends?', *Antioch Review*, 10 (1950), pp. 407–17; Daniel Bell, 'Adjusting Men to Machines', *Commentary*, 3 (1947), pp. 79–98.

32 Mills, 'The Contributions of Sociology . . .', p. 219. Mills does not specify the nature or the extent of this participation.

Notes to 4 *Proposed Solutions to Work Alienation*

1 For a brief historical survey of work attitudes in the Western world, see Adriano Tilgher, *Work, What it has Meant to Men through the Ages* (Harcourt, Brace & World Inc., N.Y. 1930).

2 Robert Blauner, *Alienation and Freedom: The Factory Worker and his Industry* (University of Chicago Press, Chicago 1964).

3 For recent literature on leisure, see: S. Pieper, *Leisure, the Basis o, Culture* (New York 1952); E. Larrabee and R. Meyersohn (eds.), *Mass Leisure* (New York 1958); N. Anderson, *Work and Leisure* (New York 1961); R. Callois, *Man, Play and Games* (New York 1961); S. de Grazia, *Of Time, Work and Leisure* (New York 1962); E. O. Smigel (ed.), *Work and Leisure* (New Haven, Conn. 1963); J. C. Charlesworth (ed.), *Leisure in America: Blessing or Curse?* (Philadelphia 1964); J. Dumazedier, *Toward a Society of Leisure* (New York 1967).

4 Henri Rabassiere, 'The Right to Be Lazy', *Dissent*, 3 (Winter 1956), p. 41.

5 Robert Dubin, 'Industrial Workers' Worlds: A Study of the "Central Life Interests" of Industrial Workers', *Social Problems*, 3 (January 1956), pp. 131–42.

6 Rabassiere, op. cit., pp. 41–2.

7 Ibid., p. 44.

8 Clark Kerr *et al.*, *Industrialism and Industrial Man* (Harvard University Press, Cambridge 1960), p. 294.

9 Ibid., p. 295.

10 Ibid., emphasis added.

11 Standard Pub. Co., Terre Haute Ind. 1904.

12 Bertrand Russell made essentially the same point in his *In Praise of Idleness* (Geo. Allen & Unwin, London 1935).

13 Lafargue, op. cit., p. 41.

14 Ibid., p. 22.

15 See also Adriano Tilgher, op. cit.

16 Quoted in Georges Friedmann, *Anatomy of Work* (The Free Press, Glencoe, Ill. 1961), p. 103. See also Ben Seligman, *Most Notorious Victory* (The Free Press, N.Y. 1966), pp. 377–84.

17 Op cit., pp. 183–4.

18 'Leisure and Work in Postindustrial Society', in *Abundance for What?* (Doubleday Anchor Books, N.Y. 1965), p. 159.

19 Ibid., p. 165.

20 Op. cit., pp. 104–5.

21 David Riesman, 'The Themes of Work and Play in the Structure of Freud's Thought', in *Individualism Reconsidered* (Doubleday Anchor Books, N.Y. 1955).

22 For a recent statement of this well-known pattern, see Kenneth Clark, 'Sex, Status, and Underemployment of the Negro Male', in A. M. Ross and H. Hill (eds.), *Employment, Race, and Poverty* (Harcourt, Brace & World Inc., N.Y. 1967).

23 Nancy C. Morse and Robert S. Weiss, 'The Function and Meaning of Work and the Job', *American Sociological Review*, 20 (April 1955), pp. 191–8.

24 Blauner, op. cit., p. 180.

25 Quoted in Friedmann, op. cit., p. 118. See Drucker's prophetic *America's Next Twenty Years* (Harper & Bros., N.Y. 1957).

26 Op. cit., p. 182. See Georges Friedmann, *Industrial Society* (The Free Press, Glencoe, Ill. 1955), for a similar alienation-curve hypothesis.

27 Friedmann, *Anatomy of Work*, Foreword.

28 *Automation: Impact of Technological Change* (American Enterprise Inst. for Public Policy Research, Washington 1963).

29 This and the data that follow were adapted from the following sources: US Bureau of the Census, *Historical Statistics of the United States, Colonial Times to 1957* (Washington 1960); US Bureau of the Census, *Statistical Abstract of the United States: 1967*, 88th ed. (Washington, 1967); US Department of Labor, Bureau of Labor Statistics, *Monthly Labor Review*, 90 (November 1967).

30 *The Sane Society* (Rinehart & Co. Inc., N.Y. 1955), p. 288.

31 *Automation and Management* (Harvard University Press, Cambridge, Mass. 1958).

32 Ibid., pp. 41 ff.

33 Ibid., p. 183, italics in original.

34 Ibid., p. 195.

35 See Water Buckingham, *Automation* (Harper & Bros., N.Y. 1961), pp. 96 ff. for a summary of the three studies mentioned here.

36 For a summary of fairly recent automation research, see Floyd C. Mann, 'Psychological and Organisational Impacts', in John T. Dunlop (ed.), *Automation and Technological Change* (Prentice-Hall Inc., Englewood Cliffs, N.J. 1962), pp. 43–65.

37 *Toward the Automatic Factory* (Yale University Press, New Haven, Conn. 1957).

38 William Faunce, among others, has noted the adverse effect of automation on work groups. See 'Automation in the Automobile Industry', *American Sociological Review*, 23 (1958), pp. 401–7. Faunce also calls

attention to other negative as well as positive features of automation.

39 See Walker, op. cit., pp. 48, 68 ff., 92 ff., 105, 213 ff.

40 Mann, op. cit.

41 *Automation in the Office* (Public Affairs Press, Washington 1961).

42 See, e.g. David Lockwood's well-known work, *The Black Coated Worker: A Study in Class Consciousness* (George Allen & Unwin, London 1958).

43 *Alienation and Freedom.* For a popular account, see 'Automation's Human Frontier: Employees Can Find New Freedom and New Dignity in the Most Up-to-Date Industries', *Country Beautiful*, 2 (June 1963), pp. 34–8.

44 See Mark Shorer's introduction to *Lady Chatterley's Lover* (Grove Press Inc, N.Y. 1959).

45 Ibid., p. 280.

46 Ibid., p. 282.

47 'Useful Work and Useless Toil', in Asa Briggs (ed.), *William Morris: Selected Writings and Designs* (Penguin Books, Harmondsworth 1962), p. 131.

48 Ibid., p. 132.

49 Ibid., p. 134.

50 Morton and Lucia White, *The Intellectual Versus the City* (Mentor Books, N.Y. 1964).

51 See Charles R. Walker, 'The Problem of the Repetitive Job', *Harvard Business Review*, 28 (May 1950), pp. 54–8.

52 Friedmann, *Anatomy of Work*, p. 46.

53 On Detroit Edison, see J. Douglas Elliott, 'Increasing Office Productivity Through Job Enlargement', in *The Human Side of the Office Manager's Job*, American Management Association, *Office Management Series*, No. 134 (1953), pp. 3–15. On Maytag, see J. F. Biggane and Paul A. Stewart, *Job Enlargement: a Case Study*, Research Series No. 25, Bureau of Labor and Management, State University of Iowa, Iowa City. 1963). On Sears, Roebuck, see the writings of James C. Worthy.

54 See e.g. M. D. Kilbridge, 'Do Workers Prefer Larger Jobs?' *Personnel*, 37 (September–October 1960), pp. 45–8; J. F. Kennedy and H. E. O'Neill, 'Job Content and Workers' Opinions', *Journal of Applied Psychology*, 42 (December 1958), pp. 372–5.

55 Charles L. Hulin and Milton R. Blood, 'Job Enlargement, Individual Differences, and Worker Responses', (University of Illinois, Urbana 1967), mimeographed.

56 'An Interdisciplinary Analysis of Job Enlargement: Technology, Costs, and Behavioral Implications', *Industrial and Labor Relations Review*, 18 (March 1965), pp. 377–95.

57 'The Problem of the Repetitive Job', p. 57.

58 William E. Reif and Peter P. Schoderbek, 'Job Enlargement: Antidote to Apathy', *Management of Personnel Quarterly*, 5 (Spring 1966), pp. 16–23.

59 Fromm argues this same point eloquently, op. cit., pp. 278 ff.

Notes to 5 *Alienation and Participation: A Review of the Literature*

1 J. R. P. French, Jr., J. Israel, and D. Aas, 'An Experiment in Participation in a Norwegian Factory', *Human Relations*, 13 (1960), p. 3.

2 Adapted from Abraham Shuchman, *Codetermination: Labor's Middle Way in Germany* (Public Affairs Press, Washington 1957), p. 6. For other scales of participation, see Delbert C. Miller and William H. Form, *Industrial Sociology*, 2nd ed. (Harper & Row Inc., N.Y. 1964), ch. 17; Rensis Likert, *New Patterns of Management* (McGraw-Hill Book Co. Inc., N.Y. 1961), pp. 242 ff.

3 For a brief historical survey of US 'partnership plans', including profit-sharing schemes, suggestion plans, wartime (I and II) joint production committees, union-opposed employee representation plans, stock distribution plans, etc., see N. Das, *Experiments in Industrial Democracy* (Asia Publishing House, N.Y. 1964), ch. 4. For the Scanlon Plan, see Frederick G. Lesieur (ed.), *The Scanlon Plan* (The Technology Press of MIT, Cambridge, Mass. 1958). I have seen no sociological research whatsoever on two interesting American economic experiments, the Merrimac Hat Company of Amesbury, Mass., owned by the United Hatters, Cap and Millinery Workers Union, or the worker-owned American Cast Iron Pipe Company of Birmingham, Alabama.

4 The original literature on these experiments is scattered but has been summarised in R. K. White and Ronald Lippitt, *Autocracy and Democracy* (Harper & Row, N.Y. 1960).

5 Kurt Lewin, 'Studies in Group Decision', in D. Cartwright and A. Zander (eds.), *Group Dynamics* (Row, Peterson, Evanston, Ill. 1953), ch. 21. For related studies or different accounts of these same studies, see Kurt Lewin, 'Group Decision and Social Change', in G. E. Swanson *et al.* (eds.), *Readings in Social Psychology* (Henry Holt, N.Y. 1947); M. Radke and D. Klisurich, 'Experiments in Changing Food Habits', *Journal of the American Dietary Association*, 23 (1947), pp. 403–9; W. Simmons, 'The Group Approach to Weight Reduction. I: A Review of the Project', *Journal of the American Dietary Association*, 30 (1954), pp. 437–41.

6 David Krech and R. S. Crutchfield, *Theory and Problems of Social Psychology* (McGraw-Hill Book Co. Inc., N.Y. 1948), p. 423. Italics in original.

7 See, e.g. J. Misumi *et al.*, 'A Cross Cultural Study of the Effect o Democratic, Authoritarian and Laissez-Faire Atmospheres in Japanes Children', *Research Bulletin of the Faculty of Education*, Kyush University, 5 (1958), pp. 41–59; Misumi, 'Experimental Studies o "Group Dynamics" in Japan', *Psychologia* 2 (1959), pp. 229–35.

8 E. B. Bennett, 'Discussion, Decision, Commitment and Consensus i "Group Decision" ', *Human Relations*, 8 (1955), pp. 251–73.

9 J. R. P. French, Jr., 'Field Experiments: Changing Group Productivity in J. G. Miller (ed.), *Experiments in Social Process* (McGraw-Hill Boo Co. Inc., N.Y. 1950), pp. 83–8.

10 Morris S. Viteles, *Motivation and Morale in Industry* (W. W. Norto & Co. Inc., N.Y. 1953), pp. 168–9.

11 L. C. Lawrence and P. C. Smith, 'Group Decision and Employe Participation', *Journal of Applied Psychology*, 39 (1955), pp. 334–7.

12 L. Coch and J. R. P. French, Jr., 'Overcoming Resistance to Change in Cartwright and Zander, op. cit., ch. 19. Originally published i *Human Relations*, 1 (1948), pp. 512–32. All page references to th former. For a spirited exchange on the subject of whether this experi ment constituted worker participation or worker manipulation, se William Gomberg, 'The Trouble with Democratic Management *Trans-action*, 3 (July–August 1966); Warren Bennis, 'A Reply', sam issue; Gomberg, 'Harwood's "Press Agentry" ', *Trans-action*, 3 (Sep tember–October 1966); Alfred J. Marrow, 'Gomberg's "Fantasy" same issue.

13 Coch and French, op cit., p. 266.

14 Ibid., p. 270.

15 J. R. P. French, Jr. *et al.*, 'Employee Participation in a Program o Industrial Change', *Personnel*, 35 (November–December 1958), pp 16–29.

16 Paul R. Lawrence, 'How to Deal with Resistance to Change', *Harvar Business Review*, 32 (1954), p. 49.

17 *Toward a Democratic Work Process* (Harper & Bros., N.Y. 1953).

18 *The Changing Culture of a Factory* (Tavistock Publications, Londo 1951), pp. 29 ff.

19 *Industrial Society* (The Free Press, Glencoe, Ill. 1955), pp. 261 ff.

20 Nancy C. Morse and E. Reimer 'The Experimental Manipulation of Major Organisational Variable', *Journal of Abnormal and Social Psycho logy*, 52 (1956), pp. 120–9.

21 Ibid., p. 122.

22 'Satisfactions and Deprivations in Industrial Life', in A. Kornhauser, R Dubin, and A. M. Ross (eds.), *Industrial Conflict* (McGraw-Hill Bool Co. Inc., N.Y. 1954), p. 105.

23 Abridged and adapted from Morse and Reimer, op. cit., p. 123.

24 Ibid., p. 127.

25 Likert, op. cit., pp. 62–9.

26 Katz, op. cit., p. 106.

27 French, Israel, and Aas, op. cit.

28 Alfred Marrow and J. R. P. French, Jr., 'Changing a Stereotype in Industry', *Journal of Social Issues*, 3 (1954), pp. 33–7.

29 Ibid., p. 36.

30 Jacob Levine and John Butler, 'Lecture vs. Group Decision in Changing Behavior', *Journal of Applied Psychology*, 36 (February 1952), pp. 29–33; also reprinted in Cartwright and Zander, op. cit., ch. 20.

31 Ibid. (Cartwright and Zander), p. 284. For another suggestive experiment—which tends to confirm the participation hypothesis—on the effects of participation by middle level managers on their job attitudes, see J. R. P. French, Jr., Emanuel Kay, and Herbert H. Meyer, 'Participation and the Appraisal System', *Human Relations*, 19 (February 1966), pp. 3–20.

32 N. Babchuck and W. J. Goode, 'Work Incentives in a Self-Determined Group', *American Sociological Review*, 16 (1951), pp. 679–87.

33 From William F. Whyte, *Money and Motivation* (Harper & Bros., N.Y. 1955), pp. 90–6.

34 Robert Blauner makes this distinction more finely by including in the former category (control over machinery) such things as the worker's control over his own time, his physical movement, and control over his technical environment. See his 'Work Satisfaction and Industrial Trends in Modern Society', in Waler Galenson and S. M. Lipset (eds.), *Labor and Trade Unionism* (John Wiley & Sons Inc., N.Y. 1960), pp. 339–60.

35 *The New Society* (Harper Torchbooks, N.Y. 1962), ch. 34.

36 Ibid., p. 301.

37 Ibid., pp. 299–300.

38 Alvin Gouldner, *Wildcat Strike* (The Antioch Press, Yellow Springs, Ohio 1954).

39 *Joy in Work* (George Allen & Unwin, London 1929), p. 202.

40 Gouldner, op. cit., pp. 50 ff.

41 Ibid., p. 68.

42 D. Katz, N. Maccoby, and N. C. Morse, *Productivity, Supervision and Morale in an Office Situation*, Part 1 (Survey Research Center, University of Michigan, Ann Arbor, Mich. 1950), p. 35.

43 Nancy C. Morse, *Satisfactions in the White Collar Job* (Survey Research Center, University of Michigan, Ann Arbor, Mich. 1953), pp. 128 ff.

44 R. L. Kahn and D. Katz, 'Leadership Practices in Relation to Productivity and Morale', in Cartwright and Zander, op. cit., p. 617.

45 I. R. Weschler, M. Hahane, and R. Tannenbaum, 'Job Satisfaction,

Productivity, and Morale: A Case Study', *Occupational Psychology*, 26 (January 1952), pp. 1–14.

46 Ibid., p. 2.

47 Adapted from ibid., p. 5.

48 H. Baumgartel, 'Leadership, Motivation, and Attitudes in Research Laboratories', *Journal of Social Issues*, 12 (1956), pp. 24–31.

49 Ibid., p. 27.

50 Adapted from ibid., p. 28.

51 F. C. Mann and H. Baumgartel, 'The Supervisor's Views on Costs', American Management Association, *Office Management Series*, No. 138 (1954), pp. 3–21.

52 Ibid., p. 11.

53 Ibid., p. 13.

54 *Some Personality Determinants of the Effects of Participation* (Prentice-Hall Inc., Englewood Cliffs, N.J. 1960).

55 Ibid., p. 34.

56 Ibid., p. 37.

57 See also F. H. Sanford, *Authoritarianism and Leadership* (Institute for Research in Human Relations, Philadelphia 1950).

58 A. S. Tannenbaum, 'Personality Change as a Result of an Experimental Change of Environmental Conditions', *Journal of Abnormal and Social Psychology*, 55 (1957), 404–6.

59 'Turnover and Employees' Feelings of Ego Involvement in the Day-to-Day Operations of a Company', *Personnel Psychology*, 4 (1951), pp. 185–97.

60 Ibid., p. 192.

61 Ibid., p. 196, emphasis added.

62 I. Ross and A. Zander, 'Need Satisfactions and Employee Turnover' *Personnel Psychology*, 10 (1957), pp. 327–38.

63 E. A. Fleishman and E. F. Harris, 'Patterns of Leadership Behavior Related to Employee Grievances and Turnover', *Personnel Psychology* 15 (Spring 1962), pp. 43–56.

64 Ibid., pp. 43–4, emphasis added.

65 D. Katz, 'Survey Research Center: An Overview of the Human Relations Program', in H. Guetzkow (ed.), *Groups, Leadership and Men* (Russell & Russell, N.Y. 1963), p. 82.

66 E. Jacobson, 'Foreman and Steward, Representatives of Management and the Union', in *Human Relations Program of the Survey Research Center: First Three Years of Development* (Institute for Social Research, University of Michigan, Ann Arbor, Mich. 1950), p. 21. See also his *Foreman-Steward Participation Practices and Worker Attitudes in a Unionised Factory* (Ph.D. dissertation, University of Michigan, Ann Arbor, Mich. 1951).

67 D. Katz, 'Satisfactions and Deprivations. . . .'

68 Ibid., p. 93.

69 D. Katz, 'Survey Research Center . . .', p. 83.

70 *Satisfactions in the White Collar Job*, p. 9.

71 Ibid., p. 135.

72 Ibid., p. 91.

73 Ibid., p. 82.

74 Ibid., pp. 138 ff.

75 'Influence: A Key to Effective Leadership in the First-Line Supervisor', *Personnel*, 28 (1952), pp. 209–17; reprinted in R. A. Sutermeister (ed.), *People and Productivity* (McGraw-Hill Book Co. Inc., N.Y. 1963), pp. 371–80. See also his 'Leadership within a Hierarchical Organisation', in A. H. Rubenstein and C. J. Haberstroh (eds.), *Some Theories of Organisation* (Dorsey Press & Richard D. Irwin, Inc., Homewood, Ill. 1960).

76 *Satisfactions . . .*, p. 133.

77 Ibid., p. 135.

78 C. M. Arensberg and D. McGregor, 'Determinants of Morale in an Industrial Company', *Applied Anthropology*, 1 (1942), pp. 12–14.

79 Lawrence, op. cit., p. 56.

80 'Leadership Practices . . .', p. 627.

81 p. 103, italics in original

82 See, e.g. Robert Blauner, 'Work Satisfaction and Industrial Trends . . .', op. cit.; F. Herzberg *et al.*, *Job Attitudes: Review of Research and Opinion* (Psychological Service of Pittsburgh, Pittsburgh 1957); Laurence Thomas, *The Occupational Structure and Education* (Prentice-Hall & Co., Englewood Cliffs, N.J. 1956), ch. 9; Victor Vroom, *Work and Motivation* (John Wiley & Sons Inc., N.Y. 1964), ch. 5.

83 Blauner, 'Work Satisfaction and Industrial Trends . . .', p. 346.

84 Ibid., italics in original.

85 Robert Blauner, *Alienation and Freedom*, p. 20.

86 Herzberg, op. cit., ch. e.

87 These three categories of what workers want from supervisors (decency, competence, and autonomy) are roughly comparable to those qualities which the Michigan Survey Research Center found important in their studies: employee orientation, the playing by the supervisor of a leadership role, and general, as opposed to close, supervision.

88 Joseph Shister and Lloyd Reynolds, *Job Horizons* (Harper & Bros., N.Y. 1949).

89 Ibid., p. 6.

90 Ibid., p. 11.

91 Ibid.

92 Ibid., p. 14.

93 Ibid., p. 13.

94 Ibid.
95 Ibid., pp. 11–12.
96 Ibid., p. 12.
97 Ibid.
98 See Kurt B. Mayer and Sidney Goldstein, 'Manual Workers as Business-men', in Arthur B. Shostak and William Gomberg (eds.), *Blue-Collar World: Studies of the American Worker* (Prentice-Hall Inc., Englewood Cliffs, N.J. 1964), pp. 537–49.

Notes to 6 *Alienation and Participation: Conclusions*

1 For an example of the sociologist's enthusiasm for destroying common sense notions, see Paul Lazarsfeld's review of *The American Soldier* partially reprinted as 'Sociology and Common Sense', in Milton L. Barron (ed.) *Contemporary Sociology* (Dodd, Mead & Co., N.Y. 1964), pp. 27–8. The sociologist Dennis Wrong has written: 'Social scientists ... greatly enjoy debunking popular myths. Some of them, indeed, appear to believe that the refutation of common sense beliefs about contemporary society provides the main justification for the existence of social science.'
2 See e.g. Douglas McGregor, *The Human Side of Enterprise* (McGraw-Hill Book Co. Inc., N.Y. 1960); Chris Argyris, 'T-Groups for Organisational Effectiveness', *Harvard Business Review*, 42 (March–April 1964); Philip Slater and Warren G. Bennis, 'Democracy is Inevitable', *Harvard Business Review*, 42 (March–April 1964); Perrin Stryker, 'How Participative Can a Company Get?', *Fortune*, 53 (September 1956); Robert C. Albrook, 'Participative Management: Time for a Second Look', *Fortune*, 75 (May 1967). For a radical criticism of this literature and more extended references, see Martin Oppenheimer, 'The "Y" Theory: Enlightened Management Confronts Alienation', *New Politics*, 6 (Winter 1967).
3 *Autocracy and Democracy* (Harper & Row, N.Y. 1960), p. 260.
4 *Personality and Organisation* (Harper & Row, N.Y. 1957).
5 M. J. Ash, 'Nondirective Teaching in Psychology: an Experimental Study', *Psychological Monographs*, 65 (1951); A. W. Halpin and B. J. Winder, *The Leadership Behavior of the Airplane Commander* (Ohio State University Research Foundation, Columbus, Ohio 1952); A. H. Halpin, 'The Leadership Behavior and Combat Performance of Airplane Commanders', *Journal of Abnormal and Social Psychology*, 49 (1954), pp. 19–22; E. P. Torrance, 'Methods of Conducting Critiques of Group Problem–Solving Performance', *Journal of Applied Psychology*, 37 (1953), pp. 394–8; L. G. Wispe, 'Evaluating Section Teaching Methods in the Introductory Course', *Journal of Educational Research*, 45 (1951), pp. 161–86.

6 'Supervision and Productivity: Empirical Findings and Theoretical Considerations', in R. Dubin *et al.*, *Leadership and Productivity* (Chandler Publishing Co., San Francisco, Calif. 1965), p. 40.

7 'Effective Supervision: An Adaptive and Relative Process', *Personnel Psychology*, 11 (1958), pp. 31–2, quoted in Dubin, ibid., pp. 41–2.

8 Ibid., p. 42.

9 Rensis Likert, *New Patterns of Management* (McGraw-Hill Book Co. Inc., N.Y. 1961), p. 245.

10 Harriet Holter, 'Attitudes towards Employee Participation in Company Decision-Making Processes: A Study of Non-Supervisory Employees in Some Norwegian Firms', *Human Relations*, 18 (November 1965), pp. 297–322.

11 See Georges Friedmann, *Anatomy of Work* (The Free Press, Glencoe, Ill. 1961), pp. 108, 125 ff.

12 See, e.g. J. E. Baker, 'Inmate Self-Government', *Journal of Criminal Law, Criminology, and Police Science*, 55 (March 1964), pp. 39–47; Daniel Glaser, *The Effectiveness of a Prison and Parole System* (The Bobbs-Merrill Co. Inc., Indianapolis 1964), pp. 217–23; E. H. Sutherland and Donald R. Cressey, *Principles of Criminology*, 6th ed. (J. P. Lippincott Co., Philadelphia 1960), pp. 490 ff; 7th ed. (1966), pp. 550–2.

13 Thomas M. Osborne, *Society and Prisons* (Yale University Press, New Haven, Conn. 1916); W. D. Lane, 'Democracy for Law Breakers', *New Republic*, 18 (8th March 1919), p. 173; Frank Tannenbaum, *Osborne of Sing Sing* (University of North Carolina Press, Chapel Hill, N.C. 1933).

14 Op. cit., p. 218.

15 F. E. Haynes, *Criminology* (The Macmillan Co., N.Y. 1935).

Notes to 7 *The Case against Workers' Management: Hugh Clegg's World of Industrial Democracy*

1 See, e.g. C. A. R. Crossland, 'What Does the Worker Want?' *Encounter* (February 1959), pp. 10–17. Clegg has also influenced foreign scholars. See, e.g. N. Das, *Experiments in Industrial Democracy* (Asia Publishing House, N.Y. 1964).

2 Blackwell, London 1951.

3 Blackwell, London 1960.

4 *Industrial Democracy*, p. 14.

5 Ibid., p. 131.

6 Ibid., p. 121.

7 Ibid., p. 73.

8 Ibid., p. 5.

9 Ibid., pp. 28 ff.

10 Ibid., p. 131.

11 Ibid., p. 133.

12 Ibid., p. 91. It is paradoxical that the Labour Government, which implicitly shares Clegg's views, is now attempting 'to integrate the trade unions in the machinery and ethos of planned capitalism', via wage restraints, increasing labour productivity, and so on, in order to lift the performance of the lagging British economy. See Tony Topham, 'The Campaign for Workers' Control in Britain', *International Socialist Journal*, 2 (August 1965), p. 473.

13 *Industrial Democracy*, p. 139.

14 Ibid., p. 126.

15 Royden Harrison, 'Retreat from Industrial Democracy,' *New Left Review*, 1 (July–August 1960), p. 34.

16 Ibid.

17 *Industrial Democracy*, p. 41.

18 Ibid., p. 22, emphasis added.

19 Ibid., p. 24.

20 *A New Approach*, p. 36.

21 Ibid., p. 91.

22 Ibid., p. 29.

23 Ibid., p. 21.

24 Ibid., p. 29.

25 Ibid., p. 22.

26 Abraham Shuchman, *Codetermination: Labor's Middle Way in Germany* (Public Affairs Press, Washington, 1957), p. 148.

27 See W. M. Blumenthal, *Codetermination in the German Steel Industry* (Industrial Relations Sections, Dept. of Economics and Sociology, Princeton University, Princeton, N.J. 1956), Research Report Series No. 94, p. 29.

28 Shuchman, op. cit., p. 152.

29 *A New Approach*, p. 94.

30 Ibid., p. 55.

31 Ibid.

32 Ibid., p. 54.

33 Ibid., p. 56.

34 Ibid.

35 Ibid., p. 98.

36 Ibid., p. 67.

37 Ibid., p. 69.

38 Ibid., p. 102.

39 Ibid.

40 Ibid., p. 67.

41 For an extended discussion of the Histadrut in the light of Clegg's

thesis, see my *Workers' Management in Comparative Analysis* (Ph.D. dissertation, University of California, Berkeley, 1966), ch. 5.

42 *Israel Economist*, 20 (August 1964), p. 143.

43 Haim Barkai, 'The Public, Private and Histadrut Sectors in the Israeli Economy', *Falk Project for Economic Research in Israel*. Sixth Report, 1961–3 (Jerusalem 1964), p. 39.

44 Milton Derber, 'Worker Participation in Industrial Management in Israel', (Institute of Labor and Industrial Relations, University of Ill. 1962), mimeographed, p. 21. Published in abridged form in *Industrial Relations*, 3 (October 1963). All page references are to the former.

45 Y. Rim and Bilha F. Mannheim, 'Factors Related to Attitudes of Management and Union Representatives', *Personnel Psychology*, 17 (Summer 1964), pp. 149–65.

46 Derber, op. cit., pp. 20–1.

47 Ferdynand Zweig, *The Israeli Worker: Achievements, Attitudes, and Aspirations* (Herzl Press, N.Y. 1959), pp. 161–3, 166, 217.

48 Ibid., p. 217.

49 Ibid., p. 219. See also H. M. Kallen, *Utopians at Bay* (Herzl Foundation, N.Y., 1958), and issues of the Histadrut publication, *Work*, for this problem and the methods attempted to combat it.

50 See my *Workers' Management in Comparative Analysis*, ch. 5.

51 For a brief discussion, see Georges Friedmann, *The End of the Jewish People?* (Doubleday & Co., N.Y. 1967), pp. 102 ff.

52 *A New Approach*, p. 77.

53 Ibid., p. 99.

54 Ibid., pp. 99–100.

55 Ibid., p. 22.

56 Ibid., p. 114.

57 This summary of works council functions is taken from Adolph Sturmthal, *Workers' Councils: A Study of Workplace Organization on Both Sides of the Iron Curtain*, (Harvard University Press 1964, Cambridge, Mass.), p. 63.

58 Ibid., p. 72.

59 Ibid., p. 76.

60 *A New Approach*, p. 54. Sturmthal doubts that councils have played this role except during World War I. See pp. 161–2.

61 Herbert J. Spiro, *The Politics of German Codetermination* (Harvard University Press, Cambridge, Mass. 1958), p. 153.

62 *A New Approach*, p. 56.

63 Ibid., p. 114.

64 Quoted in Sturmthal, op. cit., p. 159.

65 Ibid., p. 162.

66 Ibid., p. 156.

67 Spiro, op. cit., p. 172.
68 G. D. H. Cole, *Guild Socialism Restated* (Leonard Parsons, London 1920), p. 32.
69 Ibid., p. 15.
70 Ibid., pp. 32–3.
71 Ibid., p. 33.
72 Ibid., p. 34.
73 Sturmthal, op. cit., p. 169.
74 Spiro, op. cit., p. 160.
75 *A New Approach*, p. 114.
76 Spiro, op. cit., p. 160.
77 *A New Approach*, p. 27.
78 From a DGB pamphlet, quoted in Shuchman, op. cit., p. 205.
79 Ibid.
80 Ibid., p. 239.

Notes to 8 *On the Origins of Workers' Management in Yugoslavia**

1 See, e.g. Fitzroy MacLean, *The Heretic: The Life and Times of Josip Broz-Tito* (Harper & Bros., N.Y. 1957).
2 See Milovan Djilas, *Conversation with Stalin* (Harcourt, Brace, & World, N.Y. 1962).
3 Ibid.
4 Vladimir Dedijer, *Tito* (Simon & Schuster, N.Y. 1953). This work contains the best and most thorough treatment in English of the nature of the joint stock companies that Stalin attempted to establish in Yugoslavia.
5 See Robert Bass and Elizabeth Marbury (eds.), *The Soviet-Yugoslav Controversy, 1948–1958: A Documentary Record* (Prospect Books, N.Y. 1959).
6 Iliya Jukic, *Tito between East and West* (Demos Pub. Co., London 1961), p. 2.
7 *Yugoslav Communism, a Crticial Study*, prepared by Charles Zalar for the Senate subcommittee to investigate the administration of the Internal Security Act and other internal security laws, 87th Cong.: 1st Sess. (Washington 1961), p. 149.
8 Louis Adamic, *The Eagle and the Roots* (Doubleday & Co. Inc., N.Y. 1952).
9 R. Barry Farrell, *Yugoslavia and the Soviet Union, 1948–1956: An Analysis with Documents* (Hamden Shoe String Press, N.Y. 1956), p. 142.
10 *Marxism, Feeedom and the State* (Freedom Press, London 1950), p. 32.

* An earlier and abridged version of this chapter appeared in *Root and Branch* (Berkeley, Calif.), No. 2 (1963).

11 Ibid., pp. 37ff.

12 Ibid., p. 52.

13 Roberto Michels, 'Intellectual Socialists', in George B. de Huszar (ed.), *The Intellectuals* (The Free Press, Glencoe, Ill.1960), pp. 318–9.

14 See Henry Mayer, 'Marx and Bakunin: A Neglected Text', and Karl Marx, 'Marginal Notes on Bakunin's "Statism and Anarchy",' in *Etudes de Marxologie* (October 1959). I am indebted to Lewis Feuer for this reference.

15 *The End of Ideology* (Collier Books, N.Y. 1961), p. 367. See also p. 357 for Sidney Hook's early Marxist view on this point.

16 'Critique of the Gotha Program', in Lewis S. Feuer (ed.), *Marx and Engels: Basic Writings on Politics and Philosophy* (Doubleday & Co. Inc., N.Y. 1959), p. 125, emphasis added.

17 Milovan Djilas, *On New Roads of Socialism* (Belgrade 1950), pp. 9–10.

18 *The Managerial Revolution* (Indiana University Press, Bloomington, Indiana 1960), pp. 92 ff.

19 *The New Class: An Analysis of the Communist System* (Frederick A. Praeger Inc., N.Y. 1957), p. 44.

20 Using the term 'state capitalism' in a purely economic sense and not polemically, one could argue, however ironically, that the Yugoslav system more closely approximates this form than any other existing today. Hilferding once said that there could be no such thing as state capitalism because capitalism is defined in terms of a market economy and competition, both of which state ownership eliminates. (See Rudolf Hilferding, 'State Capitalism or Totalitarian State Economy', in C. Wright Mills (ed.), *The Marxists* (Dell, N.Y. 1962), pp. 334–9.) The Yugoslav system, however, does possess elements both of a market economy and competition within the framework of state or social ownership, and so could conceivably be called state capitalist were it not for the connotation which the term has acquired. The Chinese have gone a step further of late and now refer to Yugoslavia as an outright capitalist society and have developed an *ad hoc* theory of peaceful transition from socialism to capitalism (!) which is subscribed to, in part, by some American Marxists. See 'Peaceful Transition from Socialism to Capitalism?' *Monthly Review*, 15 (March 1964), pp. 569–90.

21 *The Great Soviet Encyclopedia*, quoted in Isaac Deutscher, *Soviet Trade Unions* (Royal Institute for International Affairs, London 1950), p. 123.

22 Djilas, *On New Roads . . .*, pp. 12 ff.

23 The 1958 Draft Programme of the Yugoslav League of Communists, in Bass and Marbury, op. cit., pp. 131ff.

24 Tito's speech at Pula, 11th November 1956, in ibid., p. 70.

25 Kardelj's speech to the Federal People's Assembly of Yugoslavia, 6th December 1956, in ibid., p. 91.

26 Quoted in Julian Towster, *Political Power in the USSR* (Oxford University Press, N.Y., 1948), p. 13.

27 Edvard Kardelj, 'Socialist Democracy in Yugoslavia', in Farrell, op. cit., pp. 146–60.

28 Edvard Kardelj, as quoted in Charles McVicker, *Titoism: Pattern for International Communism* (St Martin's Press, N.Y. 1957), p. 137.

29 Leon Gersković, as quoted in ibid., p. 33.

30 Jovan Djordjević, 'About Socialist Democracy', *Review of International Affairs*, 4 (1st January 1955), p. 17. For a fine statement on the alienation of the modern worker and his presumed emancipation and integration under a system of workers' management, see Edvard Kardelj, 'The Individual in the Yugoslav Social System', *Review of International Affairs*, 13 (20th March 1962), pp. 16–19, or in *Socialist Thought and Practice*, No. 5 (January 1962), pp. 5–14.

31 Ernest Halperin, *The Triumphant Heretic* (Heinemann, London 1958), p. 237.

32 T. T. Hammond, 'Yugoslav Elections: Democracy in Small Doses', *Political Science Quarterly*, 70 (1955), p. 58.

33 'Responsibility and History', in Edmund Stillman (ed.), *Bitter Harvest: The Intellectual Revolt Behind the Iron Curtain* (Frederick A. Praeger Inc., N.Y. 1959), pp. 121–2.

34 Ibid., pp. 134–5.

35 *The New Class*, p. 66.

36 Fred Warner Neal and Winston M. Fisk, 'Yugoslavia: Towards a Market Socialism', *Problems of Communism*, 15 (November–December 1966), p. 34.

37 Stephen S. Anderson, 'Economic "Reform" in Yugoslavia', *Current History*, 52 (April 1967), p. 218.

38 United Nations General Assembly, *Report of the Special Committee on the Problems of Hungary*, Eleventh Session, Suppl. No. 18 (A/3592) (New York 1957), p. 68.

39 Isaac Deutscher, *Russia in Transition* (Grove Press Inc., N.Y. 1960), p. 25.

40 David Burg [pseud.], 'Observations on University Students', *Daedalus* 89 v (Summer 1960), p. 53.

41 29th December 1967, p. 27.

42 *Russia in Transition*, pp. 56–7.

Notes to 9 *The Yugoslav Experience*

1 From a communication from G. N. Ostergaard. To my knowledge, a history of the theory and practice of workers' control in Western socialism has never been written.

2 I am indebted for this idea to G. D. H. Cole, *The Case for Industrial Partnership* (St Martin's Press, N.Y. 1957), p. 7, and to Royden Harrison, 'Retreat from Industrial Democracy', *New Left Review*, 1 (July–August 1960), pp. 32–8.

3 *Congress of Workers' Councils of Yugoslavia*, ed. of the Central Council of the Confederation of Trade Unions of Yugoslavia (Belgrade 1957), p. 38, emphasis added.

4 'The German Ideology', in Lewis S. Feuer (ed.), *Marx and Engels: Basic Writings on Politics and Philosophy* (Doubleday & Co. Inc., N.Y. 1959), p. 257.

5 'Civil War in France', ibid., p. 370.

6 'Economic and Philosophical Manuscripts', in Erich Fromm, *Marx's Concept of Man* (Frederick Ungar Pub. Co. Inc., N.Y. 1961), p. 99. See also pp. 104–5, 151, 206–7.

7 Introduction to 'Civil War in France', in Feuer, op. cit., p. 359.

8 In Feuer, pp. 481–5.

9 Ibid., p. 483.

10 'Totalitarian Imperialism', *Journal of Politics*, 20 (1958), p. 29.

11 'On Workers' Control of Production', *New International* (May–June 1951), p. 177.

12 See Leon Gerskovié,' 'On the Real Road to Socialism', *Review of International Affairs*, 1 (5th July 1950), p. 8 for a bold attempt.

13 Isaac Deutscher, *Soviet Trade Unions* (Royal Institute for International Affairs, London 1950), esp. ch. 2.

14 Ibid., p. 29.

15 Ibid., p. 62.

16 Among the major works of the guild socialist school are: G. D. H. Cole, *Chaos and Order in Industry* (Stokes, N.Y. 1920); *Guild Socialism Restated* (L. Parsons, London 1920); *Self-Government in Industry* (G. Bell and Sons, London 1917); Cole and W. Mellor, *The Meaning of Industrial Freedom* (George Allen & Unwin, London 1919); S. G. Hobson, *National Guilds*, edited by A. R. Orage (G. Bell and Sons, London 1914); A. J. Penty, *A Guildsman's Interpretation of History* (George Allen and Unwin, London 1920); M. B. Reckitt and C. E. Bechhofer, *The Meaning of National Guilds* (Cecil Palmer, London 1918). The best known history of guild socialism, written decades ago, is Niles Carpenter, *Guild Socialism* (D. Appleton and Co., N.Y. 1922).

17 Eric S. Heffer, 'G. D. H. Cole and Workers' Control', *The Review: A Quarterly of Socialist Pluralism*, 4 (1962), p. 73.

18 Cole, *Self-Government in Industry*, pp. 5, 114, 122, 154, 197. 206, 218, 255; *Guild Socialism Restated*, pp. 30, 40–1; Cole and Mellor, pp. 3–4, 25–6, 39.

19 Cole and Mellor, pp. 39–40, 42; Cole, *Self-Government in Industry*, pp. 108–10, 281, 283.

20 Cole, *Self-Government in Industry*, pp. 244, 246; *Guild Socialism Restated*, p. 61.

21 Cole, *Self-Government in Industry*, pp. 81–3, 85–6, 91–2, 242; *Guild Socialism Restated*, pp. 12–14, 31.

22 Cole, *Guild Socialism Restated*, chs. 8–9.

23 Zivko Topalović, 'Who are the Factory Owners?', *Review* (published by the study centre for Yugoslav affairs), 2 (1961), p. 91.

24 See George W. Hoffman and Fred Warner Neal, *Yugoslavia and the New Communism* (Twentieth Century Fund, N.Y. 1962). for a balanced appraisal of Yugoslavia's decentralised system of social management.

25 *Workers' Management in Yugoslavia* (Geneva 1962).

26 *New Yugoslav Law*, 1 (June–September 1950), pp. 75–83.

27 Averages compiled from the data given in 'Basic Statistics: Workers' Councils and Boards of Management in Economic Enterprises, 1952–1960', *Yugoslav Survey*, 2 (July–September 1961), p. 916.

28 *Yugoslav Life*, 9 (May–June 1964), p. 6.

29 'Basic Law . . .', p. 77.

30 Benjamin Ward, *From Marx to Barone: Socialism and the Postwar Yugoslav Industrial Firm* (Ph.D. dissertation, University of California, Berkeley 1956), p. 76.

31 Ward's data for 1954 reveal that at most there were multiple lists in only 11·5 per cent of the elections. See Ibid., p. 140. Data given for 1956 by the *Congress of Workers' Councils of Yugoslavia* indicate that multiple lists occurred in no more than 14.4 per cent of the elections in that year.

32 Benjamin Ward, 'Workers' Management in Yugoslavia', *Journal of Political Economy*, 65 (October 1957). In a reply and rejoinder, Horvat and Rašcović claim that usually all the seats are contested, but this I feel is an optimistic conjecture. See B. Horvat and V. Rašcović, 'Reply and Rejoinder', *Journal of Political Economy*, 67 (April 1959).

33 *Workers' Management in Yugoslavia*, p. 79.

34 Ibid., p. 80.

35 Ibid., p. 303.

36 The following argument is presented by Horvat and Rašcović.

37 *Workers' Management in Yugoslavia*, p. 79.

38 *Review: Yugoslav Monthly Magazine*, 4 (September 1964), p. 7.

39 A slightly different procedure, but one which also by-passes the trade union, is described in 'Election of Managing Bodies in Working Organisations', *Yugoslav Survey*, 5 (April–June 1964), pp. 2473–80.

40 Jiri Kolaja, *Workers' Councils: The Yugoslav Experience* (Tavistock Publications, London 1965).

41 ILO, op. cit., pp. 121 ff.

42 Ibid., pp. 124–5.

43 For the complex determination of personal income, see ibid., pp. 126 ff.

44 J. Davičo and M. Bogosavljević, *The Economy of Yugoslavia* (Belgrade, 1960), part 3, 'The Economic System'.

45 *Yugoslav Life*, 8 (September 1963), p. 9, and 9 (April 1964), p. 1.

46 See 'Election of Managing Bodies. . . .'

47 ILO, op. cit., p. 96.

48 Ibid., p. 97.

49 Several years ago the Yugoslav press reported that the president of the Serbian trade unions submitted to a four hour question and answer period at a large lead and zinc mine. The questions the workers put to him were the kind workers might put to their employers: Why were earnings so low? Why was the distribution of income so unequal? etc. See *Review: Yugoslav Monthly Magazine*, 1 (March 1961), p. 13.

50 Adolph Sturmthal, *Workers' Councils* (Harvard University Press, Cambridge, Mass 1964), p. 170.

51 ILO, op. cit., p. 203.

52 Ibid., p. 97.

53 Sturmthal, op. cit., p. 109.

54 Op. cit., p. 87.

55 See 'Basic Statistics . . .', for validation of the third point. I have not read any criticism, Communist or non-Communist, to the effect that the other two provisions have been violated.

56 ILO, op. cit., p. 85.

57 Ibid., p. 108.

58 Ibid., pp. 105–6.

59 Ernest Halperin, *The Triumphant Heretic* (Heinemann, London 1958), p. 138.

60 See Fred Warner Neal, *Titoism in Action* (University of California Press, Berkeley and Los Angeles, California 1958), ch. 6 for these developments, unless otherwise cited.

61 Charles McVicker, *Titoism: Pattern for International Communism* (St Martin's Press, N.Y. 1957), p. 85, emphasis added.

62 Statement by J. Davičo in International Labour Organisation, *Labor-Management Series*, No. 5, 'Workers' Management and Labor Relations in Yugoslavia', record of an informal discussion held on 16 June 1958 in connection with the 42nd session of the International Labour Conference (Geneva 1958), p. 14.

63 *Yugoslav Survey*, 8 (August 1967), p. 111.

64 *Workers' Management in Yugoslavia*, p. 92.

65 Ibid., p. 168.

66 Ibid., p. 169.

67 Ibid., p. 115.

68 Ibid.

69 Ibid., p. 89.

70 Ibid., pp. 276 ff; cf. Djuro Salaj, 'Experiences and Perspectives of Self-Government of Producers in Yugoslavia', in *Congress of Workers' Councils of Yugoslavia*, pp. 13 ff.

71 In 1960 total employment in the socialist sector was 2.8 million. See 'Rise in Employment from 1957 to 1960', in *Yugoslav Survey*, 2 (July–September, 1961), p. 795.

72 Hoffman and Neal, op. cit., p. 206.

73 ILO, *Workers' Management in Yugoslavia*, p. 33.

74 Op. cit., p. 136.

75 *From Marx to Barone*, . . . p. 141.

76 Neal, op. cit., p. 136.

77 'Basic Statistics . . .', p. 916.

78 Leonard Sayles and Georges Strauss, *The Local Union* (Harper & Bros., N.Y. 1953), pp. 143 ff.

79 Compiled and computed from 'Rise in Employment . . .', p. 799 and 'Basic Statistics . . .', p. 916.

80 For the figure on the agricultural labour force, see Neal, op. cit., p. 186; for an estimate on part time peasant workers, see McVicker, op. cit., pp. 74–5.

81 Neal, op. cit., p. 140.

82 Compiled and computed from 'Basic Statistics . . .', p. 916 and *Statistical Pocketbook of Yugoslavia* (Belgrade 1960), p. 36.

83 Op. cit., p. 211.

84 'Basic Statistics . . .', p. 916 and *Statistical Pocketbook of Yugoslavia*, p. 36.

85 *Review: Yugoslav Monthly Magazine*, 2 (April 1962), p. 7.

86 See Ely Chinoy, *Automobile Workers and the American Dream* (The Beacon Press, Boston, Mass. 1955).

87 Ward, *From Marx to Barone* . . ., p. 186.

88 Ibid., p. 187.

89 Ibid., p. 190.

90 Ibid., p. 191.

91 Hoffman and Neal, op. cit., p. 307.

92 *Yugoslav Survey*, 3 (October–December 1962), p. 1583.

93 Ibid.

94 *Yugoslav Survey*, 8 (August 1967), p. 111.

95 Op. cit., p. 391.

96 See e.g. Stephen S. Anderson, 'Economic "Reform" in Yugoslavia', *Current History*, 52 (April 1967), pp. 214–19.

97 *Yugoslav Survey*, 7 (October–December 1966), p. 4002.

98 *Yugoslav Survey*, 8 (August 1967), p. 111.

99 *Workers' Management in Yugoslavia*, p. 74.

100 See, e.g. S. Kavčič, *The Worker as Personality* (Belgrade, 1962) or E. Kardelj, 'The Individual in the Yugoslav Social System', *Socialist Thought and Practice* (January 1962), pp. 5–14.

101 Jiri Kolaja, 'A Yugoslav Workers' Council', *Human Organization*, 20 (Spring 1961).

102 'A Yugoslav Workers' Council', p. 29.

103 *A Polish Factory* (University of Kentucky Press, Lexington 1960), p. 118.

104 Ibid., p. 117.

105 'A Yugoslav Workers' Council', emphasis added.

106 *Workers' Councils: The Yugoslav Experience.*

107 Hoffman and Neal, op. cit., p. 374.

108 See *Review: Yugoslav Monthly Magazine*, 2 (May 1962), p. 14.

109 Adapted from ibid.

110 *Look East, Look West: The Socialist Adventure in Yugoslavia* (The Macmillan Co., N.Y. 1966).

111 For one of many good discussions of the 1965 reform, see Fred Warner Neal and Winston M. Fisk, 'Yugoslavia; towards a Market Socialism', *Problems of Communism*, 15 (November–December 1966), pp. 28–37.

112 For Tito's attack on Ranković and the security police at the 4th meeting of the Central Committee of the Yugoslav League of Communists in July 1966, see *Yugoslav Survey*, 7 (October–December 1966), pp. 3915 ff.

113 See *The New York Times*, 31st December 1967, pp. 1, 6; 13th January 1968, p. 8.

The Participation Literature:
A Selected Bibliography

Allport, Gordon A., 'The Psychology of Participation', *Psychological Review*, 53 (1945), pp. 117–32.

Arensberg, C. M. and D. McGregor, 'Determinants of Morale in an Industrial Company', *Applied Anthropology*, 1 (1942), pp. 12–14.

—— and G. Tootell, 'Plant Sociology: Real Discoveries and New Problems', in M. Komarovsky (ed.), *Common Frontiers in the Social Sciences* (Free Press, Glencoe, Ill. 1957).

Argyle, Michael, Godfrey Gardner, and Frank Ciofi, 'The Measurement of Supervisory Methods', *Human Relations*, 10 (1957), pp. 295–313.

—— 'Supervisory Methods Related to Productivity, Absenteeism, and Labor Turnover', *Human Relations*, 11 (1958), pp. 23–40.

Argyris, Chris, *Integrating the Individual and the Organization* (John Wiley, N.Y., 1964).

—— *Personality and Organisation* (Harper & Bros., N.Y., 1957).

Babchuck, N. and W. J. Goode, 'Work Incentives in a Self-Determined Group', *American Sociological Review*, 16 (October 1951), pp. 679–87.

Baker, J. E., 'Inmate Self-Government', *Journal of Criminal Law, Criminology, and Police Science*, 55 (March 1964), pp. 39–47.

Baumgartel, H., 'Leadership, Motivation, and Attitudes in Research Laboratories', *Journal of Social Issues*, 12 (1956), pp. 24–31.

Bavelas, A., 'Morale and the Training of Leaders', in G. Watson (ed.), *Civilian Morale* (Houghton Mifflin, Boston 1942).

—— 'Some Problems of Organisational Change', *Journal of Social Issues*, 4 (Summer 1948), pp. 48–52.

Bennett, E. B., 'Discussion, Decision, Commitment and Consensus in "Group Decision" ', *Human Relations*, 8 (1955), pp. 251–73.

Blauner, Robert, *Alienation and Freedom* (University of Chicago Press, Chicago, Ill. 1964).

—— 'Work Satisfaction and Industrial Trends in Modern Society', in Walter Galenson and S. M. Lipset (eds.), *Labor and Trade Unionism* (John Wiley, N.Y. 1960).

Blum, Fred H., *Toward a Democratic Work Process* (Harper and Bros., N.Y. 1953).

Bradford, L. and R. Lippitt, 'Building a Democratic Work Group', *Personnel*, 22 (November 1945), pp. 142–52.

Carey, H. H., 'Consultative Supervision and Management', *Personnel*, 18 (March 1942), pp. 286–95.

Coch, L. and J. R. P. French, Jr., 'Overcoming Resistance to Change', *Human Relations*, 1 (1948), pp. 512–32.

Davis, R. C., 'Factors Related to Scientific Research Performance', *Interpersonal Factors in Research*, Part I (Survey Research Center, University of Michigan, Ann Arbor, Mich. 1954), ch. 1.

Day, R. C. and R. L. Hamblin, 'Some Effects of Close and Punitive Styles of Supervision', *American Journal of Sociology*, 69 (March 1964), pp. 499–510.

Drucker, Peter F., *The New Society* (Harper Torchbooks, N.Y. 1962).

—— *The Practice of Management* (Heinemann, London 1955).

Dubin, Robert, 'Industrial Workers' Worlds: A Study of the Central Life Interests of Industrial Workers', *Social Forces*, 3 (January 1956), pp. 131–42.

—— George C. Homans, Floyd C. Mann, and Delbert Miller, *Leadership and Productivity: Some Facts of Industrial Life* (Chandler Publishing Co., San Francisco, Calif. 1965).

Faw, V., 'A Psychotherapeutic Method of Teaching Psychology', *American Psychologist*, 4 (1949), pp. 104–9.

Fleishman, E. A. and E. F. Harris, 'Patterns of Leadership Behavior Related to Employee Grievances and Turnover', *Personnel Psychology*, 15 (Spring 1962), pp. 43–56.

—— E. F. Harris, and R. D. Burtt, *Leadership and Supervision in Industry* (Ohio State University Press, Columbus, Ohio 1955).

French, J. R. P., Jr., 'Field Experiments: Changing Group Productivity', in J. G. Miller (ed.), *Experiments in Social Process* (McGraw-Hill, N.Y. 1950).

—— *et al.*, 'Employee Participation in a Program of Industrial Change', *Personnel*, 35 (November–December 1958), pp. 16–29.

—— J. Israel, and D. Aas, 'An Experiment in Participation in a Norwegian Factory', *Human Relations*, 13 (1960), pp. 3–10.

—— Emanuel Kay, and Herbert H. Meyer, 'Participation and the Appraisal System', *Human Relations*, 19 (February 1966), pp. 3–20.

Georgopoulos, B. S. and A. S. Tannenbaum, 'A Study of Organisational Effectiveness', *American Sociological Review*, 22 (October 1957), pp. 534–40.

Goode, C. E., 'Better than the Profit Motive', *Advanced Management*, 19 (1954), pp. 17–20.

Gouldner, Alvin W., *Patterns of Industrial Bureaucracy* (The Free Press, Glencoe, Ill. 1954).

—— *Wildcat Strike*, (The Antioch Press, Yellow Springs, Ohio 1954).

Guetzkow, H. (ed.), *Groups, Leadership and Men* (Russell and Russell, N.Y. 1963).

Halpin, A. W., 'The Leadership Behavior and Combat Performance of Airplane Commanders', *Journal of Abnormal and Social Psychology*, 49 (January 1954), pp. 19–22.

—— and B. J. Winer, *The Leadership Behavior of the Airplane Commander* (Ohio State University Research Foundation, Columbus, Ohio 1952).

Hare, A. P., 'Small Group Discussions with Participatory and Supervisory Leadership', *Journal of Abnormal and Social Psychology*, 48 (1953), pp. 273–5.

Herzberg, F. *et al.*, *Job Attitudes: Review of Research and Opinion* (Psychological Service of Pittsburgh, Pittsburgh, 1957).

Holter, Harriet, 'Attitudes towards Employee Participation in Company Decision-Making Processes: A Study of Non-Supervisory Employees in Some Norwegian Firms', *Human Relations*, 18 (November 1965), pp. 297–322.

Hood, R. C., 'Concern for Cost: A Participative Approach', American Management Association, *Manufacturing Series* No. 221 (1956), pp. 24–40.

Jackson, Jay M., 'The Effect of Changing the Leadership of Small Work Groups', *Human Relations*, 6 (1953), pp. 25–44.

Jacobson, E., 'Foreman and Steward, Representatives of Management and the Union', *Human Relations Program of the Survey Research Center: First Three Years of Development* (Institute for Social Research, University of Michigan, Ann Arbor, Mich. 1950).

—— *Foreman-Steward Participation Practices and Worker Attitudes in a Unionized Factory* (Ph.D. dissertation, University of Michigan, Ann Arbor, Mich. 1951).

Jaques, Elliott, *The Changing Culture of a Factory* (Tavistock Publications, London 1951).

Kahn, R. L. and D. Katz, 'Leadership Practices in Relation to Productivity and Morale', in D. Cartwright and A. Zander (eds.), *Group Dynamics* (Row, Peterson & Co., Evanston, Ill. 1953).

—— and Nancy C. Morse, 'Morale and Productivity', *Journal of Social Issues*, 7 (1951), pp. 16–17.

Katz, D., 'Satisfactions and Deprivations in Industrial Life', in A. Kornhauser *et al.*, (eds.), *Industrial Conflict* (McGraw-Hill, N.Y. 1954).

—— and R. L. Kahn, 'Human Organisation and Worker Motivation', in L. R. Tripp (ed.), *Industrial Productivity* (Industrial Relations Research Association, Madison, Wisconsin 1951).

—— 'Some Recent Findings in Human Relations Research', in G. E. Swanson, T. M. Newcomb, and E. L. Hartley (eds.), *Readings in Social Psychology* (Henry Holt, N.Y. 1952).

—— N. Maccoby, G. Gurin, G. Floor, *Productivity, Supervision and Morale among Railroad Workers* (Institute for Social Research, University of Michigan, Ann Arbor, Mich. 1951).

—— N. Maccoby, and N. C. Morse, *Productivity, Supervision and Morale in an Office Situation*, Part I (Survey Research Center, University of Michigan, Ann Arbor, Mich. 1950).

Kelly, H. H., 'Communication in Experimentally Created Hierarchies', *Human Relations*, 4 (1951), pp. 39–56.

Lawrence, L. C. and P. C. Smith, 'Group Decision and Employee Participation', *Journal of Applied Psychology*, 39 (1955), pp. 334–7.

Lawrence, Paul R., 'How to Deal with Resistance to Change', *Harvard Business Review*, 32 (1954), pp. 49–57.

Levine, Jacob and John Butler, 'Lecture vs Group Decision in Changing Behavior', *Journal of Applied Psychology*, 36 (February 1952), pp. 29–33.

Lewin, Kurt, 'Frontiers in Group Dynamics', *Human Relations*, 1 (June 1947), pp. 5–47.

—— 'Group Decision and Social Change', in E. Swanson *et al.*, (eds.), *Readings in Social Psychology* (Henry Holt, N.Y. 1947).

—— 'Studies in Group Decision', in D. Cartwright and A. Zander (eds.), *Group Dynamics* (Row, Peterson & Co., Evanston, Ill. 1953).

Likert, Rensis, *New Patterns of Management* (McGraw-Hill, N.Y. 1961).

—— C. Argyris, and H. Sheppard, 'Management Implications of Recent Social Science Research—a Symposium', *Personnel Administration*, 21 (1958), pp. 5–14.

Maier, Norman R. F., 'An Experimental Test of the Effect of Training on Discussion Leadership', *Human Relations*, 6 (1953), pp. 161–73.

—— 'The Quality of Group Decisions as Influenced by the Discussion Leader', *Human Relations*, 3 (1950), pp. 155–74.

—— and L. R. Hoffman, 'Group Decision in England and the United States', *Personnel Psychology*, 15 (Spring 1962), pp. 75–87.

Mann, Floyd C. and H. Baumgartel, *Absences and Employee Attitudes in an Electric Power Company* (Survey Research Center, University of Michigan, Ann Arbor, Mich. 1952).

—— 'The Supervisor's Views on Costs', American Management Association, *Office Management Series*, No. 138 (1954), pp. 3–21.

Mann, Floyd C. and J. K. Dent, *Appraisals of Supervisors and the Attitudes of Their Employees in an Electric Power Company* (Survey Research Center, University of Michigan, Ann Arbor, Mich. 1954).

Marrow, Alfred, and J. R. P. French, Jr. 'Changing a Stereotype in Industry', *Journal of Social Issues*, 3 (1945), pp. 33–7.

McMurry, Robert N., 'The Case for Benevolent Autocracy', *Harvard Business Review*, 36 (1958), pp. 82–90.

Misumi, J., 'Experimental Studies on "Group Dynamics" in Japan', *Psychologia*, 2 (1959), pp. 229–35.

—— *et al.*, 'A Cross Cultural Study of the Effect of Democratic, Authoritarian and Laissez-faire Atmospheres in Japanese Children', *Research*

Bulletin of the Faculty of Education, Kyushu University, 5 (1958), pp. 41–59.

Morse, Nancy C., *Satisfactions in the White Collar Job*, (Survey Research Center, University of Michigan, Ann Arbor, Mich. 1953).

—— and E. Reimer, 'The Experimental Manipulation of a Major Organisational Variable', *Journal of Abnormal and Social Psychology*, 52 (1956), pp. 120–9.

—— and Robert S. Weiss, 'The Function and Meaning of Work and the Job', *American Sociological Review*, 20 (April 1955), pp. 191–8.

Mowrer, O. H., 'Authoritarian vs "Self-Government" in the Management of Children's Aggressive Reactions as a Preparation for Citizenship in a Democracy', *Journal of Social Psychology*, 10 (1939), pp. 121–6.

Neel, R. G., *Factors Related to Productivity* (Survey Research Center, University of Michigan, Ann Arbor, Mich. 1952).

Palmer, Gladys, 'Attitudes toward Work in an Industrial Community', *American Journal of Sociology*, 63 (1957), pp. 17–26.

Pelz, Donald C., 'Influence: A Key to Effective Leadership in the First-Line Supervisor', *Personnel*, 28 (November 1952), pp. 209–17.

—— 'Leadership within a Hierarchical Organisation', in A. H. Rubenstein and C. J. Haberstroh (eds.) *Some Theories of Organization* (Dorsey Press and Richard D. Irwin, Inc., Homewood, Ill. 1960).

—— *Power and Leadership in the First-Line Supervisor* (Survey Research Center, University of Michigan, Ann Arbor, Mich. 1951).

Preston, M. G. and R. K. Heintz, 'Effects of Participatory vs Supervisory Leadership on Group Judgment', *Journal of Abnormal and Social Psychology*, 44 (1949), pp. 345–55.

Radke, M. and D. Klisurich, 'Experiments in Changing Food Habits', *Journal of the American Diet Association*, 23 (1947), pp. 403–9.

Rice, A. K., *Productivity and Social Organization* (Tavistock Publications, London 1958).

—— 'Productivity and Social Organisation in an Indian Weaving Shed', *Human Relations*, 6 (1953), pp. 297–329.

Robbins, F. G., 'The Impact of School Climates upon a College Class', *School Review*, 60 (1952), pp. 275–84.

Ross, I. and A. Zander, 'Need Satisfaction and Employee Turnover', *Personnel Psychology*, 10 (1957), pp. 327–38.

Sanford, F. H., *Authoritarianism and Leadership* (Institute for Research in Human Relations, Philadelphia 1950).

Scott, E. L., *Perceptions of Organization and Leadership Behavior* (Ohio State University, Research Foundation, Columbus, Ohio 1952).

Scott, W. H., *Industrial Leadership and Consultation: A Study of Human Relations in Three Merseyside Firms* (University Press of Liverpool, Liverpool 1952).

Seashore, S. E. *Group Cohesiveness in the Industrial Work Group* (Survey Research Center, University of Michigan, Ann Arbor, Mich. 1954).

Shister, Joseph and Lloyd G. Reynolds, *Job Horizons, a Study of Job and Labor Mobility* (Harper & Bros., N.Y. 1949).

Simmons, W., 'The Group Approach to Weight Reduction. I: A Review of the Project', *Journal of the American Diet Association*, 30 (1954), pp. 437–41.

Sutermeister, Robert A. (ed.), *People and Productivity* (McGraw-Hill, N.Y. 1963).

Tannenbaum, A. S. 'Personality Change as a Result of an Experimental Change of Environmental Conditions', *Journal of Abnormal and Social Psychology*, 55 (November 1957), pp. 404–6.

—— and F. H. Allport, 'Personality Structure and Group Structure: An Interpretive Study of Their Relationship through an Event-Structure Hypothesis', *Journal of Abnormal and Social Psychology*, 53 (November 1956), pp. 272–80.

Tannenbaum, Robert and Fred Massarik, 'Participation by Subordinates in the Managerial Decision-Making Process', in R. A. Sutermeister (ed.), *People and Productivity* (McGraw-Hill, N.Y. 1963).

Torrance, E. P. 'The Behavior of Small Groups under the Stress of Conditions of Survival', *American Sociological Review*, 19 (December 1954), pp. 751–5.

—— 'Methods of Conducting Critiques of Group Problem-Solving Performance', *Journal of Applied Psychology*, 37 (October 1953), pp. 394–8.

—— and R. Mason, 'The Indigenous Leader in Changing Attitudes and Behavior', *International Journal of Sociometry*, 1 (1956), pp. 23–8.

Turner, Arthur N., 'Foreman, Job, and Company', *Human Relations*, 10 (1957), pp. 99–112.

Viteles, Morris S., *Motivation and Morale in Industry* (Norton, N.Y. 1953).

Vroom, Victor, *Some Personality Determinants of the Effects of Participation* (Prentice-Hall, Englewood, Cliffs N.J. 1960).

—— *Work and Motivation* (John Wiley, N.Y. 1964).

—— and F. C. Mann, 'Leader Authoritarianism and Employee Attitudes', *Personnel Psychology*, 13 (Summer 1960), pp. 125–40.

Walker, Charles, *Modern Technology and Civilization* (McGraw-Hill, N.Y. 1962).

Walker, J. and R. Marriott, 'A Study of Some Attitudes to Factory Work', *Occupational Psychology*, 25 (1951), pp. 181–91.

Weschler, I. R., M. Hahane and R. Tannenbaum, 'Job Satisfaction, Productivity, and Morale: A Case Study', *Occupational Psychology*, 26 (January 1952), pp. 1–14.

White, R. K. and R. Lippitt, *Autocracy and Democracy* (Harper and Bros., N.Y. 1960).

Whyte, William F., *Money and Motivation* (Harper and Bros., N.Y. 1955).

Wickert, F. R. 'Turnover and Employees' Feelings of Ego Involvement in the Day-to-Day Operation of a Company', *Personnel Psychology*, 4 (1951) pp. 185–97.

Wispe, L. G., 'Evaluating Section Teaching Methods in the Introductory Course', *Journal of Educational Research*, 45 (1951), pp. 161–86.

Worthy, J. C., 'Factors Influencing Employee Morale', *Harvard Business Review*, 28 (January 1950), pp. 61–73.

Index